Narrative and Ps

I gradually learned that stories are necessary. As so often happens, it was a client who taught me this, a person who came to me with a self-narrative that was tragic and seemingly without hope. But with great courage, this person was able to reclaim some of the more affirming chapters in their early life, and to find ways of seeing the awful things that had happened as episodes in a 'bigger' life-story that had meaning and purpose. Somewhere during this therapy I realised that what this person was doing made most sense to me in terms of narrative processes such as telling, editing and re-writing. Around this time, I came across *Narrative Means to Therapeutic Ends* by Michael White and David Epston (1990), which provided a framework for under-standing what it means to work therapeutically with stories. I had always believed that psychology and psychotherapy are primarily cultural disciplines, that we construct personhood and identity (and our theories of personhood and identity) from the cultural resources available to us. White and Epston's work enabled me to see that narrative provided the bridge between culture and self. And this insight led back into much personal exploration, of my own experience of storytelling, my sensitivity to stories, my authority.

What is this book about? What it is saying is this: all therapies are narrative therapies. Whatever you are doing, or think you are doing, as therapist or client can be understood in terms of telling and re-telling stories. Yet there is no 'narrative therapy', there is no one way of doing this. To present 'narrative therapy' as a new brand-name product in the therapeutic marketplace (with accompanying training manual) is to misunderstand what this is all about.

If there is any common ground among narrative therapies, it lies in the intention to give the client every opportunity to tell his or her story, to really listen to these stories, and to allow space for the telling of new or different sto-ries. The importance of listening to *stories*, rather than just employing listening skills in general, or listening to or for other types of communication, is that the story represents the basic means by which people organise and communicate the meaning of events and experiences. Not listening to *stories* deprives both therapist and client of the most effective and mutually involv-ing mode of discourse available to both of them.

It is my belief that adopting a narrative perspective on therapy leads inevitably in the direction of a number of significant implications. Taking a narrative approach requires doing some re-thinking about the nature of truth, the concept of the person, the relationship between therapist and client, the knowledge base of psychotherapy. At the moment there seems to be a lot of interest being shown in the counselling and psychotherapy literature over ways of working with stories and narratives, and also a lot of confusion. It seems to me that much of the confusion arises from lack of clarity over whether the therapists concerned are inserting the concept of narrative into already existing theoretical frameworks, or are taking as their starting point a social constructionist view of the world which places a sense of the person as a story-making and story-consuming being right at the centre of its con-ceptual framework. There is a coherence to social constructionist uses of narrative in therapy, whereas writers from other traditions seem to have selectively sampled those aspects of narrative thinking that are consistent with their existing ideas, while rejecting or ignoring those elements that, for them, do not fit.

Because narrative therapies are associated with a distinctive philosophical and political position that can be characterised as social constructionist (Gergen, 1985), I have chosen in this book to give my account of some of the central notions of narrative and culture, before moving into a discussion of some of the ways in which these ideas can be applied in counselling and psychotherapy. Because I view psychotherapy not just as a process occurring between client and therapist, but also as a cultural form that encompasses research, training and organisation, the book concludes by reviewing the significance of narrative theory for these domains. In preparing this book, I have been painfully aware of how large a topic narrative therapy is, and how little I know about it. Throughout the book, there are references to what is an expanding and powerful literature on narrative, cultural psychology and allied approaches to therapy. My hope is that readers will find in this rich literature some further illumination in respect of topics to which I have not done justice.

I could not have written this book without the support and help of many friends and colleagues. I would particularly like to record my appreciation to Sue Allingham, Lynne Angus, Sophia Balamoutsou, Mike Beaney, Linda Berman, Mim Bernard, Simon Biggs, Dee Cooper, Robert Elliott, Jane Gilbert, Soti Grafanaki, Gordon Lynch, Sharon MacDonald, Linda Machin, Miller Mair, Jane Oven, Chris Phillipson, David Rennie and John Sherry. Susan Worsey and Rosemary Campbell at Sage have been unswervingly helpful and patient editors. Finally, but most important of all, I would not be anywhere without my family – my wife, Julia, and my daughters, Kate, Emma and Hannah.

1

Psychotherapy, Culture and Storytelling: How They Fit Together

Only in the middle of the twentieth century has psychotherapy and its multitude of variants (counselling, counselling psychology, clinical social work, clinical theology, self-help groups, bibliotherapy and so on) developed a solid institutional base in professional associations and universities, become accessible to significant numbers of people, and taken its place at the heart of modern society. Since that time, therapy has on the whole thrived. In most countries some degree of government control has been applied to therapy, with the introduction of regulatory bodies and licensing bestowing 'official' legitimacy to this practice. Therapy has also entered the realm of everyday awareness, to the extent that references to therapy in popular culture media such as magazines and TV series are commonplace, and are made with the tacit assumption that everyone in the audience will know what is meant.

Most people involved with therapy, either as practitioners or as clients, seem to take for granted its status as a form of 'treatment' or 'intervention' appropriate to certain types of emotional, behavioural or relationship problems. Few pause to consider the implications of the relatively recent emergence of psychotherapy, or of its classification as a type of 'treatment'. Nevertheless, the fact is that while other occupations such as farmer, lawyer or physician have been around for a long time, the occupation of counsellor or psychotherapist did *not* exist in the seventeenth or eighteenth centuries. Something happened to make psychotherapy possible. What happened? What were the factors behind psychotherapy arriving on the scene when it did, and in the form that it took?

There are basically two ways of accounting for the emergence of the psychological therapies around the late nineteenth and early twentieth centuries. One explanation points to advances in psychiatric and psychological knowledge that led to the discovery of this new form of treatment. From this perspective, therapy can be seen as part of the 'technology' of psychology and psychiatry. Doing therapy involves the application of scientifically validated theories and procedures to problems of emotional life and behaviour. This way of looking at the development of psychological therapies places them firmly within the theme of 'progress' and 'improvement' that permeates much of modern life.

The other approach to explaining the rise of therapy looks not forward with science and progress but backward toward some very old cultural traditions. From this perspective, all cultures possess ritualised ways of enabling members to deal with group and interpersonal tensions, feelings of anger and loss, questions of purpose and meaning. These rituals evolve and change over generations, and are part of the 'taken-for-granted' fabric of everyday life. Looked at in this light, psychotherapy can be viewed as a culturally sanctioned form of healing that reflects the values and needs of the modern industrial world. As such, it has not been 'invented' by scientists but has evolved from the healing practices employed in previous historical periods by ordinary people, and necessarily contains within it the residue of these earlier forms.

The vast majority of books and articles on psychotherapy are grounded in a scientific perspective. Therapists trained in any of the mainstream approaches acquire a theory of therapy that is framed in terms of abstract propositions and cause-and-effect relationships. I am assuming the reader's familiarity with at least the general shape of this literature, so will not be rehearsing in any detail the mainstream science-based account of how discoveries and advances by the like of Freud, Wolpe and Rogers laid the foundations of psychotherapy as an applied science (see Freedheim, 1992). Instead, I intend to approach the question 'why has therapy arrived now?' by examining the cultural history of psychotherapy, and by exploring the implications for theory and practice of looking at therapy as a cultural form. This discussion will review the cultural origins of therapy, the transition from religious to scientific modes of intervention, and the construction of psychotherapy as an applied scientific discipline.

My basic thesis is that stories and storytelling represent the primary point of connection between what goes on in 'therapy' – whether contemporary psychotherapy or traditional religious healing – and what goes on in the culture as a whole. From a cultural perspective, a therapy session is a site for telling certain stories in a certain way. The telling of personal stories, tales of 'who I am', 'what I want to be', or 'what troubles me', to a listener or audience mandated by the culture to hear such stories, is an essential mechanism through which individual lives become and can remain aligned with collective realities. It seems to me impossible to imagine a human culture that did not contain such a mechanism. In recent times, however, this process of 'life narration' has become deeply problematic. It is no longer clear whether existing forms of psychotherapy can provide adequate means for people to tell the stories they need to tell in the ways they need to tell them.

'People' have changed: a brief cultural history of the concept of the person

In arguing that it is important to understand psychotherapy and counselling in cultural and historical terms, I am acutely aware of the difficulties involved in any attempt to make sense of human behaviour in earlier times, or in other cultures. There seems no real escape from the dangers of both misinterpreting other ways of life by imposing frameworks of understanding derived from present-day experiences and practices, and of oversimplifying what are enormously complex matters. In acknowledging the sketchiness of the account that follows, I hope I may also stimulate others to fill in some of the detail, or even to attempt to re-draw the whole picture.

My sense of this area of inquiry is that the advanced industrial societies of Europe and North America can be understood to have undergone three main stages of cultural development. The first, and earliest stage can be characterised as *traditional* culture, which began to break down around about the eighteenth century. In traditional culture, people live in small, mainly rural communities, have relatively basic technologies to hand, and live according to an explicit set of moral guidelines mediated by religion and myth. In the *modern* era, the advancement of science and technology was associated with a gradual movement toward urban, industrial ways of life and a replacement of religion by rationality and a belief in progress. In the *late*, or *postmodern* era of the present moment, there appears to be a fragmentation of the structures and assumptions of modernity. There is an increasing questioning of the 'project of modernity', which is almost folding in on itself, or is even regarded as responsible for the destruction of the human spirit and the planet on which we live. However, it is far from clear where all this is leading. The late twentieth century is regarded by many as a time of transition. We are perhaps moving away from the age of modernity, but no one really knows where we are heading *to*. It can even be argued that 'postmodern' culture represents no more than a capacity to look back on modernity, to reflect on it, rather than a movement in any particular direction. Table 1.1 presents a summary of some of the main themes associated with traditional, modern and late/postmodern cultures.

Table 1.1   *The key characteristics of traditional, modern and postmodern cultures*

Traditional	Modern	Postmodern
Collective, family-oriented way of life	Individualistic	Awareness of 'relational' self
Self defined in terms of external factors: importance of 'honour'	Autonomous, bounded self: importance of 'dignity'	Fragmented, 'saturated' self
Belief in religion	Belief in science	Belief that knowledge is socially constructed
Moral certainty	Moral relativism	Search for moral frameworks
Static society	Commitment to 'progress'	Fear of anarchy and chaos
Localised forms of political control	Nation state	'Global village'
Agricultural work	Industrial work	Information-processing work

Although therapy is embedded in, and grows out of, the forces of history and culture, its main focus is on the detail of individual lives. The differences between the traditional, modern and postmodern worlds exist not only at the level of social organisations, institutions and forms of communication, but also at the level of the individual person. The sense of what it is to be a person is socially constructed. It depends on the relational web, the belief and kinship systems, the economic order, into which one is born. And the sense of what it means to be a person has changed. Therapy is both affected by this change and has helped to bring it about.

The feel of what it might be like to be a person in traditional times is captured in these passages from Philippe Ariès and Alasdair MacIntyre:

> The historians taught us long ago that the King was never left alone. But in fact, until the end of the seventeenth century, nobody was ever left alone. The density of social life made isolation virtually impossible, and people who managed to shut themselves up in a room for some time were regarded as exceptional characters: relations between peers, relations between people of the same class but dependent on one another, relations between masters and servants – these everyday relations never left a man by himself. (Ariès, 1962: 398)

> One central theme of heroic societies is . . . that death waits for both alike. . . . If someone kills you, my friend or brother, I owe you their death and when I have paid my debt to you their friend or brother owes them my death. The more extended my system of kinsmen and friends, the more liabilities I shall incur of a kind that may end in my death. . . . The man therefore who does what he ought moves steadily toward his fate and his death. It is defeat and not victory that lies at the end. (MacIntyre, 1981: 124)

These accounts offer a way of beginning to understand the stories that people in traditional cultures lived (and live) within: stories of 'never being alone' and stories of 'moving steadily toward my fate'. To be a person in a traditional culture is to live in close proximity to others, in spiritual and psychological as well as physical terms. For such a person the notion of an 'inner self' that forms the basis for decision-making and action (Landrine, 1992) is difficult to comprehend: 'who I am' is defined externally, through history, kinship, duty and fate.

The sense of personhood in modern society is quite different. It is perhaps helpful to differentiate two aspects of the development of a modern concept of person (Gergen, 1994). One aspect is characterised by the construction of person and relationship through the idea of *romanticism*. The romantic– modern notion of the person retains the traditional sense of the person being constituted through his or her deep ties with others, but replaces the traditonal embeddedness in community and history with relationships with others (for example, sexual or marriage partners). This aspect of modern personness is reflected in much twentieth-century psychology. For example, the focus of psychodynamic theory on inner 'self-objects' and the achievement of intimacy in relationships can be understood as examples of this movement away from a sense of person-in-community to a sense of person-in-relationship. And what accompanied this realignment of 'what it means to be me' was the discovery or creation of an inner landscape of a 'Self' with a capital 'S'. The goals of personal happiness, fulfilment, and loving and being loved by a special other, required, in the romanticist narrative, a thorough exploration and mapping of the individual, bounded Self.

The other central aspect of the modern concept of the person is a sense of the person as a *mechanism*. There is in modern life an overwhelming importance attached to rationality, control and the abolition of risk. Behind all religious stories is an encompassing macronarrative of how the individual is ultimately subject to the will and guidance of a greater power. Behind all scientific theories is a macronarrative of prediction and control: science makes it possible for human beings to be the masters of the universe. While in the nineteenth century the scientific world-view was restricted mainly to people who were actual scientists or were particularly 'progressive', during the twentieth century we have all become scientists. Through theories such as psychoanalysis, behaviourism or cognitive psychology, we are able to explain our own being in scientific, cause-and-effect terms. We are all (faulty) mechanisms.

Cushman (1990, 1995) has argued that the modern configuration of 'person-ness', the interplay of romanticism and mechanism, was generated through the efforts of mature capitalist economies to create new markets through the creation of a different type of consumer. He suggests that the sense of inner-directedness and repression of sexuality in the service of love and disciplined work noted by Albee (1977) and others was characteristic mainly of early capitalism. In later capitalist economies, the loss of family, tradition and community, particularly in the post-war middle classes, led to the a general sense of alienation: the 'empty self'. Cushman writes that:

> It is a self that seeks the experience of being continually filled up by consuming goods, calories, experiences, politicians, romantic partners and empathic therapists in an attempt to combat the growing alienation and fragmentation of the era. This response has been implicitly prescribed by a post-World War II economy that is dependent on the continual consumption of nonessential and quickly obsolete items and experiences. . . . Psychotherapy is one of the professions responsible for healing the post-World War II self. Unfortunately, many psychotherapy theories attempt to treat the modern self by reinforcing the very qualities of self that have initially caused the problem: its autonomous, bounded, masterful nature. (1990: 600–1)

Cushman's account of the conditions under which the modern notion of person-ness arose relies heavily on an analysis of the influence of the industrial revolution, the development of advanced capitalist economies and the movement toward a secular, scientifically oriented, mass urban consumer society. Behind these factors can be glimpsed yet earlier social and cultural processes, for example the slow historical emergence of consciousness (Jaynes, 1977) and the development of literacy (Ong, 1982), and the Western sense of an expressive, instrumental self (Taylor, 1989).

The construction of the modern person has brought with it a vast array of new stories-to-live-by. There are huge classes of narrative that hardly existed in traditional cultures, for example such stories as 'seeking fulfilment', 'falling in love', 'getting divorced', 'being in therapy', or 'choosing a new car'.

Yet the wheel of human culture and history turns yet again, and reveals yet another reconstruction of the person in the late/postmodern era in which we currently live. It is always difficult to capture with any confidence the sense of what is happening *now*, but the social philosopher Kenneth Gergen has perhaps achieved this task better than anyone else. His notion of the *saturated*

self effectively conveys some of the essential features of life in advanced capitalist economies at the turn of this century. Gergen (1994) describes the ways
in which people are now globalised, with the potential to have relationships
and roles in all parts of the world, thus giving endless opportunity to view one
life from a myriad perspectives. The postmodern person is bombarded by
information – satellite, cable, faxes, the Internet, mobile phones and so on.
The result of all this is fragmentation. The person is not known by any one
other or group as a consistent whole, but experiences himself or herself as different selves in different settings. A whole psychology of multiple personality
and 'sub-selves' has grown up to enable people to describe these experiences.

Perhaps the most significant new dimension of the stories people tell in
late/postmodern times lies in the extent to which these stories are permeated
by *reflexivity* (Giddens, 1991). There are so many alternative life-styles on
offer, so many channels of satellite/cable TV serving up apparently limitless
repertoires of how to be a person. Eventually, these media of communication
converge to drive home one simple message: you can choose who you are. It
is no coincidence that in recent years social psychologists have begun to
describe the phenomenon of *possible selves* (Wurf and Markus, 1991). People
in modern and postmodern times can look at who they are, and imagine
being someone else, in a way that would be impossible for someone from traditional culture.

This classification of social and cultural history into three broad stages –
traditional, modern and late/postmodern – is an oversimplification.
Fragments of traditional ways of life survive in modern times, and have
undergone a revival in some postmodern circles. However, my aim in offering
a division of cultural history into these three stages is to highlight my argument that psychotherapy and counselling are essentially *products of
modernity*. Therapy constitutes a crucial element of the cultural apparatus of
modern society. As we move further in the direction of whatever the *post* in
late/postmodernity will bring, the nature of therapy will necessarily undergo
a transformation as fundamental as that which occurred when the religious
'cure of souls' was replaced by psychoanalysis.

'Psychotherapy' in traditional cultures

The construction of what we now know as psychotherapy took place over a
long period of time, and involved the assembly of many different cultural elements. It is difficult for us to know exactly how psychological healing was
conducted in Europe in the pre-psychotherapy era. Most of the historical
accounts currently available attempt to classify and interpret traditonal healing in terms of contemporary medical and psychiatric categories. Not enough
historical research has looked at how people with emotional, relationship
and behavioural problems were actually dealt with in the centuries before
these types of problems were medicalised (although see Neugebauer, 1978,
1979). There is, however, evidence available from anthropological studies on
non-Western, non-industrialised societies. Material from both historical and

anthropological sources can be brought together to give a general picture of some of the ways that 'problems in living' can be, and have been, addressed in traditional cultures.

One of the main themes that appears in historical studies of the treatment of psychological disturbance is the importance of *religion*. In pre-industrial Europe and America, the priest or pastor, and the Church, acted as sources of help for those in psychological distress. Holifield (1983) reports that, in the Roman Catholic church, the *Catechism of the Council of Trent* (1564) was intended to instruct priests in the 'care of souls'. Holifield observes that:

> The Roman Catholic spiritual physicians had at their disposal the sacraments of the Church, including the power to judge sins, forgive them, and prescribe statutory penalties. The process required that each penitent give a detailed accounting of morally sinful transgressions. . . . Only after the recitation of sins – by a parishioner who evidenced a spirit of contrition, candor and acts of satisfaction – could the priest offer comfort with the formula of forgiveness. (1983: 18–19)

At the heart of this traditional Christian spiritual therapy was (and is) a sophisticated theoretical framework that specified the causes of disturbance (sin), a model of healthy development (stages in the road to salvation), and a set of techniques for applying these principles in individual cases (casuistry). Different churches (Roman Catholic, Lutheran, Anglican, Puritan) and individual ministers and priests within these churches each evolved their own versions of these ideas.

Holifield (1983) provides many examples of ways that Christian pastors worked in practice. If the specific religious content of these pastoral interventions is put to one side, it can be seen that what these priests were doing was strikingly similar to what a modern-day psychotherapist would do. Emphasis was placed on the qualities of the pastor, the relationship between pastor and parishioner, the expression of feeling, the examination of beliefs, the sense of movement along a developmental pathway. Throughout this process, the person seeking salvation would be expected to tell the story of his or her troubles (temptations, sins, doubts) in full detail. The debates over pastoral care that can be found in the theological literature of the eighteenth and nineteenth centuries explore themes that are familiar to contemporary readers of psychotherapy texts: the relative importance of reason and emotion, the effectiveness of therapeutic techniques. In the first half of the eighteenth century, for instance, a controversy sprang up over the significance of 'self-love' or 'self-esteem' that anticipated and pre-dated by about 200 years the idea of Carl Rogers that self-acceptance is a pre-requisite for adaptive social behaviour.

Another aspect of pre-scientific healing practices was the use of *collective ritual*. If a member of a community was suffering from what we would now label as a psychological or psychiatric disorder, it would be likely that there would be some way in which the whole community would get together to enable healing or reconciliation to occur. These healing rituals would normally contain some form of *confession*, in which the person or persons centrally involved in the 'trouble' would tell their story of what had happened, in a frank and open manner, concealing nothing. An example of this would be the use of the confessional within the early Christian church. As McNeill (1951) has shown, up until the fourteenth century confession in the Christian church tended to take place in public. Restitution for sins and the opportunity for repentance were also public activities, often relying on humiliation or punishment in front of the whole community.

A fourth element commonly found in non-medical psychological healing was the promotion of *altered states of consciousness*. Christian rituals involving fasting, singing, incense, long religious services, the reality-altering architecture of medieval cathedrals and vivid colour of stained glass, all contributed to the induction of altered states of awareness that served to release the person from the constraints and mind-set of ordinary everyday life.

The final facet of 'primitive' equivalents to psychotherapy was the participation of a powerful guide or *spiritual director*, who would facilitate and engineer the whole process. This individual would be a highly respected member of the community, who would have control over sacred spaces (such as the Church building) and sacred knowledge. Often, the spiritual leader would have a role that placed him or her somewhere on the 'edge' of the social group.

The psychiatrist Jerome Frank (1973) has proposed a generic, transcultural model of psychological healing that incorporates these elements. He argues that the fundamental experience that leads people to seek outside help is that of *demoralisation*. In most circumstances people possess the resources within their own lives and families to deal effectively with 'problems in living'. It is when these personal resources are insufficient that the individual or group becomes demoralised and hopeless and needs someone else to intervene. In all cultures, Frank would argue, the healer is a person of perceived status and moral authority, who offers an explanation of the problem and a set of procedures for alleviating what has gone wrong. The process of healing itself always involves unburdening and emotional catharsis.

The examples of non-medical psychological healing given so far have all been drawn from European Christian sources. The study of the *Ndembu* people of Central Africa by the anthropologist Victor Turner provides a description of a similar kind of process within a non-European culture, and gives a fascinating example of a process that is recognisably 'therapeutic' yet is quite unlike anything that would take place in a Western psychotherapy clinic. Turner (1964) presents the case of Kamahasanyi, an Ndembu man who was experiencing various relationship conflicts in his marriage and within his village. Kamahasanyi was exhibiting a number of symptoms, including a failure to catch antelope, sexual problems, pains in his back, limbs and chest, fatigue and withdrawal from social contact. Turner considered these symptoms to be categorisable, in Western psychiatric terms, as mainly psychosomatic and neurotic.

The particular group of Ndembu observed by Turner were followers of the *Ihamba* cult. The term *ihamba* refers to the upper central incisor tooth of a deceased hunter. These teeth were believed to contain the power of the hunter to kill animals. When a hunter died, these teeth were removed and inherited and carried by appropriate relatives to bring good fortune. However, in some cirumstances *mahamba* (the plural of *ihamba*) could become buried in the bodies of the living, causing pain and misfortune. One of the tasks of an Ndembu doctor was to perform a rite through which *mahamba* could be located and extracted from the body of a victim.

In the case of Kamahasanyi this ritual was performed by a doctor by the name of Ihembi, portrayed by Turner as:

> . . . a man about seventy years old, white-haired, dignified, but with a smile of singular sweetness and charm. He had the throaty voice characteristic of the Ndembu hunter, but he put it to lucid and eloquent use. . . . [he] belonged to a branch of the royal lineage . . .but had been permanently excluded from the succession after a bitter and unsuccessful dispute with another branch (of the royal family). . . .Ihembi enjoyed a wide reputation. In many ways he was typical of Ndembu doctors: capable, charismatic, authoritative, but excluded from secular life for a number of reasons, some structural, some personal. He was the typical 'outsider' who achieves status in the ritual realm in compensation for his exclusion from authority in the political realm. (1964: 240–1)

In the healing ritual directed by Ihembi and his assistants, all the members of the community gathered in a clearing in the bush some distance from the village. Horns were cupped on to the patient's body, to catch the offending *mahamba* when they were eventually forced out of his body. The ritual then proceeded through frequent alternation between two contrasting types of activity. There were phases of drumming, dancing and singing, in which everyone participated, culminating in trembling fits on the part of the patient. If these fits dislodged a horn, Ihembi would intervene to remove the horns and investigate them. If at that point he found nothing in the horns

> . . . he makes a statement to the congregation about why the *ihamba* has not 'come out' – which usually entails a fairly detailed account of the patient's life story – then he . . . invites village members to come, in order of sex and seniority, to . . . confess any secret ill-feeling they may have toward the patient. The patient himself may be invited as well. . . . After several hours of it, the congregation felt nothing but a unanimous craving for the removal of the *ihamba* from the patient's body. The intense excitement whipped up by the drums; the patient's trembling; mass participation in the sad–sweet or rousing hunters' cult songs, which are sung to 'please *ihamba*', followed by the spate of confessions and airing of grievances . . . all these elements make a dialogical or dialectical pattern of activity that generates strong sentiments of corporateness, reduces skepticism, and maximises sympathy for the patient. (Turner, 1964: 258–9)

From a narrative perspective, what is happening here can be interpreted as the construction of an event through which a new story can be told. During this event, the old stories of resentments and betrayals are told and heard. The depth of feeling and intimacy developed during the event, and the authority of the doctor, serve to ensure the genuineness and credibility of the stories that are recounted. Then, finally, a new story can be fashioned. It is as though everyone in the community now says: 'the *ihamba* is found, it is true that Kamahasanyi was indeed bewitched, but now everything can be different. . . .' And, as Turner reports, it seemed to work. On his return to the village a year later, he found several relationship adjustments to have taken place, and Kamahasanyi to be free of symptoms and enjoying life.

The elements of pre-scientific, pre-medical forms of emotional healing that can be observed in the case of Kamahasanyi – religious belief, collective ritual, confession, altered states of consciousness and spiritual direction – can be found in many other examples of 'folk psychotherapy' (see Kiev, 1964). However, these elements should not be understood as representing a rigid framework within which all non-industrial cultures responded to this set of issues. There are major variations in the solutions that different cultures have evolved (see Prince, 1981). Nevertheless, these healing elements do appear, in some guise, in all cultures, including modern Western industrialised societies.

But it is not enough merely to point to the similarities between the 'therapies' employed in different cultures. To make sense of our own cultural world, we need to look at how these practices have become transformed into what we know as psychotherapy. How did collective religious ritual evolve into modern forms of psychotherapeutic healing?

Psychotherapy in modern culture: the transition from a religious to a medical–scientific framework

This account, which draws mainly on the work of Cushman (1990, 1995) and Scull (1979, 1981, 1989), attributes the shaping of psychotherapy to a range of interlocking cultural factors: secularisation, the changing Western concept of self, the operation of the market economy and colonialism. These cultural factors represent different aspects of the shift from traditional to modern ways of life.

The first of these factors, secularisation, has been foreshadowed by many of the observations and arguments already put forward in this chapter. As Berger et al. (1974) have put it, the 'canopy of meaning' provided by religion has been largely eroded by science and modernity. Halmos (1965) derived figures showing that the steady decline in numbers of priests has been matched by a corresponding increase in the numbers of people employed in the various counselling and psychotherapeutic professions. The result of these trends has been that priests have been not only less available for recourse in times of trouble, but have been perceived as less and less credible as sources of help. The religious stories that previously assisted people in making sense of life dilemmas and transitions are also less well known to people now, are turned to less often, and fail to resonate with the feelings and meaning systems of those seeking help. Religious rituals, similarly, have less impact in a secular age, at least for the majority of people.

This is not the place to examine the wider reasons behind the demise of religion as an all-encompassing belief system in modern societies. The key issue of concern here is that, as religion gradually diminished in importance, there also opened up a need for something to replace it. Somebody was required to continue the work of 'cure of souls' (McNeill, 1951), even if not in a religious manner. However, religion also left behind a live cultural residue of ritual and belief that could be re-defined and re-packaged as something new, as 'psychotherapy'.

Psychotherapy did not immediately slot into the space left by religion. There was a transitional phase during the late nineteenth and early twentieth centuries, where spiritual/religious and medical/scientific approaches existed side by side in Western culture. In the beginning, the adherents of religious models of pastoral care attempted to accommodate the ideas of the new breed of psychologists and psychiatrists within a religious context (see Holifield, 1983; Scull, 1979). Over time, however, this strategy was not successful, with religious concepts becoming marginalised. The fact that some practitioners of mainstream contemporary therapies are now arguing for greater acknowledgement of the spiritual dimensions of human nature illustrates the extent and success of this process of secularisation.

A kind of mass cultural fascination with hypnosis acted as a key transition stage in the movement from religious to scientific modes of therapy. In the middle of the nineteenth century, hypnotic states were widely used in medicine, for anaesthetic purposes as well as in the new medical specialism of psychiatry. The most celebrated proponent of hypnosis was Anton Mesmer, who achieved celebrity status in Europe. Cushman (1995) has documented the importation of hypnotism to the USA in the mid-nineteenth century. Thousands of people, mainly women, were trained in hypnosis and a whole new profession was established to offer treatment for emotional problems using the technique. Cushman argues that the attraction and promise of hypnotism in nineteenth-century America lay not so much in whether it was actually effective in alleviating personal problems as in the extent to which it resonated with some of the dominant themes in American cultural life. Initially, for the mass of European emigrants, the American frontier represented the possibility of self-liberation. As the USA became an industrialised and urbanised society in the nineteenth century, the loss of the frontier meant that for many citizens the search for self-liberation and self-mastery moved *within*, toward the aim of freedom and control of one's self as a 'personality' with an 'inner life'. The frontier became an internal rather than an external landscape. Hypnosis offered an immediate, practical demonstration of the power and potential of a subconscious inner self.

By the end of the nineteenth century there was therefore a ready American audience for the new theories of the unconscious mind. Pierre Janet toured medical schools. Freud and Jung visited in 1909. American psychologists and psychiatrists such as William James, Calvin Hall, A.A. Brill and James Jackson Putnam developed and disseminated these ideas within American academic and literary circles. The emergence of the *Emmanuel* movement in Boston in 1905 was an attempt to integrate these new ideas into the Christian tradition of the cure of souls. This social movement, which was highly influential for about 10 years – not only in the USA but in other countries too – was dedicated to 'the application of psychological principles to the problem of religion' (Holifield, 1983: 202). It supported a journal, *Psychotherapy*, first published in 1908. The style employed by Emmanuel pastors is exemplified in a description offered by Holifield of the work of an Episcopalian rector in Northampton, Massachusetts:

> He began each session by asking his client to be seated in a comfortable chair before a fire and practice rhythmic breathing, muscular relaxation and visual imagery. He then led the client into 'the silence of the quiet mind' by offering 'tranquilizing suggestions', followed by healing suggestions, often interspersed with readings from the Bible or even a short 'sermon'. The purpose was to dislodge unwholesome thoughts from the subconscious. . . . The rector also sometimes used candid conversations in which his visitors were confronted with unpleasant truths about themselves, but the more frequent technique was the substitution of confident thought in place of fear and worry. (1983: 205–6)

This description, drawn from a book written in 1909, contains many elements familiar to modern-day psychotherapists: muscle relaxation, guided imagery, confrontation. In the end, however, a medical profession threatened by these developments re-exerted its domination of the 'trade in lunacy' (Scull, 1979) by withdrawing its willingness to collaborate with Emmanuel pastors, and the movement was left behind in the irresistible march toward a fully secularised psychotherapy.

The key figure in the creation of a secular psychotherapy was, of course, Freud. His approach was based in science, making use of a powerful theoretical base that drew on the modern sciences of biology and psychology, and a technique that incorporated many of the features of hypnosis and religion, but assimilating them into an essentially medicalised relationship between doctor and patient. In this new form of healing, the patient would confess all, but in a more subtle, more *private* form. The confidential, boundaried nature of the psychoanalytic consultation was a mirror of the modern, autonomous, bounded self. Psychoanalysis offered the ultimate opportunity for this self to turn in on itself again and again in its search to control and colonise the territory within.

However, psychoanalysis, Freud's icon of modernity, did not really take off until exported to the USA. In Freud's home ground of Vienna and the middle Europe of the early twentieth century, psychoanalysis had limited influence, and was largely restricted to upper-class, intellectual circles. The rise of fascism in Europe in the 1930s triggered a major emigration of psychoanalysts to the USA, a move made easier by the positive reception given to Freud and Jung on the occasion of their visit to Clark University in 1909 and the enthusiastic welcome given to psychoanalytic ideas within the advertising industry even more than in psychiatry itself. In many ways psychoanalysis and American culture were an ideal match. The need to 'have' a marketable personality, the drive to self-improvement, the empty self of a dislocated, socially mobile society, an emptiness crying out to be filled by consuming or through therapy (Cushman, 1990, 1995) – to all these problems psychoanalysis appeared to offer an answer. Moreover, this was an answer that was perfectly compatible with a market economy. The selling of psychotherapy offered no challenge to the political order.

And there followed the expansion of therapy, including new products or approaches created to fit gaps and opportunities in the market. What Kovel (1981) has called the 'American mental health industry' was in full flow. Underpinning this expansion was the theme of colonisation, exhibited through a denial of the healing rituals of others, and an absence of cultural relativism. As a result, psychotherapy remained largely a white, class-based activity, taking on itself the authority to pathologise other images of self and ways of life. One of the key features of this aspect of the cultural origins of therapy lies in the way that it encourages the adoption of a *privileged* perspective in relation to the beliefs and practices of less powerful groups. Thus, it seems easy and unremarkable for Western psychotherapists to interpret the rituals and healing stories of other cultures in terms of Western theory. Until recently, efforts to provide therapeutic services to ethnic minority groups have been seen as self-evidently appropriate, as giving 'equal opportunities', rather than as having the effect of further undermining indigenous forms of healing already weakened by the inroads of Western culture as a whole. And right in the intellectual core of therapy, in the domain of theory and research, little attention has been paid to the experience of the client, or to his or her preferences in regard to treatment. All of these characteristics of Western psychotherapy can be understood, in part, to derive from the tendency of the modern industrial enterprises to seek to dominate the world, to seek to define and control markets not only in commercial areas such as business and manufacturing but also in service industries such as education, health care, food and leisure. The fact that most Western psychotherapists see themselves as offering a universally valid model of psychological healing, rather than a merely indigenous, local model, can be understood as part of the overall drive toward 'globalisation' that lies at the heart of modernity (Giddens, 1991).

If the broad shape and structure of psychotherapy, as represented by the work of pioneers such as Freud, has been moulded by cultural forces, then so has the subsequent differentiation of therapy into a proliferation of competing 'brand name' approaches. Cushman (1990, 1995) has written extensively on the evolution of psychoanalysis, from a potentially socially critical approach that fundamentally addressed inner conflicts expressed through the bodily manifestations of 'hysteria', to a 'self' theory that attempts to remedy the fragmentation and alienation of the modern psyche as expressed through conditions such as narcissism and borderline states. Cushman associates these changes with the importation of a European Victorian set of ideas developed by Freud into the 'new world' of America. Many other writers have commented on the cultural factors and personal experiences that have influenced the thinking of other key figures in psychotherapy. For example, the approach developed by Carl Rogers can be seen to represent many of the central themes and values in American culture: optimism and hope, mistrust of experts, egalitarianism (see McLeod, 1993; Sollod, 1978, 1982). Barrett-Lennard (1996) has drawn attention to the immediate cultural location of Rogers' early theorising in the 'New Deal' intellectual and political environment instigated by Roosevelt in the 1930s. Bakan (1976) has reviewed the cultural forces that lie behind behavioural ways of thinking, for example the proclivity for boys brought up in rural farming communities to manifest a liking for mechanistic explanations and mechanical gadgets.

Counselling and therapy have continued to be shaped by social and cultural forces, even in more recent times. The development of different schools of thought and approaches in counselling and psychotherapy can be seen as a response to changing cultural pressures. Recent examples include the emergence of humanistic 'growth' therapies in the expanding economies of the 1960s, the expansion of feminist and transcultural perspectives in parallel with equal opportunities legislation, and the increased interest in time-limited counselling in a period of economic recession.

From a cultural perspective, the history of psychotherapy resembles a series of overlays of cultural practices and forms of life. Looking back, we can dimly see some of the features of traditional, pre-industrial, pre-modern forms of healing. We can also detect the first attempts to appropriate and assimilate these practices into the new, modern world by filtering them through a medical lens, through hypnosis and then through psychoanalysis. In the foreground of the picture are the various attempts to re-work the same images through self theory, humanistic psychology, behavioural and cognitive theories, and all the other varieties of therapy. The meaning of any contemporary approach to therapy is built up from a sedimentation of all these earlier layers of meaning.

However, the situation regarding the cultural origins of psychotherapy is not as simple as an 'overlay' or 'sedimentation' metaphor might suggest. Earlier forms of healing do not disappear, they do not conveniently fade into the background so that modern (or postmodern) therapies are left alone in centre stage. There are cultural residues of all the cultural practices that have been described here. In Western industrial societies there are groups of people who actively employ community rituals, religious healing, confessionals, classical psychoanalysis, hypnosis and so on. Older traditions become re-discovered and re-invented. All of these forms of healing live on, and compete for legitimacy. There exist many alternative stories about how a person gets troubles, and what can be done to help.

The construction of psychotherapy as an applied scientific discipline

As we have seen, the history of psychotherapy as a separate discipline begins with its emergence from psychiatry as a result of pioneers such as Pierre Janet in Paris and Sigmund Freud in Vienna in the 1890s. The pre-history of psychotherapy, as documented by Ellenberger (1970), was strongly influenced by the use of hypnosis as a technique for helping people who were 'insane' or 'mentally ill'. The great advance made by Freud and others was to discover that patients could be cured by someone listening to them. If the patient was given an opportunity to tell his or her story, they appeared to get better. This, at least, is the way it appears with hindsight. At the time, however, Freud and his followers struggled to fit their work into a scientific framework. All of the pioneers of psychotherapy were scientifically trained doctors, and they brought with them into the new discipline of psychoanalysis a battery of medical procedures and principles. For example, patients were classified as suffering from mental 'diseases' such as 'dementia praecox', 'obsessional neurosis' and the like. Every attempt was made to find a biological basis for psychological concepts such as 'ego' or 'id'. Training in psychoanalysis was largely restricted to those with medical backgrounds. The structure of the psychoanalytic hour replicated many of the features of the traditional doctor–patient consultation.

As psychotherapy evolved and developed, various new pieces of scientific technology were introduced. Some counsellors and psychotherapists employed psychometric assessment methods such as personality and adjustment questionnaires, projective techniques and behaviour inventories to measure aspects of the functioning of their clients. Accurate measurement brings into play the realm of mathematics, the 'queen of sciences'. Attempts have also been made to use machines in therapy, to devise technological solutions to the problems of doing psychotherapy. Down the years, therapists have used galvanic skin response (GSR) monitoring, other biofeedback devices, orgone accumulator boxes, video feedback and interactive computer programmes. None of these devices has ever really caught on. However, a flourishing technology of psychotherapy has grown up around the invention of innumerable procedures that therapists can learn and apply in response to specific client problems. Many of these procedures or techniques have been developed within cognitive–behavioural therapy: systematic desensitisation, thought stopping, eye movement desensitisation, flooding and many others. The technology of the humanistic therapies (Farson, 1978) includes 'exercises' and 'tasks' such as Gestalt two-chair work, experiential focusing, guided imagery, massage and group games.

Perhaps the most striking example of the construction of psychotherapy as an applied science lies in the domain of the kind of research that has been carried out into therapy. Psychotherapy research, like most psychological research, has largely adopted what are seen to be the methods of the natural sciences, such as accurate measurement, statistical analysis, experimentation, the search for predictive power and the role of the detached, objective researcher. As Stiles and Shapiro (1989) have pointed out, the majority of therapy studies are designed around an implicit assumption of a 'drug metaphor'. Therapy is regarded as equivalent to a drug that is administered to a patient, and the task of the researcher is to discover which drug is most suitable for which problem, and the ingredients and dosage of the drug that yield the best results. Recent studies have also considered the relative economic costs of different therapies/drugs.

It is significant that the first major figure in psychotherapy who was *not* a doctor, Carl Rogers, was also the pioneer of systematic scientific research into the processes and outcomes of psychotherapy. Freud, Jung, Perls, Moreno,

Wolpe and Beck were all doctors, and could in principle legitimate their work by reference to the scientific knowledge base of medicine. Rogers, on the other hand, was a psychologist, and needed to demonstrate the scientific basis of his new client-centred approach through research. Later generations of psychotherapists who were psychologists rather than psychiatrists, such as Meichenbaum, Ellis and Mahoney, have similarly shown great commitment to research.

The training of counsellors and psychotherapists provides other examples of the scientific legitimation of therapy. Therapy training is increasingly located in university medical or psychology departments, and so the tutors and trainers running courses are inevitably under pressure to conform to institutional expectations regarding what is taught, how it is taught, and the kinds of research that academic staff should carry out. Therapy trainees on master's or doctoral programmes are required to undertake thesis research, which again typically introduces pressure to think about therapy in terms of scientific 'variables' and models. Finally, the effectiveness of training programmes, or elements within these programmes, is examined by means of scientific research. Some training approaches, such as the Carkhuff, Ivey and Kagan models, are extensively supported by research studies (Baker et al., 1990) and claim to provide scientifically validated methods of training people in therapeutic skills.

Psychotherapy is therefore shaped in the image of science in many different ways. The theories, knowledge base, practice and training of therapists are largely framed in terms of scientific ways of thinking and reasoning. Yet, in practice, therapists *appear* to take little notice of the scientific underpinnings of their profession once they have completed training. For example, surveys by Morrow-Bradley and Elliott (1986) and Cohen et al. (1986) have shown that only a minority of practising therapists read research articles or admit that research findings have much impact on their work with clients. Clearly, the importance of science for therapy does not rely on its ability to guide the moment-by-moment decisions made by clinicians according to explicit rules. Neither therapy theory nor therapy research are anywhere near precise enough to be taken on their own as bases for action in the consulting room, under any kind of normal circumstances (although the advocates of 'manualised therapy' would dispute this point – see Moras, 1993). The value of science for therapy lies instead in two interlocking areas. First, their training provides therapists with a 'scientific' mind-set, a capacity to conceptualise client problems and therapeutic process in terms of cause-and-effect sequences and hypothesised entities or 'factors' such as anxiety, the unconscious, the self-concept, etc. Second, the apparatus of science (research, journals, data, theory) allows therapists to defend their type of healing as uniquely valid, backed up by solid evidence, more legitimate than prayer, meditation or astrology.

It is as though the rational, evidence-based, scientific side of therapy represents an outer shell that faces the rest of the world. The inner core of therapy is quite different. The construction of psychotherapy as an applied science conceals the true cultural foundations of therapeutic practice. Underneath the theoretical overlay and scientific gloss, psychotherapy is a kind of conversation, a type of meeting place, a form of social drama. In a traditional or pre-modern culture, the encounter between the person and priest, healer or shaman can be seen as an event through which a personal story became re-aligned with and assimilated into the story of the community. The person is thereby 're-moralised' (Frank, 1973), accepted back into the moral order of the culture. A similar process occurs in modern psychotherapy, but it is now much more individualised, and framed in scientific terminology. The result is that psychotherapy offers a particular type of narrative reconstruction, one that is embedded in the (largely American) cultural milieu of late twentieth-century industrial society.

The interaction between therapy and culture

Even in the very earliest years of psychotherapy, Freud's patients read his books. Now, there is a huge bibliotherapy literature that not only offers readers methods of solving their problems without going to see a therapist, but also provides those who do choose to consult a clinician an outline of the therapeutic metanarrative, the story of 'what therapy can do for you'. In addition, many millions of people in Western industrial nations have studied at least some psychology at college or university. Others have learned about therapy through magazines, novels, films and television.

Of course, not all people who consult a therapist are equally conversant with the nature of the therapy plot. As Hillman observes:

> . . . the sophisticated 'therapeutic class' who come to private therapy have their stories already formed into the therapeutic genre, that is, the story is self-reflective and focused on the 'problems' of the main character. With the 'hospital population' the shape of the story often requires coaching from the listener: there are too many characters (projections), incidents are not selected according to the economical requirements of a therapeutic plot, [and] time sequence, basic to the definition of narrative, may be altogether missing. (1975: 136)

The point here is that the therapy story may be well known to a significant proportion of the population (Hillman, 1983). As a cultural form, therapy stands in a creative tension with the rest of culture. For example, ideas and practices that start out from therapy permeate society as a whole. In one study, Pennebaker (1993b) asked people from different age cohorts, all of whom had experienced the divorce of their parents, whether they had talked about their feelings about this experience to anyone. There was a highly significant intergenerational difference in willingness to disclose this type of issue, with younger people being much more open to talking about their troubles than were older people. There are no doubt many reason why the post-war 'Baby Boom' generation is more willing to talk about difficult feelings than their parents had been, but one important factor must lie in the cultural impact of therapy during their formative years.

Therapy also assimilates and appropriates ideas and practices from the culture within which it is embedded. The initial construction of psychotherapy from pre-existing cultural elements such as the confessional, the doctor–patient relationship and hypnosis has already been noted. But as therapy has evolved, it has continued to borrow from other cultural forms of life. Psychodrama explicitly draws many concepts and techniques from the theatre. Sex therapy has appropriated techniques used by prostitutes. Progressive relaxation and Eye Movement Desensitization (EMD) have developed applications of what were originally yoga methods. Many therapists working in cross-cultural settings have integrated 'indigenous' healing rituals into their approach (see Parson, 1985). Therapists from all orientations have found ways of employing drawing, painting, sculpting and creative writing in their practice. These examples reinforce the sense of therapy as a cultural endeavour, a *cultural form* that interacts and exists alongside the many other modes of personal self-expression available to members of a culture.

But what does it imply to suggest that psychotherapy is a 'cultural form'? The concept of 'cultural form' has a number of overlapping meanings. First, it means that an activity has become taken-for-granted and widely distributed within a particular social group. It has become part of 'common sense'. Second, the activity is understood and has a distinctive 'script' within that culture. Third, a cultural form comprises not just a 'script for action' but also a set of concepts, beliefs or ideas. Users of Western psychotherapy can draw on a rich and sophisticated set of ideas to explain 'change', 'development', 'personality' and other relevant factors. Fourth, a cultural form is institutionalised, it happens in particular places, and those who control it are in some way licensed to do so. Finally, any cultural form inhabits a cultural space in which it overlaps with some cultural practices but is remote from others. So, for instance, psychotherapy is culturally positioned close to health care, education and religion. Although there are clearly many differences between psychotherapy, health care, education and religion, these cultural forms can be seen to share certain ideas, techniques and personnel. By contrast, psychotherapy is culturally more distant from sport, leisure and advertising, and a long way indeed from such cultural activities as politics, finance and farming.

What are cultural forms *for*? Cultural forms are embedded within broader cultural systems, and therefore participate in, or are open to, all of the purposes that operate within that culture. In other words, any cultural form can be a site for debates over economics (who makes money?), or power (who is in control?), or gender relations (are women given equal rights?), or values (is what happens fair?). Although psychotherapy as a cultural form appears to exist in order to help people troubled by psychological or interpersonal difficulties, it also exists to make money, to enable power to be exerted by particular groups, to express conformity or resistance to gender stereotypes, and so on. Looking at psychotherapy from a cultural perspective involves taking into consideration all of these different aspects of the phenomenon. From a cultural perspective, understanding therapy is an interdisciplinary task, requiring the application of insights from not only psychology, but also history, economics, theology, philosophy, sociology and other intellectual disciplines.

But what is the substance of therapy as a cultural form? Where can therapy be located within the huge, complex culture of modern society? The preceding discussion of cultural factors involved in the establishment of psychotherapy as an activity and profession in late twentieth-century society makes it possible to begin to extract some of the core cultural elements that underpin its success. These cultural elements can be briefly described as:

1 *A legitimacy based on science.* Unlike, for example, social work, psychotherapy has always claimed that its concepts and procedures are validated by rational scientific research and theory. At a personal level, however, many therapists strive to retain links with the non-scientific realms of religion and the humanities. This attempt to straddle the domains of both faith and science (Halmos, 1965) is undoubtedly uncomfortable, but represents a well-adapted survival strategy in a culture in which these forces are often experienced as conflicting. It also provides a creative tension that has been responsible for the continuing innovativeness and openness characteristic of much therapeutic writing. Therapy can be seen as offering a public face that is rational and scientific, while at the same time covertly supporting an 'underground' stream that is spiritual and non-rational.

2 *Drawing on the cultural resonance and power of medicine.* Although there have been strong voices in therapy opposing the medical model, the practice rather than rhetoric of counselling and psychotherapy betrays a great debt to medicine. Examples might include the use of the time-limited office appointment, close links with medical agencies, and the prevalence of the 'drug metaphor' in research (Stiles and Shapiro, 1989). The alliance with medicine has great financial benefits: one expects to pay for 'treatment' but not for conversation. The link with medicine also reinforces the perception of therapy as an enterprise based on sound scientific principles.

3 *Reinforcing cultural trends in the direction of individualism.* The examples discussed earlier suggest that in many places, and in this culture in earlier times, the problems of the individual were dealt with in a collective manner by the whole community. Contemporary therapeutic practice, with the partial exception of family therapy, clearly does not operate in this manner. The person is viewed as a discrete, separate and autonomous individual. The importance of the concept of privacy in therapy is further evidence of the significance of individualism. Counselling or psychotherapy is a private act, carried out in an enclosed, private space, available to groups of people who expect and can afford privacy in their lives.

4 *Becoming a specialist product.* The centrality of market economics as an ideological force in current culture has been reflected in the powerful movement in therapy to become more highly professionalised and marketable as a product within its own distinctive niche. Despite the values of

egalitarianism and empowerment espoused by many humanistic and radical therapists, and the existence of self-help therapies and attempts to
'give psychology away' (Miller, 1969), therapy is becoming more and more
a service offered by a trained, accredited and certificated professional
expert in an office, approachable only through a receptionist. Far from
being 'given away', therapy is actively marketed, promoted and sold.

5   *The denial of morality.* The privacy of the therapy hour is accompanied
by a retreat from engagement in public moral debate. Many writers on
modern culture have drawn attention to the erosion of public spaces in
which moral debate can take place, and the trivialisation of the moral
debate that still exists through 'soundbites' and other types of distorted or
sensationalised media coverage of moral issues. The decline in moral discourse can probably be attributed to the lack, in most Western societies, of
a cohesive set of religious beliefs or other traditions (MacIntyre, 1981)
within which moral argument can take place. Therapists are meant to be
morally neutral. Science is supposed to be 'value-free', and a counsellor or
psychotherapist is an applied scientist. Most therapists work hard to create and maintain a therapeutic 'frame' that is morally neutral, into which
their own beliefs and values do not intrude. Their intention in doing this
is to enable the client to arrive at his or her own moral judgements.

Psychotherapy as a cultural form reflects some of the major themes and tensions in contemporary society. The essentially *private* nature of most
psychotherapeutic transactions is the key to understanding its cultural significance. Partly, this concern for privacy goes hand in hand with a concept of
self as something layered, with an external, somewhat 'false' shell concealing
or protecting an inner core that is construed as dangerous, violent and sexual
(psychoanalysis) or loving, sensitive and creative (humanistic psychology).
This way of making sense of the self implies that the person needs a very safe,
private space to enable the inner, 'true' self to emerge. The privacy of therapy
is also associated with the social conditions under which therapy can thrive.
A society needs to be wealthy enough to afford spaces for privacy, and to support the kind of social mobility and urban anonymity that makes
confidentiality possible.

Psychotherapy is a cultural form or arena in which people are given permission to tell their personal stories of troubles, in the presence and with the
assistance of another person with special skills and status in relation to this
task. To this extent, therapy is similar to the examples of traditional, religion-
based healing discussed earlier. However, the story told by the therapy client
becomes constructed in a particular fashion. It is to a large extent stripped of
its social and cultural context and moral content, and used instead as the
basis for identifying 'underlying' pathological structures existing within the
individual. The therapy that is on offer in the late twentieth century is a
reflection of the times: the person is a mechanism to be fixed, an individual
unit, a consumer, a stranger, a statistic. Here is the paradox of modern therapy. For many people, the therapy room offers the only place where they can

be truly heard, where they can tell their story and be accepted. This is what makes therapy such a powerful element of modern life, such an attractive product. Yet, for the most part, the telling of the story does not work in the way that it did in the past, it does not function to re-integrate the person into a somehow bigger, shared narrative that binds together the members of a culture. There is a gap between what the 'mental health industry' (Kovel, 1981) promises, and what it can deliver. As the structures and forms of life of modernity become more transparent and open to question and revision, this gap has become more visible.

Psychotherapy from a postmodern perspective

The nature and cultural position of therapy is beginning to shift, as part of a broader movement toward postmodern forms of practice. Earlier in this chapter, some of the key characteristics of postmodernism were identified: globalisation, reflexivity, the replacement of 'grand narratives' by 'local knowledges'. There are many trends within contemporary psychotherapy that are consistent with this set of ideas. For example, one of the most striking developments within counselling and psychotherapy has been the erosion of the influence of the major schools of therapy and their gradual replacement by an eclecticism or integrationism in which individual or small groups of practitioners assemble concepts and techniques into their own personal *bricolage*, thereby creating a set of interlocking local knowledges rather than a 'universal' theory. Behind this tendency is a commitment to pluralism: there is no fixed 'truth'. Moreover, clients just as much as therapists have recourse to a range of therapy narratives. The ideas of Freud, Jung, Rogers, Skinner (and Skynner) and many others now permeate everyday discourse, undermining the sense of the therapist as the modern, expert technician. Finally, the colonialism of mainstream psychotherapy is increasingly challenged by voices from other cultures, and from traditions previously submerged within the dominant culture. Having worked hard to establish itself as a rational, research-based discipline, worthy of a place in the academy, therapy is now finding that many of the most exciting new developments are in areas where therapy practice has been transformed by the addition of new ideas from feminism, political activism, religion and spiritual practice, and indigenous healing ritual.

The notion of a *profession*, an occupational group licensed by the State to exert a monopoly over a sector of human service (such as medicine or law), is a thoroughly modern concept. The institutionalisation, through legislation, of craft and guild activities into professions has been one of the driving forces of the modern project. Psychotherapy and counselling are late professions, having joined the club toward the end of the modern era at a point where the strength of professional control over key areas of life is chipped away by political and economic pressure and by increased consumer participation and choice.

Psychotherapy is also increasingly reflecting the contemporary awareness that the good life cannot be constructed within a moral vacuum. Morality, banished from the early 'psychotherapy' of the Emmanuel movement and other nineteenth-century religious groups, is edging back into therapy discourse. In recent years, there appears to have been a greater readiness to acknowledge the moral dimension of psychotherapy (Sugarman and Martin, 1995). In part, this change has come from the growing influence of feminist approaches to therapy, which are grounded in an explicit political stance and set of values. From a different direction, other theorists and practitioners have been exploring the relationship between psychotherapy and various systems of religious belief. Yet others have been evolving an avowedly radical or 'critical' perspective on therapy (Cushman, 1995).

The radical relativism associated with much late twentieth-century thought, the sense that we inhabit a constructed world, is implicit in the concept of therapeutic *metanarrative* recently introduced by Omer and Strenger (1992). They suggest that the theory of therapy espoused by a therapist acts as a kind of general or overarching story through which the client learns to frame his or her life narrative. Every reflection or interpretation made by a therapist acts as a vehicle for the therapist to communicate, bit by bit, a story of what life is about. Schafer has summarised some of the more widely used psychoanalytic therapy metanarratives:

> *Freud's 'Darwinist' story*: Begins with the infant and young child as a beast, otherwise known as the id, and ends with the beast domesticated, tamed by frustration in the course of development in a civilization hostile to its nature.
>
> *Freud's 'Newtonian' story*: [The mind is a] machine characterized by inertia; it does not work unless it is moved by force. It works as a closed system; that is, its amount of energy is fixed, with the result that storing or expending energy in one respect decreases the energy available for other operations: thus on purely quantitative grounds, love of others limits what is available for self-love, and love of the opposite sex limits what is available for love of the same sex. The machine has mechanisms, such as automatically operating mechanisms of defence and various other checks and balances.
>
> *Melanie Klein's story*: The child or adult [is] in some stage of recovery from a rageful infantile psychosis at the breast . . . our lives begin in madness, which includes taking in the madness of others, and we continue to be more or less mad though we may be helped by fortuitous cicumstances or by analysis.
>
> *Kohut's story*: Tells of a child driven in almost instinctlike fashion to actualize a cohesive self. The child is more or less hampered or damaged in the process by the empathic failures of caretakers in its intimate environment. Its growth efforts are consequently impeded by reactive and consoling grandiose fantasies, defensive splitting and repression, and affective 'disintegration products' . . . bits and pieces of the shattered self striving to protect itself, heal itself, and continue its growth. (Schafer, 1980: 30–5)

What Schafer is getting at here is asking 'what was Freud doing?' Was Freud constructing a scientifically based theory? Or was he promoting a particular type of story about what it means to be human? And it can be seen that there can be many variations on each of these stories. For example, a follower of Winnicott or Langs would have his or her own version of the psychoanalytic story. Nevertheless, each therapist has a story to tell about how life should be lived, and cannot help but convey this story to clients. As Schafer points out, some psychotherapists, such as Freud himself, may espouse two (or more) interlocking metanarratives, reflecting different cultural themes that influence their work. Humphreys (1993) has argued that self-help groups also possess and disseminate metanarratives, the '12 steps' story of Alcoholics Anonymous being the best-known example. The concept of therapeutic metanarrative subtly edges therapy away from the domain of science: therapy theory is just another story.

These are, then, some glimpses of the impact of late/postmodernism on counselling and psychotherapy. The postmodern impulse is to deconstruct therapy, to strip away its claims to privileged scientific knowledge/power/certainty and to reveal the core of therapy as an arena for telling personal stories.

The transformation of storytelling

The cultural shifts that have been described, from traditional to modern to late/postmodern, have been associated with different forms of therapeutic healing. What we know as 'psychotherapy' is very much a product of modernity. However, it seems to me that to understand the changing nature of therapy it is not sufficient merely to place it in a historical and cultural context. If therapy is a form of storytelling, an occasion for the client/patient to be the author and narrator of the story of his or her life, then it is necessary to consider how the experience of storytelling has itself evolved and been transformed during this period of time. What I am suggesting here is that what happens in therapy can be regarded as a reflection of much broader cultural changes in the way that people participate in a 'storied world'. Social change and technology have fundamentally altered the ways that stories are told and heard.

The study of historical change in making and telling stories is clearly an immense topic. Table 1.2 offers a summary of some of the more significant contrasts between the ways that stories have been used in the three cultural eras under consideration. What is perhaps most striking is the extent to which therapy as a form of storytelling displays many of the features of that other distinctively modern narrative form, the novel. Like novels, therapy stories are often concerned with the attempts of a singular hero/self to find meaning and fulfilment in the face of restrictive social conditions. Novels and therapy stories are also typically constructed around a linear time-frame, making connections between past and present within the span of an individual life. Novels, like therapy sessions, are like little cultural modules that can be purchased and slotted into a life for some period of time, then discarded. Finally, the novelist, like the therapist, is in the position of a privileged narrator, enjoying an omniscient 'God's eye' view of events.

Table 1.2 *Storytelling in traditional, modern and postmodern periods*

Traditional	Modern	Postmodern
Oral culture	Literary, print culture	Television and Internet culture
Participatory, communal storytelling	Passive, individualised story-reading	Possibilities of pseudo-interaction with electronic media; revival of oral tradition
Narrative embedded in a collective moral–religious framework	Narrative located in secularised everyday reality	Globalised everyday reality
Relatively limited stock of mythic/religious stories	Wide range of stories available	Seemingly limitless narrative choice
Heroic themes	Romantic themes – ordinary person as hero	Ironic themes – rejection of possibility of hero
Circular, repetitive story structure: use of musicality and poetry	Linear, logical story structure (e.g. detective novel)	Disruption, experimentation and deconstruction in relation to narrative structures
Stories embedded in a culture	Stories explore cultural difference, but characterise other cultures as dangerous or primitive	Celebration and assimilation of stories from other cultures
Personal or family problem stories shared in community arena	Problem stories told in confidence to one other person	More public disclosure of problem stories: testimony, survivors speak out, Oprah Winfrey show
Problem stories understood in moral–religious terms	Problem stories conceptualised in scientific terms	Range of different ways of making sense of problem stories
Narrative unity and coherence sought at communal level	Narrative unity and coherence sought at individual level	Questioning of possibility of narrative unity

By contrast, storytelling in traditional cultures has a quite different quality. Here, storytelling is characteristically a shared, communal experience. The same stories are carried through a life, heard again and again at different points in the life-course. Stories are transmitted by voice, with the effect that perhaps story and voice are to some extent merged in the remembering of the tale. Collective stories in traditional cultures, for example myths, are framed within a time-span that vastly transcends individual lives. Therapeutic or healing stories can only be told to some person or group whom the person has known and will continue to know: there are no anonymous strangers who can promise confidentiality.

And now, at the edges of the culture of modernity, the way stories are told reveals further differences. Film and television genres disrupt linear time-frames: the idea of the 'flashback' developed from cinema. Tellers of stories and their audiences are often well capable of deconstructing the story that is being told; stories are permeated by reflexivity and irony. At the same time there is a basic separation of storyteller and audience. Mythic stories are no longer mutual experiences where the audience can 'join in'. Contemporary mythic stories are relayed by CNN and viewed by millions. And the story is told less by the word than by the image. The modes of telling therapeutic or healing stories in contemporary culture have been influenced by all this. Therapy is becoming globalised, with therapists all over the world delivering the same standardised interventions gleaned from the same treatment manual. But at the same time the consumer of therapy has become much more sophisticated, and is able to deconstruct both his or her story, and that of the therapist, in what can become almost a parallel reflexive commentary on the 'therapy' itself.

Conclusion: narrative and the cultural foundations of psychotherapy

An understanding of the positioning of psychotherapy in contemporary culture brings into focus some important implications. The first of these is that psychotherapy is not and cannot be a *universal* human enterprise. Certainly, it can be demonstrated that in all human societies people experience 'problems in living' that are dealt with through a combination of listening, re-framing, catharsis, interpretation and behaviour change (Frank, 1973). Nevertheless, there is no escape from the fact that the activities that we know as counselling and psychotherapy are the indigenous remedies of people in Judaeo-Christian urban industrial societies: therapy is part of Western indigenous psychology. There are many cultures in which therapy as we know it has never taken hold or has had only a marginal impact.

A cultural perspective on psychotherapy highlights the paradoxical relationship between individual change and social cohesion. This is a paradox which many therapists acknowledge, but few successfully resolve. For an individual client, psychotherapy may be of immense value, while at the same time contributing to the erosion of community or social cohesiveness. For example, a student oppressed by examinations and uninterested tutors is helped to survive his course through the efforts of a college counsellor. How often is the anger or betrayal felt by such a student fed back into the political process of the university? Cushman puts it in this way:

> The patient is diagnosed as empty and fragmented, usually without addressing the sociohistorical predicament that caused the emptiness and fragmentation . . . thus, through the activity of helping, psychology's discourse and practices perpetuate the causes of the very problems it is trying to treat. (1990: 600)

What Cushman identifies here as the 'sociohistorical predicament' is not that different from the heroic 'debt', 'fate' and 'liability' that MacIntyre (1981) saw in the lives of people in medieval society. But, whereas a person in a traditional culture would attempt to make sense of whatever the 'problem' was by placing it in a narrative that went far beyond the bounds of the individual to encompass ancestors and the very origins of the clan, a modern person would do no such thing. In the modern narrative of the self, the 'problem' is located within the structure of the individual personality, as if the individual could be regarded as a microcosm of the world.

The longing to understand the past that fuels modern therapies such as psychoanalysis is also clearly visible in traditional healing practices and religions, but in the latter the past is defined as the history of the community as communicated through myth and story. In modernity, individuals have little access to an orally transmitted past beyond the details of the lives of their grandparents (McKay, 1993). The personally known past is therefore restricted to a personal history located within a vague family history. Beyond that, there is only official, written-down generalised history provided by the authorities. Many people in the modern world have experienced the consequences of losses due to war, migration, social change within recent generations. They may have lost a way of life, a place, a culture. Therapy does not deal with these issues: the past begins in childhood.

Thinking about the cultural evolution of counselling forces us to take the long view. Therapy has only been around for 50 years or so. The pace of social change seems to be becoming more and more rapid. Right now, counsellors and psychotherapists have consolidated around a well-defined professional identity, and have claimed a niche within the helping professions and medicine. But what will therapy be like in another 50 years? Can we be sure that the therapeutic stories that serve us well now will be equally relevant throughout that period of time?

Therapy is one of the ways in which a culture keeps itself in existence as a system of thought and action. It is also a means by which individual members of that culture engage with the question of what it means to be a person at the specific time and place in history in which they find themselves. The main mode of operation of therapy is through the telling of stories. Clients or patients come in and, one way or another, tell their story and discover or construct new stories to tell. Therapists do not usually disclose stories of their own personal troubles, but instead offer their clients more general, almost mythic, stories of how people change or what life can be like. Implicit in the therapist's story is an image of the 'good life'. Narratives of fulfilment, self-improvement and self-management are, of course, everywhere: movies, novels, advertising hoardings, glossy magazine questionnaires. But what better way to seed these stories deep in the cultural soil than by giving people opportunities to acquire these stories through intimate conversations in which they can try out therapeutic narratives, versions of the good life, as templates for their own lives?

Recognising the cultural foundations of therapy shifts the focus of attention. The therapeutic encounter is no longer merely 'treatment', but can be seen as a conversational and narrative event, one of the many types of storytelling performance arenas available to members of a culture. Understanding therapy in this way requires a brutal shift in perspective for many people trained in the methods and assumptions of modern psychotherapy, a shift from *internal* to *external*. The philosopher Alasdair MacIntyre takes the view that a person is 'essentially a story-telling animal'. He wrote that 'I can only answer the question "What am I to do?" if I can answer the prior question "Of what story or stories do I find myself a part?"' (MacIntyre, 1981: 216). The stories that, for the most part, construct our lives are 'out there', they exist before we are born and continue after we die. The task of being a person in a culture involves creating a satisfactory-enough alignment between individual experience and 'the story of which I find myself a part'. The job of the therapist is to help the person to do this, particularly at times of crisis or conflict when the alignment has been lost. A narrative perspective inevitably takes therapy in the direction that Lynch describes as 'moving out' into the stories of a culture rather than 'moving in' to individual personal experience: 'the therapeutic process as an outer journey into the language and symbols of a particular culture' (1996: 7).

In recent years, many therapists have started to become interested in narrative and storytelling as ideas that allow them to make sense of what happens in therapy. Chapters 3, 4 and 5 in this book review the ways in which therapists have employed narrative concepts. However, it seems to me that the majority of therapists using narrative have only the most limited appreciation of the implications of what they are doing, in terms of the multiple meanings associated with the concept of narrative. It seems useful, therefore, to take the opportunity to look more closely at the nature of narrative and storytelling. What is a story? What is happening when someone tells a story? These issues are examined in the next chapter.

2

Narrative Knowing: The Nature and Function of Storytelling in Therapy

The aim of this chapter is to examine in more detail the nature of narrative and storytelling. In the previous chapter, it was argued that the emergence of the modern world, with its emphasis on science, rationality and order, had the effect of diminishing the legitimacy of personal storytelling as a way of communicating. In modern life, much of the important information about a person is represented in an abstract form, in numbers. From a historical perspective, therapy can be regarded as a rearguard action against the erosion of opportunities to tell personal stories. The therapist is a person who is guaranteed to listen to whatever story the client will tell, will believe the client's stories, will take them seriously. But what is a story? What does it mean to tell a story? What is happening when people tell stories? To appreciate the significance of stories for therapy, it is necessary to understand the unique richness of storytelling as a way of knowing.

The psychologist Jerome Bruner is the writer who has perhaps done most to draw attention to the gap between the kind of knowledge of the world that can be gained through stories, and that obtained through science. Bruner has had a long and distinguished career as a theorist and researcher in the USA and Britain, making significant contributions in the fields of social psychology (Smith et al., 1956), developmental psychology (Bruner, 1983) and cognitive science (Bruner et al., 1956). He is perhaps best known for his efforts to integrate the biological–structuralist developmental theories of Piaget with the more explicitly socially based ideas of the Russian psychologist Lev Vygotsky. In recent years, however, Bruner has returned to a theme that permeates the whole corpus of his work, that of constructing a 'cultural psychology'.

At the heart of Bruner's notion of a cultural psychology is his distinction between *paradigmatic* and *narrative* knowing. Paradigmatic knowing is rooted in scientific modes of thought, and represents the world through abstract propositional knowledge. Narrative knowing, by contrast, is organised through the stories that people recount about their experiences. For Bruner, although both narrative and paradigmatic ways of knowing are essential facets of the human capacity to make sense of the world, relatively little is understood about the narrative mode. In attempting to be scientific, psychologists and other researchers have focused almost entirely on paradigmatic, propositional knowledge, and have dismissed narrative knowing as irrational, vague, irrelevant and somehow not legitimate.

The decline of narrative knowing

Communication through telling stories is a basic human activity. The Bible and other religious texts consist of sets of stories that teach moral lessons. The values and sense of identity of social groups have always been transmitted from generation to generation through legends and myths. At an everyday level, we are surrounded by stories: gossip, news reports, novels, cinema, TV soaps.

One of the distinctive features of the modern world, however, has been the tendency to ignore and diminish the significance of stories. We can easily recognise the entertainment value of stories, but we do not take them *seriously*. In our culture, stories are generally regarded as *fiction*. In other words, a story may be fascinating or enthralling, but there is always a question over whether it is *true*, or whether it is 'only a story'. Not knowing whether to believe a story is truth or fiction makes it difficult to act on the information conveyed by the story.

In the modern world, characterised by urbanised industrial societies, it is only scientific knowledge that can claim to be true, and can therefore serve as the basis for reasonable action. The growth of science and technology over the last 200 years has been associated with a gradual loss in legitimacy of stories as a way of communicating truths about the world, to be replaced by a belief in the validity of scientific procedures as means of arriving at reliable and accurate knowledge.

It is not difficult to understand why this has happened. Science and technology have made huge contributions toward giving people control over the physical world. There has been the promise, if not always the reality, that scientific advances will improve the quality of life. Science has produced, in fields such as medicine, transport and communications, technological inventions that seemed like new 'wonders of the world' to those who had grown up without them: radio, contraceptive pills, a photograph of planet Earth, a supermarket.

To participate in a scientific world we have all had to learn to think and communicate scientifically; we have needed to be socialised into a realm of abstract propositional knowledge. Think about what is involved in carrying out a scientific/technical task such as designing and manufacturing a car. To design the engine block, for example, requires being able to think about abstract entities such as 'volume', 'weight', 'density', 'tensile strength' and 'heat'. These variables are related to each other in complex formulae. The formulae enable the designer to *predict* how a particular type of engine block will perform under specific conditions. There are procedures for measuring each variable, and thus testing the exact truth of formulae or models.

Scientific ways of knowing are familiar and taken for granted by most members of modern societies. Yet scientific knowing relies on a set of distinctive assumptions and procedures. First, there is no need to take social context into account. It can be assumed that the relation between heat and metallic structure in an engine block design, once established, is universally true at all times and places. The formula will not change, will not depend on who runs the experiment. Scientific statements are abstract, general truths, describing the associations between variables rather than describing any one specific object or example. Second, scientific knowledge is not communicated in ordinary, everyday language, but is formulated through sets of propositional statements such as 'if x, then y', or 'a + b = c'. Third, there is no ambiguity in scientific propositions, or as little ambiguity as possible. The aim is to predict with a high degree of certainty what will happen. You want to know that the engine block will not blow up after the first 1,000 miles.

So, scientific thinking is abstract, impersonal, free of social context, logical and predictive. A story, by contrast, is a form of thinking and communication that recounts some concrete event that has already happened. A story is contextualised in a social world known to teller and audience. Stories convey intention and feeling. Stories are essentially grounded in oral culture; scientific thinking depends on the existence of writing and print (Ong, 1982). The design of an engine block can be expressed in a set of scientific formulae. The members of the design team will have their own stories to tell about how they arrived at these formulae.

The rediscovery of narrative

Scientific thinking seems to work well for designing engine blocks and other technological wonders. But does it work so well when applied to human affairs? What happens when we think scientifically about ourselves, our relationships, the societies we have created? This is perhaps the central issue that has dominated social science and psychology since these disciplines emerged in the late nineteenth century. It is also a question that is critically important to the practice of psychotherapy. In psychotherapy, the client tells stories about himself or herself, while the therapist employs supposedly scientifically based theories and interventions in order to facilitate change.

Psychology as an organised body of knowledge is founded on scientific, propositional knowledge. Psychotherapy, an area of practice that draws heavily from psychology, has also attempted to ground itself in this type of knowledge. An increasing number of critics (Gergen, 1985; Mair, 1989a; Rennie, 1994b; Shotter, 1975) argue that there are severe limitations in the extent to which ideas and methods of natural science are appropriate to the study of people. But how else can we develop a reliable understanding of how people act and feel? The answer that has begun to emerge is a sense that an appreciation of people as active social beings requires attention to the way personal and cultural realities are constructed through narrative and storytelling.

The 'narrative turn' in psychology and social science gained pace and momentum in the 1970s and 1980s. A chronology of the main contributions to this field can be found in Table 2.1. It can be seen that the earliest writings focused on general philosophical issues, and only more recently has 'narratology' been applied to more practical areas such as education, research method and psychotherapy. While it is certainly true that the literature of narrative perspectives in psychology and social science has been influenced by, and indeed has been part of, a more general impetus toward postmodern forms of social analysis, there is also perhaps a more mundane explanation for the growth of interest in narrative and storytelling. Social scientists began to become aware of what was staring them in the face – that people structure experience through stories.

Table 2.1   *The development of a narrative approach: some key texts*

Philosophy
Wiggins, J. B. (ed.) (1975) *Religion as Story* MacIntyre, A. (1981) *After Virtue: A Study in Moral Theory* Polkinghorne, D.E. (1988) *Narrative Knowing and the Human Sciences*
Psychology
McAdams, D.P. (1985) *Power, Intimacy, and the Life Story: Personological Inquiries into Identity* Bruner, J.S. (1986) *Actual Minds, Possible Worlds* Sarbin, T.R. (ed.) (1986) *Narrative Psychology: The Storied Nature of Human Conduct*
Linguistics
Labov, W. and Waletzky, J. (1967) 'Narrative analysis: oral versions of personal experience' Polanyi, L. (1982) 'Linguistic and social constraints on storytelling' Gee, J.P. (1986) 'Units in the production of narrative discourse'
Other social science disciplines
Mishler, E.G. (1986) *Research Interviewing: Context and Narrative* Kleinman, A. (1988) *The Illness Narratives: Suffering, Healing and the Human Condition* Birren, J.E. et al. (eds) (1996) *Aging and Biography: Explorations in Adult Development*
Psychotherapy
Schafer, R. (1980) 'Narration in the psychoanalytic dialogue' Spence, D.P. (1982) *Narrative Truth and Historical Truth: Meaning and Interpretation in Psychoanalysis* White, M. and Epston, D. (1990) *Narrative Means to Therapeutic Ends* *Journal of Constructivist Psychology, Journal of Cognitive Psychotherapy* – special issues on narrative approaches, 1994

The phenomenology of narrative

In beginning to gain a sense of what is involved in making and using stories, it is perhaps valuable to start by examining some of the ways that this form of communication is experienced – the *phenomenology* of narrative. One of the immediate distinctions that can be made is that between stories and narratives. A story is an account of a specific event. Much of the time, however, stories are linked together, so that between separate stories are linking passages that reflect on the stories, categorise them, comment on their veracity and so on. The term 'narrative', then, is more loosely defined than the term 'story'. A 'narrative' is a story-based account of happenings, but contains within it other forms of communication in addition to stories. The word 'story' is much more widely employed in common usage than the word 'narrative', because a 'story' is a more accessible, immediately graspable entity that people deal with at an everyday level. The idea of 'narrative' is more often found in academic discourse. However, the ordinary-language notion of 'narrator' captures some of the meaning of 'narrative'. A narrator tells a story, but in doing so offers something over and above the bare story, for example asides, or by announcing 'the end'.

There is a variety of ways that stories are marked out in ongoing conversation or writing as comprising discrete, bounded communicational units (see, for example, Young, 1986). The experience of participating in a story, as teller or audience, is typically that of being caught up in it while it is being told. This phenomenon is perhaps most obvious in situations where, for example, a skilled storyteller might be recounting a story to a group of children, who would be 'lost' in the story, or 'spellbound'. The same sort of thing happens in all storytelling events. It is as though the human capacity for reflexivity, of being able not only to experience something but to monitor that experience and reflect on what it might mean, is largely suspended when a story is being told. Too much reflection during the story will break the 'spell', and either teller or hearer will 'lose the thread' and the story will break down. Reflection is usually carried out after a story is finished.

A final aspect of the phenomenology of stories is that they are *structured*. There appears to be a pattern or template into which all stories must fit, with the consequence that violations of this pattern are experienced as strange or incomplete. At its simplest, the notion of story structure can be understood as signifying not much more than that a story has a beginning, a middle and an end. However, several writers have suggested that 'good' or 'well-formed' stories tend to share a rather more complex structure or 'story grammar' (for example, Stein and Glenn, 1979; Labov and Waletzky, 1967).

An examination of the phenomenology of stories reveals the existence of stories as marked-off units, the spontaneity and relative unreflectiveness of the storytelling process, and the existence of a story 'grammar' that few people could explicitly identify but that everyone intuitively uses. All of these features tend to suggest that the 'story' is a basic building-block of human communication. This insight is reinforced by research into the development of narrative competence in childhood.

Acquiring the ability to tell stories

The capacity to narrate arrives early, almost as soon as the child acquires the use of language. Bruner and a group of his colleagues (Bruner and Lucariello, 1989; Feldman, 1989) carried out a fascinating study of the language development of a little girl, Emily, between the ages of 22 and 36 months. Their method was to place a tape recorder in her bedroom in order to capture what she said when she talked to herself as she went to sleep each evening. Many of Emily's monologues could be clearly identified as stories, and over the period of the study these stories became better structured and more complex. She appeared to be using narrative both to 're-create' her world and to solve problems. The research carried out by Trevarthen (1995) has focused on the first year of life, when the child does not use language as such, but communicates with caretakers using a rich repertoire of sound and movement. These studies have mainly involved analysis of video recordings of mother–infant interaction. Trevarthen observes that the communication between a baby and (usually) his or her mother possesses a narrative quality. The mother will perform dance, movement and song with the baby, for example clapping songs, drawing on traditional rhymes but also adapting contemporary popular music. Trevarthen suggests that the way that the mother intuitively plays with music and poetry in this way helps to build up an understanding of, and capacity to use, the basic *structure* of storytelling:

> . . . micro-analysis of videos reveals that the mother's performances not only excite the interest and emotions of the infant, who watches eagerly, anticipates with 'dread' and laughs with joy at appropriate places. They also give the infant a rhythmic 'story' to learn, with introduction, build-up, climax and resolution. (1995: 10)

Trevarthen makes the point that, in his view, narrative competence emerges from the 'innate musicality' of infants, and he recommends that there is a strong case for shared musical experience to be given priority in pre-school education. The relationship between storytelling and associated forms of self-expression and communication such as poetry and music will be discussed in later chapters, in the context of therapy. Here we may note how fundamental music, song and poetry are to the development of the child, and how early in life they emerge.

The story as a model of the world

J.S. Bruner (1986, 1990, 1991) has attempted to identify the core features of storytelling as a way of conveying meaning. The key question for Bruner is to understand how a story 'operates as an instrument of mind in the construction of reality' (1991: 6). We are all intuitively aware of what makes a good story. We construct stories spontaneously and without much reflection. Nevertheless, within this apparent simplicity there are a number of processes occurring that enable the story to communicate meaning at a number of different levels. Bruner in fact suggests that there are certain key features of narrative as a form of representing the world, such as the capacity to order experience in sequences. These features are specified in fairly technical terms in Bruner (1991) and discussed in a more accessible form in Bruner (1990). The account of Bruner's ideas offered here simplifies his complex and wide-ranging exploration of these issues, and the reader is encouraged to refer to the original sources to gain a fuller appreciation of what is meant.

Sequentiality

A story consists of a sequence of events. Within the story there may be reference to several distinct actions or feeling states. Yet, as Bruner (1990: 43) puts it, 'these constituents do not . . . have a life or meaning of their own'. The meaning of each event is given by its place in the overall sequence or plot. To make sense of a story, then, the listener must extract the plot from these constituent elements. This aspect of narrative communicates a sense of experience as a process (every action is preceded by something, and leads on to something else). The sequentiality of the story as a form of communication carries a sense of 'nextness': each bit of the story, each segment of action or feeling, somehow points toward an emerging future. A sense of the history is also conveyed through any story. The sequentiality of the story implies a past that is becoming transformed into a future. As Neimeyer puts it:

> . . . narrative has both a historical dimension (in the sense of selectively recruiting past events, whether real or imagined) and an anticipatory thrust (in the sense of reaching toward a conclusion or end point that is posited with more or less clarity and conviction. (1994: 238)

Narrative is therefore the mode of communication and representation that best captures the experience of temporality, of living in time. Edward Bruner stresses this aspect of narrative in writing that:

> . . . narrative structure has an advantage over such related concepts as metaphor or paradigm in that narrative emphasises order and sequence . . . stories give meaning to the present and enable us to see that present as part of a set of relationships involving a constituted past and a future. (1986: 153)

Accounting for departures from the ordinary

There is a basic difference between experiences that are 'narrativised' or made into stories, and those that are not. Everyday life is mainly constituted of 'ordinary' events or 'taken for granted' routine experiences. On the whole, these events do not make 'good' or 'interesting' stories. Bruner suggests that stories are often told to manage or explain departures from the expectable or 'canonical' norm. For example, 'I went to the shop and bought a newspaper' is merely a description of a culturally expectable sequence of behaviour. However, 'I went to the shop to buy a newspaper and the shop was empty . . .' becomes the basis for a story about what I did next, how it all ended and so on. 'Buying the newspaper' needs no explanation. 'Entering an empty shop' violates an implicit cultural norm, and calls for some kind of explanation. The point here is that part of the meaning of any story arises from the tension created between the exceptional events that are being recounted, and the ordinary routines that have been breached. A story, then, relies on, and hints at, an implicit set of social or cultural rules, and each story that is told reinforces this shared set of rules. But the story is itself a means of problem-solving, of reconciling the tension between the exceptional and the expected.

Communicating subjectivity

A story imparts information about the inner world of the storyteller or the person(s) about whom the story is being told. A story is not just a chronicle of events over time, but will include statements about intentionality ('so I decided to . . .'), feeling states and beliefs. Bruner (1986: 25) uses the term 'subjectification' to describe this aspect of narrative: 'the depiction of reality not through an omniscient eye that views a timeless reality, but through the filter of the consciousness of protagonists in the story'. The story gives entry not only into a 'landscape of action' but also into a 'landscape of consciousness'. An important dimension of the meaning of a story therefore lies in what it has to say about the identity, intentions and feelings of the person telling it.

Ambiguity

Stories refer to specific, concrete events. Although general principles can be abstracted from a narrative (e.g. the 'moral' of the story), the convention of storytelling is that what is recounted has taken place at a particular time and place. However, these events may have actually happened, or they may be imaginary, or they may comprise a combination of the imaginary and the real. Bruner (1990: 52) points out that no language imposes sharp grammatical distinctions between true stories and imaginary ones; making the distinction between fact and fiction is no easy matter. To some extent, the factualness of a story may be signalled by indicators of the *genre* within which it can be categorised. The genre of illness-stories-told-to-the-doctor would signal not only a certain style of storytelling, but also communicate the idea that the information contained within the story was as close to straightforward fact as possible. On the other hand the genre of fairy stories strongly signals make-believe. Any story beginning with 'Once upon a time . . .' is received by competent members of Western cultures as fiction. It is necessary to note that marking a story as belonging to a particular genre conveys meaning over and above the claimed truth status of the narrative that is being delivered. For example, genre signals may indicate the relationship between teller and listener, and may impose constraints on the kinds of events that can be reported.

The ambiguity of stories is heightened by what J.S. Bruner (1986: 26) calls *subjunctivising* devices. The idea of subjunctivising refers to the introduction of implicit meanings within a story, of using the structure of a story to 'mean more than we say'. Frequently, the teller of a story will not directly describe what happened, but will recount events in a way that forces the reader/hearer to make presuppositions about what has happened. For instance, in the 'I went to the shop to buy a newspaper and it was empty . . .' story introduced earlier, the reader is led to the supposition that 'on every previous visit to the shop there was someone behind the counter', without any such statement being made explicit. Other common ways of phrasing this story, such as 'I had just planned to drop in to the shop to . . .' or 'I was keen to buy a paper . . .' introduce alternative means of making the meaning of a story more open-ended, of giving the listener more to 'fill in' with his or her presuppositions about what the teller might mean. The use of metaphor, as in 'I walked into the shop and it was like a bad dream . . .' introduces yet more opportunity for the opening out of multiple meanings. J.S. Bruner suggests that the use of these and other storytelling techniques reflect the fact that narratives are 'trafficking in human possibilities rather than in settled certainties' (1986: 28).

The fact that a storytelling event is itself a performance situated in a particular time and place contributes to the ambiguity of the story. The narrative that is told is always to a greater or lesser extent shaped by its audience. As the anthropologist Edward Bruner puts it:

> . . . narratives change, all stories are partial, all meanings incomplete. There is no fixed meaning in the past, for with each new telling the context varies, the audience differs, the story is modified, and [we] . . . discover new meanings. (1986: 153)

The existence of ambiguity as a fundamental property of stories has the effect of forcing the reader or listener to engage in an active process of meaning-making whenever a story is offered. There can be no one definitive 'reading' of a story. Different audiences will interpret a story differently according to their interests and point of view. This feature of narrative is very obvious in literary studies, where dozens of critical interpretations can be constructed in response to one novel. But it happens also in everyday storytelling, in which a listener may interrupt the teller to seek clarification, or may fail to get the 'point' of the story as intended by the teller. The experience of active engagement by the therapist in the story told by the client is perhaps better portrayed by Edelson (1993) than by anyone else.

Story-construction as problem-solving

A story can be seen as a particular way of representing experience, but it can also be a means of resolving dilemmas and tensions. There are a number of ways in which this may occur. As has already been discussed, one of the features that makes a story 'tellable' is associated with the mismatch between the exceptional and the ordinary. An experience in which something has happened that is unusual or notable is likely to be the basis for a story. Routine, predictable sequences of action do not make good stories. As Jerome Bruner puts it, the story provides a structure for accounting for such experiences: 'the function of a story is to find an intentional state that mitigates or at least makes comprehensible a deviation from a canonical cultural pattern' (1990: 49–50). An example of this process can be observed in the case of Carl, where a client describes the thing that is troubling him as 'not [being] able to tell my close friends . . . my feelings or express my feelings to them', and then goes on to tell a story, exemplifying this problem. It is worth noting that this particular story is basically a monologue, in which Carl himself is searching for a way of 'making comprehensible' the puzzle of why he can't tell his close friends his feelings. Toward the end of the storytelling sequence, he begins to move closer to a solution of this puzzle. He can see that, somehow, his difficulty in situations like this is exacerbated by a sense of being 'forced' by the other. This particular story was related by the client within the first minutes of therapy. A fuller analysis of it (and other stories told by this client) can be found in McLeod and Balamoutsou (1996):

Counsellor: Well, you can start wherever you want to, whatever thing you want to talk about.

Client: Well, I want to talk about, um, one problem I am struggling with for a long time. In some situations I am not able to tell my close friends . . . my feelings or express my feelings to them, because I think if I tell them what I feel like in this moment that might hurt them and they might not be my friends any longer. It's very uncomfortable to feel like that.

Counsellor: So, that . . . I can see that it's not a general thing. It's on particular occasions, you have strong feeling or emotion about something . . . and you feel that it would kind of drive them away.

Client: I can give you an example. Two weeks ago one of my friends called me from Holland. I am going back to Holland again in the middle of September and we decided to rent this flat together and share this flat together. Now, when I was in Holland I was talking to her and mentioning to her 'where can I find some work?' and 'I don't know where I can find work'. So I'm not quite sure where I can find work and what I can do. Then she mentioned she knows a person who was a teacher in a school. I am a teacher. Well, I was a teacher. I can ring this person and I can ask her if I could have some hours of teaching. And I said I can do that. Then I came back here and a couple of weeks ago she called me and asked me 'did you ring this person?' and I said 'no' and I have this feeling . . . eeerh . . . why can't she not let it happen in my way, to let it happen for myself? Why does she force me to do that? I couldn't say to her 'I really appreciate your concern but frankly I don't like, I don't think I will do that'. Because I have this fear that she might reject me then. So I didn't tell her that. I feel she forces me.

In co-constructed narratives, the listener or audience may feed their own alternative accounts into the story that emerges, or may seek clarification by asking questions. So, the act of telling a story makes available a communication structure that not only conveys a sense of a world of uncertainty and ambiguity, but also provides a means for reducing dissonance and re-establishing a sense of control and order, by assembling an account that becomes more complete or ordered through the process of being told.

Another way that stories may have a problem-solving function is through re-casting chaotic experiences into causal sequences, thereby helping the person to gain an understanding of how and why something happened. This kind of use of storytelling can be found in situations of danger or trauma. When a fire-fighter attends a major incident, for example, he or she will typically experience an intense, fast-moving 'slice' of the action. At the conclusion of the incident, members of the crew will be left with a range of problems to solve: 'where, how and why did the fire start?', 'why did that piece of the building collapse?', 'would there have been a different outcome if we had done things in a different way?', 'did I personally do the right thing at the right time?' These are very important questions for emergency services personnel personally and professionally committed to achieving high standards. Docherty (1989) has described the practice of 'jigsawing' in fire crews, where members of a fire-fighting team piece together their individual accounts of what happened in order to create a coherent story of the event.

Fire-fighters' stories are created around events that most people would consider extraordinary and unusual. However, everyone has experiences that are perplexing and somehow 'unfinished' until they can be told to someone else, written in a diary or in some other way 'narrativised'. Putting them in story form is an effective method of sorting out and making sense of what happened.

Re-telling stories is also a means of problem-solving. Each time the story is re-told the teller gains the opportunity to revisit that set of experiences, to assimilate into the narrative elements of experience that have hitherto remained unnamed or have not fitted into the sequence.

The social construction of narrative

Clearly, stories are told by one person to another. There is a teller and there is an audience of some kind. These are obvious points to make, but they are also important. As a way of knowing, narrative implies a *relational* world. A story exists in a space between teller and audience. It may be created by the teller, but is always created in relation to a particular audience, so it is as if to some extent the recipient(s) of the story draw it out of the teller. A story is a performance (Langellier, 1989). Even a story written alone, such as a novel, has an implied audience.

The most immediate social function of storytelling is to enable one person to be known by another. Telling a story is a way of telling someone else about yourself, of being open to receiving their empathic response (or not). The story of 'my problems' or 'my life' is a very direct way of being known. However, even an apparently externalised story, such as 'how the goalkeeper was sent off in the football match' conveys a great deal about the person telling it, in the way it is told, the feelings and values imputed to characters in the story, the 'moral' implied by the story, and through the very fact that the teller chose to recount *this* story.

Jerome Bruner has pointed out that stories are often told around areas of social conflict. Among the features that make a story memorable and entertaining are the suspense and tension generated by accounting for 'departures from the ordinary'. As a form of communication, a story is structured in such a way as to provide the possibility for reducing at least some aspects of the tension, by offering a 'resolution' or 'moral' that brings the exceptional back closer to the expected order of things, or by offering a prescription for action.

Stories also convey direct and indirect information about the social and cultural location of the teller. This is done in two ways. First, it is usual for the beginning of a story to situate the events in time and place (for example, 'it was when we were driving to the golf course, and the car broke down . . .'). This narrative device encodes within a story clues as to the social and cultural context of the speaker (for example, 'I play golf', 'I own a car'). However, there are other signs of social status and role that are conveyed by the style in which the story is told. In his studies of stories told by middle-class and working-class children, for example, Bernstein (1972) found that working-class children recounted events using a 'restricted code', giving relatively little explanatory information about the motives and roles of the people in their stories. Middle-class children, by contrast, employed an 'elaborated code' characterised by a greater frequency of explanatory data. Bernstein suggested that working-class children might be regarded as living in an environment in which it would be reasonable to take for granted that anyone they spoke to shared the same set of experiences and assumptions. Middle-class children, on the other hand, would have more exposure to a diversity of audiences who would not have access to this kind of direct intersubjective experience, and would need the teller to explicitly 'spell out' what he or she meant. Another stylistic factor that appears to be associated with social identity is the degree to which a story follows a linear form. People who have been successfully socialised through Western education tend to produce 'well-formed', logically structured stories, while those who have not may often tell episodic stories that go back and forward in time. Finally, voice quality and accent are powerful markers of social difference and place.

Stories convey meaning about the social context and identity of the teller and audience. However, stories also have an *effect* on that identity and context. For example, when a member of a group tells a story, he or she is asserting their right to be a member, and if the story is long, compelling and monopolises the conversational space, the story may have the result of establishing or maintaining the dominance of the speaker. Alternatively, if a person has habitually told personal stories around the theme of 'I am a failure', and then begins to recount tales of personal success and achievement, the new stories will have the effect of challenging the image of the person held by those around him or her, and may well produce change in the way they behave toward the teller. Someone who is associated with narratives of success is more likely to be invited to join projects and ventures than is someone who specialises in narratives of failure.

This idea of a story (or, indeed, any type of conversation) as not merely a form of representing information and experience, but as a form of social and interpersonal *action* has been highlighted in the work of philosophers such as Ludwig Wittgenstein and Kenneth Gergen. It is an idea that is crucially important for an understanding of storytelling in counselling and psychotherapy. The client telling a story is not only *reporting* on a set of events, but is at the same time *constructing* a social identity. Many therapy clients are socially isolated and lacking social support, and for them the very experience of telling, of being considered worthy enough to be heard, is a step in the direction of a new sense of who they are. The creation or discovery of fresh stories in therapy is not merely a matter of *insight*: these new stories are then used back in the everyday world to construct different patterns of relationship and feeling.

Perhaps the most significant social dimensions of narrative lies in the fact that we live in a 'storied world' (MacIntyre, 1981; Mair, 1989a, b; Sarbin, 1986). Membership of a family, a social group or a culture depends on knowing the stories that carry the traditions and values of that particular set of people. Each story that is constructed draws on a huge stock of pre-existing stories.

Communicating feeling and emotion through narrative

Stories can function by giving a means of contextualising or locating feelings
and emotions within a broader framework of meaning. Sarbin (1989a,b) argues
that there has been a tendency for emotions to be considered by psychologists
and other scientific observers as spontaneous automatic reactions that are
experienced as internalised in the physiology of the person's body. This way of
understanding emotion effectively *reifies* feeling: for example, anger or fear is
a 'thing', a 'lump', or 'it' inside. This way of looking at emotion is consistent
with the notion of an 'autonomous, bounded self' described in Chapter 1,
and also with the predilection for psychologists to seek to explain human
experience and action in terms of objectifiable, measurable, biological dimensions or variables. However, Sarbin points out that an analysis of the ways
that words and phrases describing emotion are *actually used* in everyday life
reveals that emotional states are usually located within narratives. Sarbin,
along with other writers on emotion such as Averill (1991), Baumeister et al.
(1995) and de Rivera (1991), starts from a position that persons are fundamentally social beings, and that 'emotion' must be viewed within a social
and interpersonal perspective.

Sarbin offers an example:

> Albert Jones, a steamfitter, was engaged in a heated quarrel with Donald Miller, a
> co-worker, over responsibility for a botched-up job. Employing Anglo-Saxon exple-
> tives, Miller pointedly insulted Jones with a well-rehearsed digital gesture. Without
> hesitation, Jones struck Miller on the head with a fourteen-inch pipe wrench. When
> Jones subsequently explained his actions to a police officer, he said, 'I just felt the
> anger surging up in me and I exploded.' (1989b: 188)

This case, taken from a police file, demonstrates how stories are used to
'emplot' emotions: passions are 'storied'. This particular event has been constructed as an 'anger' story, in which a difference of opinion leads to an
argument that leads to violence. 'Anger' is used to explain what happened.
More than this, within the context provided by a story, an emotion such as
anger supplies a moral justification for action. Sarbin writes that:

> . . . anger, grief, shame, exultation and jealousy are rhetorical acts intended to con-
> vince others or oneself of one's moral claims . . . in the service of preserving or
> enhancing one's moral identity. (1989b: 192–4)

So, in the Jones/Miller story, Jones is able to preserve his sense of himself as
a reasonable person, and his public reputation, by the rhetorical device of
attributing his violent conduct not to any general tendency to harm others or
moral weakness but to a situational and transient 'surging' and 'explosion'.

The suggestion here is not that that emotions do not exist, that people
pretend to have feelings for self-justificatory purposes (although this can
happen too). Emotions are real enough. What Sarbin is doing is to identify a
particular kind of relationship between emotion and narrative. If one of the
crucial dimensions of the sense of self is to be found in the emotions and feelings a person experiences, then what Sarbin is proposing is that these feelings
and emotions are not merely autonomous 'lumps' of experience. Nor, for

that matter, are emotions merely mediated by perception and cognition, as a theorist such as Lazarus (1984) might suggest. Emotions are connected to other roles and meanings in a person's life through the medium of the stories in which they are embedded.

The theory of emotion developed by de Rivera (1989, 1991; Lindsay-Hartz et al., 1995) illustrates the intrinsically 'storied' nature of emotion. Lindsay-Hartz, et al. characterise emotions as 'transformations of an individual's relationship to objects, persons or events in the world' (1995: 274). They suggest that an emotion comprises four distinct components. First, there is the 'situation', the way the individual interprets or construes a given event. Second, emotion involves 'transformation', represented by change in the person's way of being in the world, including his or her experience of their body, and sense of space and time. Third, an emotion implies an 'instruction', or impulse to act in a particular way. A simple example of an 'instruction' might be the pull to flee associated with feelings of fear, or the pull to be close to another that accompanies feelings of love. Finally, these three parts of an emotion, taken together, have a 'function' in terms of expressing, maintaining or preserving core values. In a series of research studies, de Rivera and his colleagues invited participants to describe experiences of emotions such as guilt, shame, anxiety or depression. An interviewer probed for detail, to facilitate as full an account of the emotion event as possible. The research team then constructed abstract, general descriptions of the different emotions, based on the interview material. These abstractions of the 'core meanings' of types of emotion were tested on further groups of research participants, who were asked to judge the extent to which the summary descriptions matched their own experience of the particular emotion, and also whether reading the summary descriptions triggered new insights for participants.

The summary descriptions of shame and guilt generated in the Lindsay-Hartz et al. (1995) study are reproduced in Tables 2.2 and 2.3. What is striking about these descriptions is not only their compellingness but their *narrative* quality. It is clear that to achieve a comprehensive statement of the experience of, for instance, 'feeling guilty', a person must eventually recount or construct a 'guilt story'. Any account of guilt merely in terms of a single element (for example, 'I felt bad about myself', or 'I just wished I had never asked him to do it') can, in comparison with a narrative account, offer only a partial and incomplete understanding.

The work of Scheibe (1986) on adventure exemplifies this kind of process in action. Scheibe does not consider specific emotions such as anger or grief, but examines instead the broader category of 'adventure' experiences. Behaviour experienced as 'adventurous' is associated with a wide variety of feeling states. Joy, delight, satisfaction, despair, frustration, sense of community and many other feelings are evoked by adventurous activities such as sport, gambling, bringing up children, war, business, crime and politics. Scheibe (1986: 131) asserts that 'people require adventures in order for satisfactory life stories to be constructed and maintained'. Different people may draw upon different sources of adventure. However, each type of adventure

Table 2.2   *Summary description of guilt*

Emotion component	Content
Situation	We experience this emotion when *there is a violation of the moral order for which we take responsibility with our conviction that we could and should have done otherwise and that there then would have been no violation.* A violation of the moral order involves something bad and wrong happening or involves us doing what we should not or not doing what we should. The moral order, consisting in part of particular moral values, is implicitly upheld by members of a community to which we belong, and we must uphold such values to belong to that community. Since we are responsible for the violation of the moral order. . .
Transformation	. . . when we are experiencing this emotion, our way of being in the world involves a dynamic tension. We feel like a bad person, yet know that while we did a bad thing, we are not really bad. We feel out of place and feel lost and alone, unconnected with other things or persons. We feel unsettled and not at peace. We may become stuck repeatedly thinking about our past actions or past events, unable to leave such thoughts behind, yet unable to come to terms with them in the present. In terms of our past actions, our motivations are clouded. We may not be entirely certain why we did a bad thing or what we actually did was wrong.
Function	Wanting *to uphold the moral order and be reconciled* with the community and be *forgiven*, and *believing that we have some control* over events. . .
Instruction	. . . we attempt *to set things right* and in some way repair the breach in the moral order.

Source: Lindsay-Hartz et al. 1995

Table 2.3   *Summary description of shame*

Emotion component	Content
Situation	We experience this emotion when, upon viewing ourselves *through the eyes of another, we realize that we are in fact who we do not want to be and that we cannot now be otherwise.* We usually try to avoid being who we do not want to be. Yet, we have somehow not avoided this, often because we have been unaware of the implications of our acts or have not understood something about ourselves that is now revealed to us.
Transformation	Being who we do not want to be, we *shrink* in relation to our previous image of ourselves and we are *exposed* before the other. As we shrink, a single characteristic or action seems to define the whole of who we are; we are worthless; and our view of the world may shrink to one small detail.
Function	Upholding our *ideals about who we want to be and maintaining our commitment to a social determination of who we are*. . .
Instruction	. . . we wish *to hide* in order *to get out* of the interpersonal realm and escape our painful exposure before the other.

Source: Lindsay-Hartz et al. 1995

gives the person a ready supply of stories through which to create an identity both in the form of an on-going self-narrative but also a narrative that is shared with, and co-constructed with, other people. Adventurous activities also furnish a reference group of others willing to listen to these stories, as in groups of anglers 'swapping' tales of fish caught and fish that got away.

The experiential theory of Gendlin introduces another perspective on the means by which stories and feelings interrelate. Gendlin (1962, 1969) has drawn attention to the existence of the bodily 'felt sense', through which the implicit meanings of events, relationships and situations are represented. It is through the symbolisation of this felt sense in words and images that meaning becomes explicitly rather than tacitly knowable. For Gendlin, the presence of a state of flow in which felt meanings are readily symbolised and articulated is a sign of optimal psychological functioning. However, it is common for people to avoid areas of inner feeling that they sense are painful or in some way 'forbidden', or to be socialised into functioning at an intellectualised, over-cognitive manner that makes only minimal reference to inner feeling states. Gendlin's description of the interaction between felt sense and symbol provides the basis for making sense of the way in which a story can move a person toward, or away from, feeling. Some stories fully capture the 'felt sense' of an event, while other stories do not resonate with the same intensity with this inner feeling. It is important to acknowledge that Gendlin's approach does not explicitly draw on a narrative perspective. In his research and practice, feeling may appear to be symbolised only through individual words, phrases or images rather than through stories. However, closer examination of his case examples reveals that the focusing events he describes in fact occur in the context of storytelling processes.

Stories move people. Watching a film, reading a novel, listening to someone recount an episode in their life, are all narrative events that may result in having feelings that were not in awareness before that particular story was told. From an experiential perspective, the audience for such a story will engage in the meaning of the story by allowing the themes or images of the narrative to resonate with appropriate areas of inner feeling. Conversely, the person telling a story, particularly a story recounting personal experiences or troubles, can shape the story to move closer to, or further away from, such feeling states. It is usually the intention in psychotherapy to create conditions and expectations of sufficient safety for the client to be able to tell stories that open up previously warded-off areas of feeling. In everyday life, the existence of numerous social taboos against expressing certain kinds of feelings in public leads to different kinds of stories being told. For example, someone who has a life-threatening disease might use a therapy hour to tell stories of fear and anger, while continuing to narrate cheerful or 'heroic' stories to family members or friends.

So far, stories have been presented as ways of regulating feelings in the service of the individual's prevailing sense of self or personal identity. It is an error to over-individualise this process. Feelings are of course experienced by individuals, and are very much personally 'owned' through being experienced as 'in' the person's body. However, much of the time these feelings are collective, are shared. The literary critic and cultural analyst Raymond Williams (1961) used the phrase 'structure of feeling' to describe the way that people in specific social groups at particular times in history tend to feel the same about things. For Williams, who wrote about the history of English literature, the structure of feeling was exhibited through the novels read by people in certain historical eras. In contemporary society, the media of mass communication have created other story forms that shape collective ways of feeling, such as films or television news coverage. The stories that resonate across the modern world – for example the stories of those held hostage in Beirut – bind together the feelings of millions of people.

Stories and the sense of self

It is important to emphasise the affective side of narrative, both because it is neglected in the work of many recent theories of narrative, and because feelings and emotions are so central to the personal meaning of stories and to the place that stories have in the sense of self of a person. At the heart of the personal meaning of stories is the process of constructing an on-going 'self-narrative'. Several writers have proposed that the notion of self can be understood as referring to a 'storied self', that the identity experienced by an individual is constituted through the stories he or she tells about himself or herself.

Polkinghorne (1991: 143) points out that 'the self concept has traditionally been structured as a thing . . . as a collection of properties'. So, for instance, in Rogers' writings on the self-concept he proposes that:

> The self-concept, or self-structure, may be thought of as an organized configuration of perceptions of the self which are admissible to awareness. It is composed of such elements as the perceptions of one's characteristics and abilities; the percepts and concepts of the self in relation to others and to the environment; the value qualities which are perceived as associated with experiences and objects; and goals and ideals which are perceived as having positive or negative valence. (Rogers, 1951: 136–7)

This sense of a self as comprising a collection of 'properties' or 'elements' is reinforced in the 'Who are you?' test, a commonly used technique for gaining self-concept data in which the person is asked to generate as many answers as possible to the question 'Who am I?' (see Burns, 1979). Typically, a person will respond with a list of the social and physical properties such as 'I am British, I am a man, I am a father, I am tall, etc.' Polkinghorne argues that these approaches to the self-concept ignore the existential notion that the 'self' is not experienced as a static 'entity' but as a process of becoming. From this perspective, the self-concept requires a narrative structure, since this is the only way in which events over time can be integrated into a cohesive unity.

For Polkinghorne, the person's concept of self can best be understood as comprising a self-narrative that tells the story of the whole of a life. This self-narrative gives coherence to the multiplicity of episodes, events and relationships experienced in the course of a life to date, including the prospective anticipation of its ending. The person has access to a rich cultural stock of narrative plots in the form of novels, films, fairy stories and religious stories that can be employed in the construction of a coherent self-narrative. Polkinghorne uses Rollo May's idea of *personal myth* to capture the sense of an overarching life-story: 'a myth . . . is a story having the power to provide life with meaning' (Polkinghorne, 1991: 145).

These ideas represent a return to the notion of the 'storied world' discussed earlier. In the exploration of the social meaning of stories, it was suggested that there exists a set of mythic stories reflecting the fundamental moral and existential issues faced in a culture. Now, it can be seen that these mythic stories also serve as resources in the construction of individual personal identity. The person can find a story that enables him or her to gain a sense of his or her life as a meaningful whole.

It is clear that different people use quite different strategies for creating coherence across the mass of memories that could potentially be included in a self-narrative of this kind. Gergen and Gergen (1993) have examined the contrasting narrative structures employed by women and men in constructing autobiographical stories.

Writers influenced by psychoanalytic ideas have placed a great deal of emphasis on the role of children's stories in the construction of self-narratives or personal myths. Their assumption is that personality is shaped by early experience and that stories heard early on in life, before the child possesses much of a capacity to detect and question the moral message implicit in the story being told to him or her, have the potential to provide a prototypical template for all later self-stories. It is as though the child unconsciously learns to identify with a character or relationship pattern depicted in a story, and continues to view the world in this way through adulthood (unless psychotherapy or other crises intervene) (Berne, 1975; Bettelheim, 1976). Another version of this model can be found in Csikszentmihalyi and Beattie (1979), who attribute adult mythic stories to specific, consciously remembered key events in early life.

The notion of the coherent self-narrative or personal myth is appealing, and has seized the popular imagination (see McAdams, 1993), but has serious limitations as a framework for understanding self. Implicit in the idea of self-narrative are the assumptions that such a thing as a unitary self exists, that it is somehow desirable to achieve a coherent sense of self, and that the self is bounded and autonomous. All of these assumptions reflect ideas of self prevailing in Western culture, as Cushman (1995), Landrine (1992) and many others have pointed out.

The view that there can exist a personal myth that captures a coherent sense of self cannot, therefore, be accepted as a universal truth. It is a conception of self that is part of the ideology of individualism prevalent in much of Western culture. Perhaps it would be more accurate to locate this conception of self more explicitly within Western masculinist culture, with its emphasis on hero myths. It is easy to see how this idea of the bounded, autonomous individual fits into the achievement-oriented, militarist, consumer society that has been created in the modern world. However, it is possible to generate other ways of viewing self without necessarily venturing into non-Western cultures. Even within the main currents of psychological theory there can be found images of a multiple-storied self rather than a single-story self. Mair (1977), for example, talks of a 'community of selves'.

From this point of view, then, the self can be seen as encompassing a multiplicity of narratives, attached to different situations and relationships, places and people. The compatibility of this view of self with that of the 'unitary', personal myth conception is a matter for research and debate. One important issue concerns the conditions under which people present themselves as unified or as 'distributed' selves. The 'distributed' or 'indexical' sense of self occurs when the person defines self in terms of external relationships and situations rather than in terms of an inner autonomous core. There are clearly occasions, for example being interviewed for a job, or writing an autobiography, that call out for life events to be integrated into a unitary pattern. Perhaps in most everyday life situations there is less pressure to present a 'mythic' self, and more tolerance of discontinuity of self-feeling.

The moral landscape of narrative

A story can provide a guideline or 'script' for how to behave in social situations. This aspect of narrative can be seen, for example, in religious parables. The story of the 'Good Samaritan' instructs the listener or reader in how to behave when confronted by someone in need. By contrast, violent videos and TV programmes have been widely criticised for telling stories that will influence impressionable viewers to behave violently. One of the interesting features of stories as guides to action is that they do not supply explicit rules on how to act. Stories are more than literal 'scripts' that determine everything that an actor will do. As discussed earlier, a story is always interpretable; there is always enough ambiguity to necessitate the reader engaging actively in constructing the meaning of the story from his or her own point of view. Thus, violent movies do not direct the audience to be violent. Most watchers will retain enough critical distance from the narrative to enable themselves to be selective in choosing whether or not to copy the behaviour of fictional characters.

As Labov and Waletzky (1967) have pointed out, every story has its 'moral', its message about where the events being recounted fit into the moral landscape inhabited by the storyteller. Among the many other aspects already examined, stories have the function of conveying a sense of a moral order. Often, the dramatic impact of a story hinges on some violation of what is right or wrong.

What is a story?

A central concern for psychological studies of storytelling has been the problem of creating a definition or understanding of storytelling as opposed to any other form of communication. Studies addressing this issue have typically presented subjects with a text and asked them to judge whether or not it could be classified as a 'story', or to rate its 'storiness'. Using these techniques, Stein and Policastro (1984: 147) concluded that texts must include an 'animate protagonist' and 'some type of causal sequence' to be considered a story. Polanyi (1982) proposes that a story relates an event in past time, and that the telling of a story must have a 'point'. Brewer and Lichtenstein (1982) have focused particularly on the communicational or social function of stories, which they regard as basically that of *entertainment*. For Brewer and Lichtenstein, a story can be defined as a form of communication structured in such a way as to produce surprise, suspense, curiosity and enjoyment in the hearer or reader. J.S. Bruner (1986), drawing on the work of the literary critic Kenneth Burke, proposes that narrative requires five elements: an actor, an action, a goal, a scene, and an 'instrumentality'. However, the dramatic or suspenseful quality of a good story is provided by a sixth essential element: 'trouble'. What makes a story worth telling is the tension or imbalance between the five main elements. For example, an actor may not possess the instruments to achieve his or her goal.

Other researchers struggling with the definition of story have introduced the notion of the 'story grammar'. For example, Mandler (1984) suggested that a traditional story begins with a setting, followed by an episode or series of episodes, within each of which a protagonist reacts to events and strives to achieve a goal. Stein and Glenn (1979) propose that the grammatical structure for stories includes six main elements: (a) the setting; (b) the initiating event; (c) the internal reaction or response of the protagonist; (d) the attempt/action on the part of the protagonist to deal with the situation; (e) the consequences of this action; and, finally, (f) the reaction to these events, or moral of the tale. Various studies (reviewed by Mancuso, 1986) indicate that this type of story 'grammar' is acquired by the age of three, and that it is more difficult to read and recall stories in which these elements are missing or in the wrong order. By contrast, Labov and Waletzky (1967), working with spoken rather than written language, suggest that the grammatical structure of stories found in everyday dialogue consists of six key elements. First of all, the teller offers an 'abstract', in effect a summary of the story. Woven into this may be 'orientation' information, in which time, place and persons are identified. There then follows the 'complicating action', which comprises the core of the narrative, and takes the form of a series of clauses describing 'what happened next'. There is then a 'resolution', which conveys the result of the action, an 'evaluation', in which the teller conveys the point of the story, and, finally, a 'coda', which returns the speakers to their present, here-and-now situation. Table 2.4 displays the way in which the story told by a client (introduced earlier – see p. 37) in therapy might be analysed in terms of the Stein and Labov models.

It can be seen from the analysis of this narrative in story grammar terms that the *evaluation* component of the story tends to be given particular emphasis in 'problem' stories told in therapy. As Labov has written:

Table 2.4   *Story grammar analysis of Carl's story*

1   Setting/Orientation
Two weeks ago one of my friends called me from Holland. I am going back to Holland again in the middle of September. . . .

2   Initiating event/Complicating action
. . . we decided to rent this flat together and share this flat together. . . .

3   Internal response/Complicating action
I was talking to her and mentioning to her 'where can I find some work?' and 'I don't know where I can find work'. So I'm not quite sure where I can find work and what I can do.

4   Attempt (by friend)/Complicating action
Then she mentioned she knows a person who was a teacher in a school. . . . I can ring this person and I can ask her if I could have some hours of teaching.

5   Consequence(s)/Resolution
And I said I can do that. Then I came back here and a couple of weeks ago she called me and asked me 'did you ring this person?' and I said 'no' and I have this feeling . . . eeerh. . . .

6   Reaction/Evaluation
. . . why can't she not let it happen in my way, to let it happen for myself? Why does she force me to do that? I couldn't say to her 'I really appreciate your concern but frankly I don't like, I don't think I will do that.' Because I have this fear that she might reject me then. So I didn't tell her that. I feel she forces me.

> The evaluation of the narrative forms a secondary structure which is concentrated in the evaluation section but may be found in various forms throughout the narrative. (1972: 369)

From the perspective of this kind of analysis, it is possible to view therapy as a process in which client and therapist work together to 'unpack' the evaluation of the social events that constitute the client's stories, and thereby arrive at a more satisfactory 're-evaluation' of them.

Story grammar models offer a powerful means of analysing story structures. A story grammar framework makes it possible to examine the way that a story is marked off from other types of discourse. Also, the sense of a story consisting of a *sequence* of actions is foregrounded in this approach, and it can be seen how the meaning of a story builds to a climax or resolution/evaluation/moral. There are also some significant limitations to the story grammar approach. It does not seem at all obvious that storytellers from different backgrounds necessarily share the same set of grammatical rules. For example, Riessman (1988) carried out a detailed analysis of women's narratives about their marriage and divorce. She gives particular attention to the case of Marta, a young American-Hispanic woman. Riessman is able to show that Marta's story represents a powerful and moving account of her troubled relationship with her former husband. However, she also points out that 'some [theorists] might argue that Marta's account is not, strictly speaking, a narrative at all' (1988: 158) because it was structured in episodic fashion rather than conforming to the linear, rational, temporally ordered structure taken as normal in Western industrial–capitalist cultures. Riessman urges caution in assuming that story grammars based on studies of members of dominant American social groups can readily be applied to other groups. A similar conclusion was reached by Michaels (1991), in a study of the stories told by primary school (first grade) children in 'sharing time' or 'show and tell' sessions, where they are invited to talk freely in front of all their classmates about a personal experience or object. Michaels describes the struggles of Deena, a 'very bright, highly verbal six-year-old Black girl' to generate stories that were acceptable or comprehensible to her white teacher. Other research on cross-cultural aspects of storytelling has tended to confirm the culturally bound nature of existing models of story grammar. For example, Minami and McCabe (1991) found that Japanese chidren told stories that tended to reflect the characteristics of *haiku*. Invernizzi and Abouzeid examined the story comprehension of children in Ponam Island, Papua New Guinea, by asking them to write down what they remembered of a story that had been read to them. They found that the Ponam children 'wrote detailed, factual recalls that to a Western eye, would appear to miss the point' (1995: 8). However, the story details remembered by the Ponam children, and the form in which they reported these details, were consistent with the cultural and environmental demands of Ponam life.

In conclusion, then, it perhaps makes sense to take the view that, while stories are structured in consistent ways, the 'rules' of structure, the 'grammar' of a story, is highly dependent on cultural context and tradition.

It can be seen, even from this brief overview of the relevant literature, that there exist quite different ideas about what we mean by the idea of a 'story' or a 'narrative'. The situation is made even more complex by the tendency on the part of some writers to use the concept of 'narrative' as a general term to refer to all, or virtually all, forms of human sense-making and communication. The clearest example of this kind of approach is perhaps found in the paper by Howard (1991) in which he argues that thinking, including scientific theorising and mathematics, should be regarded as forms of storytelling. He goes as far as suggesting that 'human thought . . . is nothing but storytelling' (1991: 189). For Howard, narrative is a 'superordinate' category, with the implication that other forms of communication and mental activity must be seen as species of storytelling rather than as a distinct type of thought and expression that sits alongside other modes. Whereas J.S. Bruner (1986) makes a broad distinction between 'narrative' and 'paradigmatic' ways of knowing, Howard asserts that for human beings there is only one way of knowing, which is narrative. Howard's position has been vigorously challenged by other narrative theorists (Russell and Luciarello, 1992; Vogel, 1994), who point out that the concept of narrative loses meaning if there is nothing that is *not* a story: 'if all is narrative, the term *narrative* conveys a distinction without a difference' (Vogel, 1994: 249). In other words, if the notion of narrative is to *make a difference*, it is necessary to be able to use it in a way that classifies some events or phenomena as 'stories' and other events or phenomena as 'not-stories'. The key point here is that it does not seem helpful to attempt to deal with the question 'what is a story?' by taking the line that 'everything is a story'.

The position taken in this book follows the view of Neimeyer that it makes most sense to restrict usage of the *narrative* to discrete story-telling events:

> ... many of the processes that transpire in psychotherapy – information gathering, coaching in communication skills, advice giving, problem solving, most psychological testing – are nonnarrative processes, although they may, in some more abstract sense, be part of a script or culture tale of what constitutes therapy or helping. Moreover, one can easily enough identify acts of human mentation that are nonnarrative. For example, mathematical processing and logical processing lack the plot structure that defines narrative, and even important feeling states are not stories, although they may be triggered or conveyed by stories. Even Kellian construing, viewed in its irreducible essentials of simultaneously dimensions of comparison and contrast, is not narrative in this sense, though it may be a precondition for the construction of narratives that weave together the events and thematic constructs the individual construes. Thus, I believe it is conceptually possible to identify reasonably distinct storytelling episodes or processes in [therapy]. (1994: 238)

Narrative, then, is a category of thought and discourse that can usefully and reliably be differentiated from other forms of cognition and communication. Yet the question remains – what is it that makes *narrative* distinctive? What are the defining characteristics of the story form?

The problem of arriving at an adequate definition of a story, or of narrative in general, has been discussed very fully by Stein (1982). In her view, it is not possible to specify a unique set of features or attributes that can be used to identify a story. In arriving at this conclusion, she draws on the theory of categorisation of natural objects (that is, objects found in the everyday world) developed by Rosch and her colleagues (Rosch and Mervis, 1975). Rosch argues that, in everyday life, people do not categorise things in terms of the strict application of a set of logical criteria, but operate on the basis of *prototypical* examples. For example, if asked to define what is meant by the term 'bird', most people might begin by saying that 'a bird has feathers, it flies, it lays eggs . . .'. But it is clear on further reflection that we would classify an ostrich as a bird, yet it does not fly. Clearly, then, the basis for defining something as 'bird' does not rely on a single set of defining features. Rosch has found that people faced with this type of cognitive task rely on an image of a 'typical' bird. Some birds will be 'good' or core examples of the category while others (like ostriches) occupy a place more toward the edge of the category. The boundary of most natural categories is 'fuzzy', so that an object such as a bat may be viewed as a bird or a mammal depending on the context.

Stein uses this theoretical framework to bring some sense to the many different and competing definitions of 'story'. Her view is that all the features listed by various researchers (well-formed structure, suspense, an active protagonist, a resolution . . .) are perhaps best taken as characteristics of 'good' prototypical stories. A story that possessed all of these features might even be perceived as a 'very good' story. Nevertheless, the idea of a 'story' is so integral to human experience that it is possible to strip away many of these features, or combine them in different permutations, and still produce something that people will recognise as a story, or will make into a story.

It seems to me that Stein's idea that context determines whether or not we regard a piece of communication as a story is particularly relevant to the understanding of storytelling in counselling and psychotherapy. In therapy, it is as though the client is building up a multiply layered account of his or her life, in which many different stories or story-lines are interwoven. In this situation, a single remark or word can sometimes be part of a story that began several sessions ago. To try to understand storytelling in therapy using strict formal definitions of story grammar or structure would result in losing sight of the type of fragmented storytelling process that is in fact characteristic of much therapy. After a while in therapy, it can be as if both therapist and client are aware of an *implicit* story, which links together the words that are said. Spence (1982a) describes this process as the achievement of a *privileged competence*, where client and therapist are participating in a much wider set of meanings and shared understandings than could be appreciated by an outside observer.

I have found it valuable to use the term 'narrative' to refer to the therapeutic discourse as a whole, and the word 'story' to refer to accounts of specific incidents. The therapeutic narrative, then, can be viewed as an attempt by the client to 'narrativise' a problematic experience through the production of a series of stories connected by linking passages and therapist interventions (see McLeod and Balamoutsou, 1996). It is possible, in therapy discourse, to identify discrete storytelling 'events' without needing to be prescriptive about the defining features or precise boundaries of these events. Research that will be reviewed in the next chapter shows that clients, therapists and external observers are well able to identify storytelling episodes within the flow of the therapy conversation. However, in therapy, and usually also in other storytelling settings, specific stories are embedded within a broader 'narrative'.

Returning to the issues discussed in earlier sections in this chapter, it is perhaps worth summarising some of the principal aspects of the function of storytelling. As a form of communication, a story functions to impart several different types of information. A story communicates:

1 A description of an event, including data about time, place and behaviour.
2 An expression of subjectivity, intentionality and identity – 'this is who I am'.
3 An expression of relationship – 'this is the story I choose to tell to *you*'.
4 Data about the teller's understanding of his/her social world: 'this is what I would expect, but look what happened yesterday . . .'.
5 An expression of feeling.
6 The location of events within a moral order.

As a form of thinking, or in more general terms 'sense-making', a story serves the following functions for the teller:

7 Bringing order, sequence and a sense of completion to a set of experiences.
8 Problem-solving, by providing a causal explanation for something that happened.
9 Development of a sense of perspective, by placing a singular event into its broader context.

It is the nature of storytelling that all of these functions can be accomplished in parallel within the same story. Moreover, there is a high degree of spontaneity in storytelling. The person recounting a story is not consciously aware of expressing information about self, problem-solving and so on. If, in telling a story, we 'catch ourselves' 'giving away' too much, and as a consequence attempt to censor a story once it is underway, there is great danger that the story will not work, it will fall flat, drift off. 'Good' stories seem, almost, to tell themselves.

Earlier in this chapter (see p. 37), the story told by a client at the start of therapy was introduced. This particular piece of narrative is fairly brief, but is nevertheless typical of the way that clients talk in therapy when invited to describe their 'problem'. It is a readily understandable form of communication between someone in distress and someone from whom they hope to gain help. A narrative perspective reveals the richness of information conveyed by this simple story. Table 2.5 breaks down the story into some of its component meanings. It can be seen that, through the medium of this story, the therapist is being offered a great deal of information about the client. Also, the client is in all probability 'saying more than he knows'. In other words, he is unlikely to be aware of just how much he has disclosed about himself so soon. It is, in my view, one of the central tasks of therapy to *retrieve* the meaning implicit in the stories that clients (usually) and therapists (sometimes) tell.

Table 2.5   *Information conveyed by Carl's story*

---

1 *Event description.* Event took place two weeks ago, returning in September; Holland as an important place in his life; what happened when they talked.

2 *Expression of intentionality and identity.* Intending to: return to Holland, seek a job, do things in his own way. Identity: I am . . . a teacher, someone with friends.

3 *Expression of relationship.* [*To therapist*] I am willing to tell you something personal about myself. [*To friend*] We can make decisions together (but now . . .) You are forcing me. There is something I can't say to you .

4 *Social world.* There are jobs available. A man and a woman can share a flat together. I expect others to give me space.

5 *Expression of feeling.* I'm not sure . . . I have a questioning feeling . . . I fear rejection . . . I feel forced.

6 *Moral landscape.* I must make my own decisions and not be forced by someone else to go against my own inclinations.

7 *Ordering experience.* This is the series of events that led up to my feeling of fear of rejection.

8 *Problem-solving.* I know what I *could* say to her. The core of the problem is my sense of being forced.

9 *Development of a sense of perspective.* Not explicitly stated, but implicit link with other occasions of 'feeling forced'.

Summary and conclusion

This chapter has introduced a framework for understanding narrative and storytelling in therapy. This framework will be further articulated in subsequent chapters, as the contributions of various theorists and writers on narrative approaches to therapy are examined in detail. The main aim of this chapter has been to demonstrate that narrativisation and storytelling represent a powerful, complex and subtle medium for conveying meaning. Any attempt to oversimplify the nature of narrative by imposing a fixed or narrow definition of 'what is a story' is likely to be counterproductive, at least in the domain of counselling and psychotherapy. While it may be necessary in cognitive or linguistic research to operationalise the concepts of narrative and story, in psychotherapy it is essential to retain as holistic and multidimensional a notion of story as possible, based in everyday, common-sense notions of storytelling. Every story that a person tells carries information about action, purpose, identity, feeling, intentionality, and the world within which the storyteller lives. These dimensions of meaning are bound together, and are not easy to extract. At the heart of psychotherapy is the *retrieval* of meaning, the reflective discovery and assimilation of the meanings implicit in the stories told by the client in the setting of the therapy room. Once the meaning implicit in a story has been captured and understood, client and therapist can work together to create new meaning and forms of action. The ways that different schools of therapy have set about this task are addressed in the following chapters.

3

Narrative in Therapy:
Psychodynamic Approaches

The message of the first two chapters has been that we are surrounded by stories. Our talk, any talk, is saturated in narrative. However, although the field of counselling and psychotherapy in part reflects the storied nature of human life, the practice of therapy frequently constitutes a denial of much of the full significance of stories. The next three chapters review the ways that ideas about narratives and stories have been employed in therapy. The work being discussed here can be broadly divided into two broad approaches. First, there are numerous examples of narrative concepts, and narrative-informed methods, being used in an almost incidental manner, being subsumed into theoretical frameworks that do not fundamentally characterise the person as a storytelling being. Within this school of thought the most important groupings are around the *psychodynamic* and *constructivist/cognitive* uses of narrative in therapy. These therapies can be described as *foundationalist*, in that they employ narrative and story as a means of gaining access to supposedly more 'foundational' levels of psychological reality. Second, there are examples of therapists who have placed narrative right at the heart of their scheme of things, who have created an explicitly 'narrative therapy'. This second group of writers and clinicians can be described as *constructionist* in orientation: experience is socially constructed (Gergen, 1985). Although the work of constructionist 'narrative therapists' represents a more coherent approach to the role of narrative in therapy, it is also clear that it draws heavily on earlier uses of narrative. Constructionist therapies cannot be adequately understood without reference to what has gone before. Some aspects of the new narrative therapies also need to be seen as constituting an explicit rejection of earlier uses of narrative ideas. Other aspects are similar to psychodynamic and constructivist uses of narrative. The narrative therapies are still growing and developing as a body of theory and practice, and are in a state of tension not only with long-established therapeutic approaches, but also in relation to broader cultural forces, such as postmodernism.

The recent explosion of interest in narrative makes it impossible to contain and review all the relevant literature in the space available here. What I have attempted to do is to take representative examples of the uses of narrative in therapy theory and practice, and to describe these in a manner that allows the distinction between foundationalist and constructionist approaches. The difference between these streams of thought is that the former is, in J.S. Bruner's (1986) words, 'paradigmatic' in intent (that is, stories are useful in yielding access to underlying structures and factors), whereas the latter regards the story or narrative as the primary vehicle for knowledge and understanding, and is therefore committed to an essentially 'narrative' way of knowing. The use of stories in psychodynamic/psychoanalytic therapy is discussed in this chapter. An account of the new wave of cognitive/constructivist narrative therapies is given in Chapter 4.

Encouraging the client to tell their story: narrative as a source of clinical data

Perhaps the basic and original use of the story in therapy is to gather information about the client. In many versions of psychodynamic therapy, it would be usual for the therapist to begin work by taking a 'history' of the client, gathering information about the 'story' of his or her life (in psychodynamic therapy) and the particular patterns of behaviour that were causing trouble. However, although the client participating in this type of assessment interview might well recount many stories, the life data being conveyed would not necessarily be encoded or recorded in story form. Rather, what the client said would be reduced to categories seen by the therapist as being of particular interest. For instance, a psychodynamic therapist might be looking for examples of triangular relationships, developmental issues, and transference themes, with the aim of arriving at a formulation or diagnosis. The material gathered in the assessment would find its way into the patient's file, but what could be found there would be more the therapist's version of the client's story, rather than the story as told by the person himself or herself. As we will see later, one of the trends in constructionist narrative therapy has been to encourage people to 'author' their own life-stories, rather than participating in 'authorised' versions produced by 'authority' figures (White and Epston, 1990). From this perspective, history-taking in assessment interviews can have a unhelpful impact on therapy, by signalling the authority of the therapist right from the start.

Much of what a therapist does in the course of therapy can be viewed as creating an environment in which the client is enabled to tell his or her story without interruption or judgement. Techniques such as free association or empathic reflection can be seen as aids to storytelling, ways of encouraging the client to create narrative accounts of significant experiences. Again, however, in most therapy situations the therapist will not work with the story itself but will use the narrative to gain access to what are considered to be more fundamental emotional or behavioural structures. For instance, a client-centred therapist might listen to a story for evidence about the level of self-acceptance of the client, or a psychodynamic therapist might listen for data about object relations and attachment patterns.

Thus it seems that, while a therapy session provides a unique arena for telling stories, these tales are not usually responded to as stories, but are treated as sources of evidence in relation to the supposed underlying personality structures expressed through the story. There is little or no explicit acknowledgement of the specific characteristics of narrative as a distinctive form of communication or way of knowing.

There are also several examples of narrative being used to generate clinical data through assessment tools. The most celebrated of these devices is the Thematic Apperception Test (TAT) (Murray, 1938), which consists of a set of picture stimuli. The patient is asked to invent imaginative stories in response to these pictures, and these protocols can be analysed in terms of constructs such as 'need for achievement'. More recently Lahad (1992) has devised a set of instructions to elicit stories about how a person copes with stressful situations in his or her life. Finally, a measure of attachment style has been developed based on the narrative structure of the life-stories told by patients being administered the Adult Attachment Interview (see Holmes, 1993).

The idea of the core, repetitive life narrative

The notion that there is an underlying unity to the stories a person tells about his or her life represents a basic theme in psychodynamic therapy. Ultimately, this idea derives from Freud, who regarded all of emotional and relational life as grounded in the template provided by the story of Oedipus. One of the primary tasks of therapy, as a consequence, is to uncover this core 'life-story' and give the person an opportunity to gain insight into it and control over its effects. An important element of the concept is the idea that the story repeats itself in different relations the person has at different points in his or her life. The assumption of thematic unity to an individual life implicit in this theory is, of course, highly consistent with the Western cultural construction of the 'bounded, autonomous self' discussed in Chapter 1.

Some of the attempts to conceptualise a core life-story place the origins of this structure firmly in the earliest years of life. One of the most extreme versions of this approach is the 'nuclear scene' model created by Tomkins (1979, 1987). An account of the childhood origins of a core life-story that suggests a more gradual developmental process is offered by Berne (1975) and Steiner (1974) in their concept of 'life script'. According to Berne and Steiner, the child acquires a life script in early life, mainly through listening to fairy stories and other childhood stories that serve as answers to the child's search for answers to questions such as 'who am I?' and 'what happens to someone like me?'

Other psychoanalytically informed writers have focused their attention more on the ways that core life-stories are expressed in adult life, rather than speculating about childhood origins. One of the most influential theories in this area has been the Core Conflictual Relationship Theme (CCRT) framework for narrative analysis developed by Luborsky and his colleagues (Luborsky and Crits-Christoph, 1990). In this approach, stories told by clients in therapy about their relationships are regarded as conforming to a structure in which each story expresses a *wish* (for example, 'I want to be angry with my mother'), which leads to a *response of other* (such as 'she will reject me') and finally results in a *response of self* (for example, 'I will feel depressed'). The research carried out on this model confirms that clients exhibit the same CCRT patterns in the stories they tell about significant others, such as their parents or spouse, as they do in their interaction with their therapist, thus supporting the Freudian idea of transference. Effective therapy is associated with therapists' accuracy in interpreting CCRT patterns. Finally, the relationship stories told by clients change as a result of therapy, with positive outcome stories being more common at the end of therapy than at the beginning. The CCRT model is one of the strongest examples of how psychoanalytic practitioners and theorists have integrated narrative concepts into their approach, but without changing their basic method or theoretical assumptions.

Another theorist who makes use of narrative ideas in the service of a fundamentally psychodynamic approach is Hans Strupp. In his model of time-limited dynamic psychotherapy, Strupp argues that a therapist working within time limits must actively seek a *dynamic focus*, which is defined as:

> . . . a working model . . . of a central or salient pattern of interpersonal roles in which patients unconsciously cast themselves, the complementary roles in which they cast others, and the maladaptive action sequences, self-defeating expectations, and negative self-appraisals that result. (Strupp and Binder, 1984: 68)

This description of a dynamic focus looks remarkably like a description of a problem story, and in fact Strupp and Binder write that 'the primary psychological mode of construing life experience . . . is narration: the telling of a story to oneself and others' (1984: 68). They regard the dynamic focus as organised and communicated by the patient/client as a schematic story characterised by four main elements: acts of self, expectations about others' reactions, acts of others toward self, and acts of self toward self (see Table 3.1). This story is continually re-enacted in the client's life as a series of repetitive 'self-propagating vicious circles' (1984: 73). Client and therapist are seen as needing to be involved in a joint narration and re-narration of the central dilemmas and issues in the patient's life, with the aim of constructing a new story that is more 'intelligible and purposeful'.

Table 3.1 *The Strupp and Binder model of narrative structure*

---

1 *Acts of self.* Include all domains of human action, such as affect and emotion (e.g. 'I wish my wife would pay more attention to me'), cognitions (e.g. 'I can't stop thinking about how ugly and inferior I am when I meet someone attractive'), perceptions and overt behaviour. Acts of self vary in the degree to which they are accessible to awareness.

2 *Expectations about others' reactions.* The imagined reactions of others to one's own actions, for example: 'if I speak up, I imagine that she will disapprove of me'. May be conscious, preconscious or unconscious.

3 *Acts of others toward self.* Observed acts of others viewed as occurring in specific relation to acts of self, for example, 'when I asked for the money he ignored me'.

4 *Acts of self toward self (introject).* How one treats oneself (self-controlling, self-punishing, self-congratulating, self-destroying), for example, 'when my husband praises me I feel guilty and remind myself of my shortcomings'.

Table 3.1   *Continued*

Typical focal narrative

Presenting problem. The client, Frances, complains of depression and marital difficulties.

Acts of self. Frances assumes a passive interpersonal position in which she refrains from disclosing her inner self, avoids social contact by withdrawing or procrastination, defers or submits to others' wishes, and spends much time in private thinking and wondering rather than in active communication.

Expectations of others' reactions. Frances expects that other people will ignore or reject her. She validates this expectation with recollections of being ignored or rejected by her mother and by various significant others.

Observed reactions of others. Others find Frances' passivity unappealing and do not spontaneously recognise her distress and come to her aid. However, Frances does not see this as an understandable reaction to her passivity, but instead interprets this as evidence that others are actively rejecting and ignoring her.

Introject (how she treats herself). Frances views herself as helpless in a hopeless situation. Rather than endure the imagined negative reactions of others, she inhibits and controls herself and refrains from asserting her desires or complaints (hoping that this interpersonal passivity will make her mere presence more palatable to others).

Source: Strupp and Binder, 1984: 77–8

Luborsky, Strupp and many other therapists have found value in their various versions of the notion of a unitary, repetitive, core life-story that represents the 'basic fault' in the client's personality. Perhaps the most radical version of this approach has been Gustafson's (1992) categorisation of life-stories into three main types. Whereas Luborsky and Strupp have proposed conceptual frameworks or structures that can sustain a multiplicity of different plot-lines, Gustafson argues that the stories that people tell and live are essentially organised around a small set of alternative solutions to the problem of personal and interpersonal power. He proposes that some people develop a pattern of relating to others that is basically *subservient*. Others adopt a pattern of *bureaucratic delay*, while a third group evolve an *overpowering* style of relating to others. A paradox in Gustafson's work is that, while he has constructed a model of life-narrative that is oppressively oversimplified, his own writing is among the most creative and humane within the psychiatry and psychotherapy literature.

The central theme in the work of this group of psychodynamic writers is, as mentioned above, the assumption that it makes sense to characterise a life in terms of a single story. Spence (1987) refers to this therapeutic strategy as the 'singular solution'. It is clearly valuable to have a means of bringing order or coherence to the complex material presented by a client or patient in therapy. Nevertheless, it is also important to be aware of some of the implications of this way of seeing persons. Omer (1993b) has argued that there can be a danger of oversimplifying the complexity and richness of a life by reducing it to a core narrative theme. He points out that in traditional long-term therapy the sense of achieving an adequate understanding of the overall life-history of the client would be considered as the *end-point* of therapy. By contrast, in contemporary brief therapies, the formulation of a 'life-sketch' is an *early* event in treatment, and in some clinics a person might not be taken on as a client unless a plausible life script or narrative can be identified at the assessment phase. Omer is concerned that this inevitably leads to 'quick caricature' that is imposed on the client. Another objection to the way that the life-story concept has been used has come from deShazer (1985), who points out that all too often such models lead therapist and client to generate 'problem-focused' stories. DeShazer regards it as more helpful to concentrate on the 'solution-focused' stories in the client's repertoire – accounts of how and when the client was able to achieve satisfying outcomes in relationships. DeShazer is here offering a contemporary version of the classic humanistic critique of psychoanalysis: that it pathologises individuals, has little room for the creative, problem-solving aspects of the person. The client life-sketch reproduced in Table 3.1 above provides an example of the kind of remorselessly pessimistic narrative that appears to be intrinsic to this mode of therapy. Spence (1987) himself adds another powerful objection to the use of 'singular solution' frameworks for understanding clients' lives. He argues that a singular solution can only be achieved by 'smoothing' what the client has said, by ignoring or downplaying statements that do not fit. Spence takes the view that unsmoothed, 'raw' clinical data are always open to a multiplicity of alternative interpretations.

It is notable that recent work in narrative therapy (for example, White and Epston, 1990; Penn and Frankfurt, 1994) does not assume the existence of a core, repetitive life-story. The trend in this current work is to expect the client to be able to generate a multiplicity of alternative story-lines. In this respect, narrative therapists have been explicitly influenced by postmodern thinkers who have emphasised the fragmentation of identity in contemporary culture, and have criticised the modernist notion of the singular 'true self'. These approaches are examined in more detail in Chapter 5.

Mythic stories as sources of life-narratives

Some psychodynamic theorists who have espoused the core life-story model have also developed explanations for where these stories come from. Most of the work in this area has identified 'mythic' stories such as fairy tales, Biblical stories and Greek myths as providing a stock of culturally shaped story-lines that individuals draw on when constructing an identity. The attraction of these stories is their 'mythic' nature; they have been told and re-told so often that they have come to express fundamental truths about life and existence.

The founder of Transactional Analysis, Eric Berne, and the celebrated psychoanalytic writer Bruno Bettelheim have both explored the formative power of fairy tales in early development. Both take the view that the child is able unconsciously to select the fairy story that best makes sense of his or her life situation. There exists an extensive literature on the psychoanalytic significance of fairy tales (Cath and Cath, 1978; Rinsley and Bergmann, 1983).

Other theorists active in this area have argued that all mythic stories and tales can be reduced to one core story. The two writers most widely known for this strategy are Joseph Campbell and Sigmund Freud. In his analysis of myths from many cultures, Campbell (1949) found that these stories could be reduced to a single 'hero' myth, in which the protagonist undertakes a hazardous journey (for example, into Hades) in pursuit of truth and meaning. Freud, by contrast, saw the Greek story of Oedipus Rex as providing a structure for making sense of a wide variety of human relationships.

These approaches to unearthing mythic sources of, and parallels to, the stories told by therapy clients have usefully informed the narrative therapies insofar as they point in the general direction of trying to understand the general stock of cultural resources that play a part in the construction of personal identity. On the other hand, there are a number of points at which narrative therapists have been critical and cautious about this kind of use of myth.

The first problem with the mythic frameworks that have been discussed is that they are over-reliant on 'classical' stories that are accessible to middle-class members of the dominant White Anglo-Saxon cultural group, but are less relevant to other people. For example, Bagarozzi and Anderson (1989), describing an approach to therapy in which they asked clients to explore stories that have had meaning to them, report that their clients tend to choose stories drawn from cartoons, films and television more than from traditional fairy tales. The lesson here is that it is not appropriate to assume that a particular set of classical stories and myths will necessarily have meaning for people participating in a highly diverse modern cultural milieu.

A second issue that arises when making connections between clients' lives and mythic stories is the validity of supposing that a story or fairy tale has had an actual causal effect on the person, for example by being heard in childhood and thereby influencing the way the person-when-child came to think about himself or herself. In the majority of cases it is impossible to know whether a person did actually fall under the spell of 'Little Red Riding Hood' or any other fairy story when they were four or five years old. All that can be known is that as an adult they find that the story somehow makes sense of the course their life has followed. A fairy story or other mythic story may be more a way of making sense *now* than it is a developmental event *then*. The fairy story remains emotionally significant for the person, but in a less deterministic manner.

A third, and more serious objection to the use of mythic stories in therapy arises whenever it is implied that such a story might have a fixed meaning, and that therefore it is something specific and fixed in relation to a client's life. From the philosophical perspective adopted by social constructionist approaches to narrative, the meaning of any event or story is socially constructed, and is framed and understood through socially prevailing definitions of reality. This point refers back to the issue of narrative *ambiguity* discussed in Chapter 2.

The use made by Freud of the story of Oedipus illustrates the multiplicity of meaning that can be extracted or read into even a well-known mythic story. Hillman (1975: 132) has characterised the Oedipus myth as 'Freud's one plot', the basic story-line that underpins all Freud's psychoanalytic case histories. Emde and Oppenheim (1995) suggest that Freud's individual-focused reading of the text of Sophocles' fifth-century BC drama of *Oedipus Rex* can be supplemented by other, more interpersonal or communal interpretations. Freud re-told this drama through the eyes of one of its characters, Oedipus, in the following way:

> Oedipus, son of Laius, King of Thebes, and of Jocasta, was exposed as an infant because an oracle had warned Laius that the still unborn child would be his father's murderer. The child was rescued, and grew up as a prince at an alien court, until, in doubt as to his origin, he too questioned the oracle and was warned to avoid his home since he was destined to murder his father and take his mother in marriage. On the road leading away from what he believed was his home, he met King Laius and slew him in a sudden quarrel. He came next to Thebes and solved the riddle set him by the Sphinx who barred his way. Out of gratitude the Thebans made him their king and gave him Jocasta's hand in marriage. He reigned long in peace and honour, and she who, unknown to him, was his mother bore him two sons and two daughters. Then at last a plague broke out and the Thebans made enquiry once more of the oracle. It is at this point that Sophocles' tragedy opens. The messengers bring back the reply that the plague will cease when the murderer of Laius has been driven from the land. (1900: 261–3)

Freud used this account of Oedipus to arrive at the conclusion that:

> [Oedipus'] destiny moves us only because it might have been ours. . . . It is the fate of all of us, perhaps, to direct our first sexual impulse toward our mother and our first hatred and our first murderous wish against our father. Our dreams convince us that this is so. King Oedipus, who slew his father Laius and married his mother Jocasta, merely shows us the fulfilment of our own childhood wishes. (Freud, 1900: 263–4)

The classic Freudian reading of Oedipus is therefore a story of repression and guilt over the expression of sexual impulses within the family.

An alternative re-telling of the same story could place more emphasis on the provocativeness of Laius, who cruelly abandoned his baby son, his feet tied together (Oedipus means 'swollen feet'), and who picked a fight with him at the crossroads many years later. In this version of the story, Jocasta is an accomplice in the mistreatment of Oedipus. As Emde and Oppenheim (1995) observe, the story now becomes one of child abuse, neglect and seduction.

A further re-telling of the story offered by Emde and Oppenheim considers the fact that the whole tale centres around the theme of a search for secret knowledge. The story is a means of examining 'what is shared and not shared' within a community. Oedipus is someone who is excluded from essential information about his origins and about the nature of his relationships with others. This reading of the story transforms it into an account of Oedipus' search for meaning in his life, in the face of other people's efforts to deny him access to relevant realms of meaning.

Emde and Oppenheim (1995) are psychotherapists using their re-interpretation of the story of Oedipus to legitimate a more socially aware approach to therapy. Other writers and theorists have also engaged in critical re-appraisals of foundational myths (for example, Zipes, 1979).

The work of Dan McAdams: integrating psychodynamic narrative themes

The body of theory and research produced by Dan McAdams and his colleagues (McAdams, 1985, 1991, 1993, 1994) represents a significant attempt to bring together many of the key ideas used by narrative psychodynamic therapists. While recognising the importance of early exposure to mythic, fairy-tale narratives, McAdams draws on the writings of Erik Erikson in constructing a model of development that spans the entire life-course, rather than being principally determined by events in the first years of life. He is interested in identifying the personal myth that brings coherence to all the stages in a life. The sense of his approach is captured well in the instructions he gives to participants in his research. He begins his structured life-story interviews by stating:

> I would like you to begin by thinking about your life as if it were a book. Each part of your life composes a chapter in the book. Certainly, the book is unfinished at this point; still, it probably already contains a few interesting and well-defined chapters. Please divide your life into its major chapters and briefly describe each chapter. You may have as many or as few chapters as you like, but I would suggest dividing it into at least two or three chapters and at most about seven or eight. Think of this as a general table of contents for your book. Give each chapter a name and describe the overall contents of each chapter. Discuss briefly what makes for a transition from one chapter to the next. (McAdams, 1993: 256)

The interview continues with a series of questions that open up particular aspects of the 'book', and then closes with a review of the life as a whole:

> Looking back over your entire life story as a book with chapters, episodes and characters, can you discern a central theme, message or idea that runs throughout the text? What is the major theme of your life? (McAdams, 1993: 263–4)

It is clear that the person invited to tell his or her story in this way will be likely to produce an account that is presented in linear chronological order, and influenced by fictional and autobiographical literature to which he or she has been exposed. The life-stories that McAdams gathers in his research are therefore 'cleaner' than those generated in therapy. Indeed, his research has tended to focus on people who are in the main well-adjusted and generative rather than on people who are troubled and seeking help. Nevertheless, his framework for understanding life-stories or myths is certainly relevant to the tasks of therapy. In his analysis of the 'plot-lines' that emerge in the life-stories that people create in his research, McAdams (1985) has found a number of metaphoric themes that occur over and over again: life is a journey, a battle, and so on. These typical plot-lines for life-stories are:

1   Establishing a garden, or building a home: creating order from chaos.
2   Engaging in a contest or fighting a battle: protecting the integrity of the self against external threat.
3   Taking a journey: moving forward, searching, fleeing a difficult past.
4   Enduring suffering: overcoming external pressure, surviving tests of loyalty.

5 Pursuing consummation: seeking transcendence.

Like other psychodynamically oriented theorists, McAdams is interested in the mechanisms of mental and emotional life that lie behind the story. The narrative is taken to be a surface, the contours of which suggest underlying forces and structures. For McAdams, the basic motivational structure underpinning personal stories is the tension between *agency* and *communion* in a person's life. The agency–communion distinction was originally made by David Bakan (1966), and has subsequently been a highly influential idea within North American psychology. Agency motivation refers to a striving to be in control of the environment, to achieve success and mastery, to be powerful, autonomous and separate from others. Communion, by contrast, refers to a striving to develop close relationships, to become immersed in something 'bigger' than the self, to have a sense of 'we' rather than 'I'. Love and intimacy are key values for people with a high need for communion. For McAdams, personal stories express the position adopted by the person on an agency–communion dimension. More than this, however, the characters within stories represent ways in which agency and communion can be enacted within a life. In McAdams' model, these characters are called *imagoes*. An imago is regarded as being a 'personified and idealized concept of the self' (McAdams, 1993: 122). These imagoes are mainly constructed during adolescence and early adulthood. McAdams suggests that it is helpful to gain insight into the imagoes around which a personal myth is organised:

> . . . we come to understand ourselves better by a comprehensive understanding of the main characters that dominate the plot of our story, and push the narrative forward. With maturity, we work to create harmony, balance, and reconciliation between the often conflicting imagoes in our myth. (1993: 123)

Table 3.2 gives a list of some of the types of imago frequently identified by McAdams in his research studies. While the concept of imago remains a cornerstone of his theory, he is careful to stress that the set of labels he provides cannot capture the uniqueness of characterisation within individual myths: one person's Warrior may be very different from that evolved by another person. He also warns against any tendency to reduce personal narrative to characterisation alone, pointing out that a story may be viewed from a variety of different perspectives.

The final component of McAdams' theory involves the role of significant stories that somehow capture the critical moments in a person's life. These are described as *nuclear episodes*, and include peak and nadir experiences, turning points, and significant memories (in early childhood, adolescence and adulthood).

McAdams is not primarily a therapist, but his approach to personal narrative combines many of the core elements of psychodynamic thinking: a powerful and sensitive way of 'reading' stories to uncover unconscious meaning, an awareness of life-course, developmental issues, an appreciation of the ways that internal 'objects', characters or 'imagoes' mediate between the individual and his or her experience of significant others.

Table 3.2   *Characterisation in personal myth: types of imago*

Agency-oriented
The Warrior (Ares)
The Traveller (Hermes)
The Sage (Zeus)
The Maker (Hephaestus)

Communion-oriented
The Lover (Aphrodite)
The Caregiver (Demeter)
The Friend (Hera)
The Ritualist (Hestia)

Imagoes high in both agency and communion
The Healer
The Teacher
The Counsellor
The Humanist
The Arbiter

Low in agency, low in communion
The Escapist
The Survivor

Source: McAdams (1993)

Research into psychodynamic approaches to narrative

In recent years, an increasing amount of research has been been directed at the problem of understanding the process of counselling and psychotherapy, at making sense of what occurs on a moment-by-moment basis during therapy to bring about helpful outcomes. Some process researchers have begun to examine the role of storytelling and narrative in therapy. The studies by Luborsky and Crits-Christoph (1990) are examples of this trend. Essentially, this research group have refined the psychoanalytic concept of transference by identifying the ways that transference reactions of patients are expressed in stories.

Another psychoanalytically oriented set of studies into the role of narratives in therapy process has been carried out by Bucci (1993). In her model, ideas from cognitive psychology are introduced to explain the existence of discrete phases in the process of therapeutic change. Specifically, Bucci proposes a 'multiple code' model of human information processing, in which people are capable of employing three distinct and separate modes of processing data about the world. The first is known as 'subsymbolic' and is basically a non-verbal, visceral, motoric way of knowing. It is at this level of processing that emotional meanings are coded and stored. The second mode of representation is verbal, and draws upon the human capacity to think logically, to categorise and classify, and to create semantic, symbolic networks of meanings. These two principal modes of information processing are derived from research in cognitive psychology conducted by Paivio (1986) and others. The unique contribution of Bucci has been to postulate a third mode of representation, which she characterises as *referential activity*. In this type of information processing, the person is involved in making links and connections between the non-verbal/affective and verbal/symbolic domains of experience. For Bucci, the key task in therapy is to help the client to engage in effective and appropriate referential activity, which is seen as forming a bridge between the painful or warded-off feelings and images that led the client to seek therapy, and the kind of reflective self-understanding associated with good therapeutic outcome. The movement between these different modes of representation in therapy is seen as a cyclical process:

> . . . the referential cycle has three main phases: each phase is characterized by dominance of a particular type of connecting process: nonverbal, referential or verbal. The patient first attempts to retrieve private emotional experience – the passion, the terror, the rage – in a halting, indirect and lonely quest, then connects the private nonverbal representations that have surfaced to the communicative verbal mode, and finally reflects on this in the shared therapeutic discourse. Optimally, the collaborative contemplation of this material, within the intensity of the therapeutic relationship, will lead to the opening of new emotional structures, thus continuing the cyclical progression on a deeper level. (1993: 4)

The significance of this model from a narrative perspective is that referential activity in therapy often takes the form of storytelling (in psychonanalysis this might frequently be a dream-story). As Bucci (1995: 104) has written: 'the telling of a story is precisely the expression of an emotion schema, or parts of a schema, in verbal form.' Thus, Bucci's multiple code theory provides a framework for understanding the role of stories in therapy – sites for the linking of verbal and non-verbal modes of knowing. Bucci and her colleagues have developed methods of measuring intensity of referential activity on a moment-by-moment basis throughout the process of therapy. Their instruments include both rating scales used by observers, as well as objective (computer-assisted) counts of quantifiable linguistic features of therapy transcripts. Referential activity is assessed in terms of four dimensions: *concreteness* (sensory quality and reference to bodily experience); *imagery* (the degree to which the language evokes corresponding experience in the reader or hearer); *specificity* (the amount of detailed explicit descriptions of persons, objects, places or events); and *clarity* (how well the linguistic image is focused). Research employing these measures has produced substantial evidence to support the multiple code model.

The multiple code process model developed by Bucci clearly has its roots in psychoanalytic thinking, as a version of Freud's primary–secondary process theory, and also in biologically based cognitive science. It does not claim to offer a constructionist perspective on the role of narrative in therapy. The model does not include any sense of the person as an intentional agent operating in a socially constructed world. Nevertheless, it does contain within it some ideas that can be brought to bear on how and when narratives occur in therapy, and on the characteristics of helpful narrative events. These ideas are explored further in later chapters.

Other voices within the psychoanalytic tradition: the work of Roy Schafer

The American psychoanalyst Roy Schafer has been a key figure in the emergence of a narrative approach to therapy. Like Donald Spence (whose contribution is discussed in Chapter 5), Schafer has taken the sensitivity to the client narrative that is characteristic of good psychoanalytic practice, and placed it at the centre of his style of doing therapy. Schafer's ideas on narrative need to be understood in the context of his earlier endeavours (Schafer, 1976) to establish an 'action language' for psychoanalysis. He argues that the theory of mind as a mental apparatus is obsolete and unhelpful, and proposes to replace it with an understanding of human beings as active agents, constructing a psychological world in which they live. In this respect, Schafer has much in common with constructivist theorists (see Chapter 4), although he does not appear to have made any attempt to locate himself within that tradition: his writing is firmly grounded in psychoanalytic theory and practice. For Schafer, narration is the way in which the person constructs a description of an action or sequence of actions. He is interested in how the client or patient employs an active process of narrat*ing*, tell*ing*, present*ing* a story-line to create and maintain an inner emotional life and set of relationships. His model of narrative therapy was introduced in a paper in 1980, and has been extended in his 1992 book, *Retelling a Life: Narration and Dialogue in Psychoanalysis*. The title of this book (and its contents) reinforce Schafer's continuing identification with psychoanalysis, and in fact he can be highly critical of other approaches to therapy.

Schafer takes as his starting point the idea that people create *story-lines* to account for important events and phenomena that they encounter in their lives. In therapy, both client and therapist are engaged in constructing story-lines, often drawing upon a well-known stock of possible stories. One of the most intriguing aspects of Schafer's writing lies in the way he is able to take well-known psychoanalytic phenomena and re-frame themes as story-lines. An example is his discussion of defence mechanisms:

> . . . in using the [concept] of *defense*, a warlike storyline is established, and in the interest of narrative consistency and coherence the [therapist] makes a commitment to follow that storyline. Such terms as *abwehr, warding off, attack, infiltration, breakthrough, collapse, strengthening*, and *rebuilding* may be used: terms that have figured prominently in conventional psychoanalytic discussions of defense, and all of which may be said to be entailed and regulated by commitment to the same bellicose storyline . . . the term *resistance* (a close relative of defense) establishes a commitment to the same adversarial storyline. (Schafer, 1992: 47)

The point Schafer is making here is that the 'relationship is war' story-line implied by concepts such as 'defence' and 'resistance' is only one type of story that might be told about a therapeutic relationship. Indeed, there may be times when it would be more helpful to construe the same events in terms of a more 'impartial' or 'affirming' story-line.

The therapeutic approach developed by Schafer is one of adopting a high level of sensitivity to narrative, an ability to understand what is happening in therapy as an interplay between client and therapist story-lines. The story-line that is in the foreground of therapy is the self-narrative or self-story-line of the client. Given that this narrative of self is troubled, confused or in some other way felt by the client to be unsatisfactory, the task of the therapist is to facilitate the emergence of an alternative story-line. The therapist achieves this goal through a transformational dialogue that acts to *destabilise, decon-struct* and *defamiliarise* the client's consciously presented narrative of self. Some of the ways that these processes can operate within psychoanalysis (Schafer, 1992: 157–9) are set out below:

- Free association enables the elements of the narrative to surface
- Frequent sessions facilitate the construction of a continuous story
- One-hour sessions allow the story-line to 'double back on itself' creating a story that grounds current defences in the 'danger situations of early childhood'
- The mechanisms of defence stabilise and maintain the 'problem story': analysis of defences destabilises this story
- The analyst focuses on the contradictory and incoherent aspects of the client's narrative
- The analyst begins to re-tell the client's story, and to 'bring the analysand into the process of retelling'
- 'Working-through' can be seen as a process of repeated defamiliarisation.

It is hard to tell how influential Schafer has been in psychoanalytic circles. His project appears to be one of initiating a revolution in psychoanalysis, of reformulating the philosophical and conceptual foundations on which analysis is built. However, in doing so he arrives at a form of therapy that bears many similarities to the constructivist therapies to be described in Chapter 4 and the social constructionist approaches discussed in Chapter 5. The impression is of an original and creative thinker who has developed a framework for understanding psychoanalysis. To use Schafer's own terminology, he has produced a 'master narrative' that subsumes and explains the 'master narrative' of Freud. Whether his colleagues will choose to follow him into this new territory remains to be seen.

Conclusion: the uses of narrative in contemporary psychodynamic therapy

In this chapter, the use of narrative in a range of psychodynamic therapies has been examined. It can be seen that concepts of narrative and story have played a significant role in the work of several important theorists. However, it is also clear that what these approaches have been doing has been to use stories as a means of gaining access to other areas of experience, such as relationship themes, or other unconscious content, which are regarded as representing the basic subject matter for therapeutic work. In mainstream psychodynamic therapy, listening to stories is a means to an end. The story itself is of relatively little intrinsic interest to the therapist. Mainstream contemporary therapy in this respect reproduces the tendency in modern culture to give more credence to abstract, scientific–paradigmatic modes of knowing, and to marginalise the concrete, contextualised knowing provided by narrative.

The culture in which we live has closed down many of the possibilities for telling personal stories. We inhabit a densely storied world, but in the main find ourselves acting as the passive recipients of waves of stories transmitted by television, newspapers and novels. Perhaps one of the central forms of social control in modern times has been achieved through the massive expansion in non-participant narrative. Each year an average member of a modern urban–industrial society will consume, at a superficial level, many hundreds of transient, distanced stories that have relatively little personal meaning and are barely recollected once heard or seen. At least therapy provides an opportunity to tell one's own, personal story in all its detail. This is probably the great appeal and yet the disappointment of therapy. There can often be a sense of relief and a feeling of profound affirmation for a person that his or her story has been heard, that it can be told, that it is acceptable and can be taken seriously, that it makes sense to someone else. The disappointment lies in the fact that most forms of therapy do not provide any means through which the person can locate their own personal narrative in the wider stories of their culture. Therapy can enable a person to find meaning within the set of events and experiences that make up their individual life history, but does not in itself give access to the broader set of meanings that make up a culture. Indeed, in promoting a genre of over-psychologised, individualised, a-historical stories, therapy as it currently operates has probably contributed to the erosion of these bigger stories. In Chapter 6, we turn to the work of a group of therapists who have attempted to construct forms of practice that attempt to address this problem. Before then, however, it is necessary to examine the ideas of the cognitive/constructivist school of narrative therapy.

4

Constructivist Narrative Therapies

The field of cognitive therapy has undergone something of a transition in recent years. The early key figures in the approach, Beck and Ellis, had been trained in and influenced by psychoanalytic ideas, and brought into the new cognitive therapy the notion that psychological problems stemmed from unconscious mental *content*, such as 'irrational beliefs'. At the same time, other pioneers of cognitive change techniques, notably Bandura and Meichenbaum, had essentially grafted cognitive concepts on to a behavioural approach to therapy. However, the subsequent development of cognitive therapy over the last 20 years has led in a direction that has become known as *constructivism*, giving greater emphasis to the human capacity actively to construct meaning through cognitive processing of information. In many ways, this new movement can be seen as a version of the personal construct psychology that George Kelly produced in the 1950s, but with a more solid base in cognitive research.

It could be argued that the originators of cognitive approaches to counselling and psychotherapy, figures such as as Beck, Kelly and Ellis, created theories that were no more than loosely connected to actual theory and research within cognitive psychology; later generations of cognitive therapists have attempted to base their therapeutic models more explicitly within a research tradition. In doing so, some cognitive therapists have particularly looked toward experimental studies of the role of narrative in development, learning and language use. The key idea within cognitive approaches to narrative is the concept of a story as a form of *representation*. Modern cognitive psychologists tend to assume that people represent the world not through static 'pictures' or images in their heads, but through *schemas* or *scripts*, that can be understood as dynamic sequences of actions that can be taken in relation to external objects. For example, an object such as a bottle is not mentally represented as a kind of internal picture of a bottle, but is encoded in terms of potential action sequences such as 'graspable', 'pouring', or even 'drinkable from'. This sense of representation occurring through action schemas can be seen most clearly in the context of language acquisition in young children, in which objects are initially encoded and remembered in terms of what can be *done* with them, whether they can be sucked, bashed or made noise with. In everyday adult life, the structured web of schemas with which we make sense of the world is expressed in the stories that we tell. The person constructs and conveys meaning through narrative. Cognitive/constructivist therapists, therefore, regard stories as a means of gaining access to, and facilitating change in, fundamental underlying schemas and scripts.

Basic principles of change in constructivist narrative therapy

The implications for therapy of cognitive research into narrative have been explored by Bamberg (1991), Russell (1991), Russell and van den Broek (1992), Russell et al. (1993) and van den Broek and Thurlow (1991). The more general contours of a cognitive narrative therapy have been articulated by Neimeyer (1994), Viney (1990, 1993), Vogel (1994) and, notably, Goncalves (1994). However, in this body of work, the most fully developed approach is to be found in the writings of Robert Russell, particularly in his seminal paper with Paul van den Broek (1992) entitled 'Changing narrative schemas in psychotherapy'. Here, Russell and van den Broek argue that narrative is a 'fundamental form of schematic representation' (1992: 344) that enables the individual to organise experience. Narratives differ along dimensions of structural connectedness, degree of subjectivity and linguistic complexity (Russell's research into these variables is described more fully in the following section). One of the tasks of the therapist is to be sensitive to the way the client portrays his or her world and life using these elements (see also Bamberg, 1991). Change or transformation in narrative schemas is viewed as occurring through two main processes of *differentiation* and *integration*. First, rival narratives, different but equally plausible stories told about the same events, must be generated. This is essentially a process of differentiation. The client who previously could tell only one 'problem story' finds with the assistance of the therapist that he or she has available alternative accounts of his or her troubles. Second, one of the competing narratives comes to be seen as more compelling, as:

> (a) more coherent, more accurate and/or widely applicable (i.e. representing courses of conduct, feelings and beliefs that would be considered positive achievements for a larger number of protagonists than the conduct represented in the other narrative), and (b) able to subsume the subordinate narrative in a fashion that permits it to be illuminated and integrated within the superordinate narrative. (Russell and van den Broek, 1992: 348)

This is the integration stage of the process of therapeutic change. The client emerges from this process with a new story that includes within it the kernel of his or her previous narrative. Russell and van den Broek point out that it is crucial that the therapist focuses on new narratives that fulfil criteria of coherence, accuracy and applicability without departing too dramatically from the narrative schemas currently employed by the client. They draw on Vygotsky's notion of 'zone of proximal development' to clarify this issue. The Russian developmental psychologist Vygotsky (1978) suggested that effective learning should neither require that the person merely demonstrate what he or she can already achieve, nor should it it set goals that are so difficult that the individual repeatedly fails. Instead, a teacher (or therapist) should operate in a territory defined by the learner's 'current highest level of achievement'.

The process of narrative change described by Russell is essentially that of generating contrasting schemas. A similar idea is put forward by Vogel (1994) when he talks about *perspective by incongruity*, a term borrowed from the literary critic Kenneth Burke (1966, 1969). Incongruity can be understood as constituting a kind of 'radical metaphor', where the everyday way of thinking and talking about a topic or problem is subverted by the introduction of a fundamentally new way of depicting it. A therapeutic example might be the use of the 'fixed role' techniques in personal construct therapy (Fransella, 1985), which involves the client generating and then acting out, a social role that is 'orthogonal', is essentially different from their own. Vogel suggests that many of the most influential psychological theories, such as psychoanalysis and behaviourism, can be experienced by the client as 'perverse and absurd' but nevertheless have the effect of challenging the way that he or she experiences self.

In the same vein, Efran (1994) argues that the purpose of therapy is to help the person to break free of the 'abstractions' that can come to dominate the way the person perceives the world. The therapist operates outside the social and cognitive rules that prevail within the life of the client, and in doing so can help him or her to *see* things differently.

It is of some interest that, while the constructivist theorists discussed here all attribute narrative change to a process of cognitive conflict, Russell regards the most effective type of conflict as that which is 'proximal' or incremental. Vogel and Efran, on the other hand, appear to suggest that change arises from the client's experience of confronting much more fundamental and radical incongruities in how they construct a personal world.

Constructivist models of stages of narrative change

It is clear that the identification in constructivist therapy of competing or incongruent narratives is embedded in a broader therapeutic process. Several writers have attempted to give an outline of this process in constructivist terms. Recently, for example, Meichenbaum (1995) has moved his original formulation of cognitive behaviour modification in the direction of a narrative constructivist approach to therapy. In the first phase of therapy, the goal of the therapist is to build a relationship that will facilitate the client's capacity to tell his or her story. The therapist then helps the client to 'normalise' his or her reaction to stressful events, to build a 'healing theory' of what happened and why it happened. Throughout this process, Meichenbaum advocates close attention to the metaphors used by the client, as indicators of the core emotional meanings implicit in the client's stories.

A more complex model of narrative change is proposed by Goncalves (1994, 1995a, 1995b). He suggests that there are five discrete stages or tasks involved in the transformation of the client's self-narrative in constructivist therapy: recalling, objectifying, subjectifying, metaphorising and projecting. Although Goncalves' model may appear to depict a rather fixed framework, his clinical examples suggest that in practice the approach is sensitively attuned to the needs of specific clients. Goncalves describes the ultimate goal of his approach as that of empowering the client to use narrative techniques to 'develop a continuous sense of actorship and authorship in his/her life' (1995b: 158). What is striking about Goncalves' work is a continuing effort to introduce incongruity and conflict into the client's way of construing the world. Over and over again, the client is invited to re-tell the story of key events in different ways: objectively, subjectively, metaphorically. The five stages of Goncalves' model are:

- Phase 1. *Recalling narratives.* Identification of memories of important life events, using guided imagery exercises to facilitate recall. Homework assignment involving writing key stories from each year of life. Review of collected life-stories to select a 'prototype' narrative.
- Phase 2. *Objectifying narratives.* Re-telling important narratives in ways that 'bring the reader into the text', for example through giving greater attention to sensory cues: visual, auditory, olfactory, gustatory, tactile. Collecting documents and artefacts (e.g. photographs, music, letters) that will further 'objectify' the story by defining its external referents.
- Phase 3. *Subjectifying narratives.* The aim of this stage is to increase the client's awareness of his or her inner experience of the narrative. Exercises are used in which the therapist triggers recall of a significant story and then asks the client to focus on the inner experience of the event through instructions such as 'allow yourself to be aware only of what you are experiencing now' or 'try to to pick one of your thoughts and uncover the thought that is behind it until you reach what seems to be your most basic thought'.
- Phase 4. *Metaphorising narratives.* The client is trained in methods of generating metaphoric associations to stories, and then the origins of these images in his or her life are explored.
- Phase 5. *Projecting narratives.* The client is given practice in constructing alternative metaphors, drawn from literature and art. These new root metaphors are implemented within sessions and then in everyday life.

(Goncalves, 1995b: 145–7)

The constructivist approach to narrative change developed by Lynne Angus (Angus, 1996a, 1996b; Angus and Hardtke, 1994) presents a cyclical rather than stage-based model. Angus argues that there are three modes of narrative processing: external, internal and reflexive. These correspond to the main tasks of therapy:

> First of all, the client and therapist focus on the remembrance of past events and the description of current events in order to 'fill the gaps' of what has been forgotten or never fully acknowledged, and hence not understood. Second, client and therapist undertake a detailed unfolding and exploration of associated perceptions, sensations, emotions and thoughts such that the lived experience of the event can be engaged and perhaps articulated for the first time. The third goal entails the reflexive analysis of the related experiences and circumstances of 'what happened' such that a new meaning or understanding is formed which either supports or challenges the implicit beliefs about self and others that underscore the dominant macro-narrative. (Angus, 1996a: 3)

Research carried out into this model (discussed in more detail below) suggests that, in good outcome therapy, the therapist actively initiates shifts from either external or internal to reflexive processing of the narrative. Angus, like Meichenbaum and Goncalves, emphasises the role of metaphor in bringing about narrative change (Angus, 1992, 1996b; Angus and Rennie, 1988, 1989). The collaborative identification and use by both client and therapist of a 'core metaphor theme' draws the therapist into the client's story, provides a focus for reflection, and can lead to 'reframing and understanding of new possibilities' (Angus, 1996b: 82).

Research into constructivist processes

One of the distinctive features of cognitive therapy has been a willingness to use research to inform and advance clinical practice. The growing interest in narrative exhibited by constructivist therapists has stimulated a number of research studies that serve to illustrate the advancing 'edge' of constructivist thinking on this topic. To date, these studies have focused on the process of constructivist narrative therapy rather than on its outcomes.

Russell et al. (1993) have constructed a framework for coding three levels of narrative organisation: structural connectedness, representation of subjectivity, and complexity. The notion of *structural connectedness* arises from research in cognitive and developmental psychology, which has demonstrated that individuals (at least, individuals in dominant Western cultural groups) are better able to understand and remember stories that follow a sequence such as 'setting–initiating event–internal response–attempt–consequence–reaction' (Stein and Glenn, 1979). This kind of 'story grammar' comprises a causally connected, temporally ordered sequence of events that constitutes a well-rounded and complete story. *Representation of subjectivity*, the second dimension of the Russell et al. (1993) model, reflects the idea that a story communicates not just a series of events, but also conveys information about the point of view of the teller. For example, a story can be told in the present or past tense, in the first or third person, and so on. As J.S. Bruner (1986) puts it, one of the key functions of stories is to convey the 'landscape of consciousness' of the narrator. The third dimension of the Russell et al. (1993) model is that of *complexity*. Stories can vary according to the lengths of sentences, density of adjectival and adverbial descriptors, and other linguistic variables. It is likely that these factors are important in psychotherapy. As Russell et al. (1993: 342) suggest, 'if clients tell truncated, sparse narratives with little degree of conceptual variation and linguistic complexity, therapists not only might note the client's reluctance to reveal details but also might wonder about the possible poverty of the client's experience and lack of psychological mindedness'. So far, this category system only appears to have been applied in one study, to the analysis of transcripts of sessions of child psychotherapy. The findings of this study (Russell et al., 1993) also yielded a further feature of narrative production in therapy: the degree of *attunement* of the therapist to the client's narrative. This dimension was foreshadowed in the client's coding scheme without being explicitly coded, but emerged in the client's analysis.

Another system for coding and analysing narrative processes in psychotherapy discourse has been developed by Angus and Hardtke (1994). Their Narrative Process Coding Scheme (NPCS) requires that raters first divide therapy transcripts into topic segments, defined as blocks of text that include both client and therapist statements relating to discrete topic areas, themes or issues. These topic segments are then further subdivided and coded in terms of modes of narrative processing. Three types of narrative processing are identified: focusing on external events, focusing on internal experiences, and reflexive analysis. When a narrative sequence is primarily focused on *external events*, the therapeutic discourse comprises descriptive material recounting 'what happened'. *Internal* sequences occur when the client or therapist articulates subjective experiences, feeling states or emotional reactions. Finally, *reflexive* sequences represent attempts to understand or interpret the meaning of events. In a study comparing transcripts from poor and good outcome therapies, Angus and Hardtke (1994) found that positive outcomes were associated with higher numbers of topic segments in each session, substantially higher frequencies of reflexive processing, and lower frequencies of internal processing sequences.

Although the work of Rennie has been primarily addressed to developing a framework for understanding the client's experience of the therapy, his research has also generated valuable insights into what happens when a client embarks on telling a story to his or her therapist. Although Rennie does not explicitly place himself in the cognitive–constructivist tradition, his approach is sufficiently compatible with constructivism to be discussed here. In the studies carried out by Rennie, recordings are made of therapy sessions, and the client is invited to listen to (or watch) the tape and report on what he or she was experiencing at the time of the actual session. This 'stimulated recall' method is increasingly used to gain access to the 'interior' of therapy (Elliott, 1991). The recall interview yields a mass of qualitative material that is then analysed in terms of themes or categories of experience reported by the client. The initial studies carried out by Rennie (1990) mapped the totality of categories and themes experienced by clients in individual sessions. Later analyses have focused in on more specific dimensions of the client's experience, including the client's experience of 'storytelling'.

Rennie (1992) found that, on average, clients were aware of eight discrete 'storytelling' episodes in each session of therapy. Clients reported that, prior to embarking on telling a story, they had experienced tension, or what Rennie (1994a: 237) termed an 'inner disturbance'. When giving their account of what they were actually experiencing during the storytelling episodes, the research participants talked about two phases in the process of producing a story: *distancing from disturbance* and *storytelling as a therapeutic experience*. Telling a story in therapy appeared to be a means of initially maintaining distance from the inner disturbance while still exploring a personal issue. Distancing from the inner disturbance sometimes took the form of 'delaying entry' into deeper feelings. Clients reflecting on this phase of the storytelling episode observed that they had been 'stalling', or 'skating over the main point'. On other occasions, clients reported a form of distancing that could be described as 'belief management', which involved telling the story in such a manner as to reduce its potential to threaten the image of self that they wished to convey to the therapist. For example, one client used a story of a job interview to create a false impression of being confident and in control. She acknowledged on the recall interview that:

> ... this belief management had been motivated by the fear that if she had admitted the truth, she would have gotten upset, which could have taken several days to over-come. The therapy session had occurred on a Friday; she had a lot of work to do, and she could not afford the risk. (1994a: 239)

The sense here is that, in this first phase, the client starts to construct a story that is an acceptable version, a narrative that will communicate some of his or her world to the therapist, but which allows the client to remain emotionally safe.

However, the participants in this research related that, as they told the story, and once they had finished it, they were aware of a number of therapeutic effects. First, there was a feeling of emotional relief. It was as though the tension associated with the story, arising from the necessity to balance different elements, became resolved as the story was completed. Clients reported that, toward the end of the story, they felt an urgency about completing it without interruption. The tension inherent in the storytelling process could only be resolved if every piece of the narrative could be fitted into place. A second therapeutic process arose from the way that telling the story re-evoked the experience of the initial event: 'once into the story, they were flooded with images, memories and associations' (Rennie, 1994a: 239). Even if the client had begun the story with an intention to avoid the inner disturbance, the storytelling process appeared inevitably to lead back into it. The third therapeutic process mentioned by clients was that they were aware that, while they were telling the story to the therapist, they were internally processing some of the implications and meaning of what they were saying. Rennie noted here that 'the spoken story is often only an outcrop of a richer, inner story' (Rennie, 1994a: 240). Behind the narrative, the client could 'try feelings and realizations on for size in private'.

The findings of the Rennie (1994a) study of client experience of storytelling need to be understood in context. Clients participating in the research were required to review a tape of a whole session and report on their experience of everything that happened. They were not asked specifically to focus on stories, and in fact accounts of storytelling events comprised a relatively small proportion of the overall protocol. Also, 'storytelling' was a category defined by clients, which might not encompass all the different types of narrative event that might be envisaged. Despite these limitations, the study provides a powerful representation of the complexity and therapeutic impact of telling stories, and reflects many of the themes introduced in Chapter 2. The story told in therapy is experienced by the client as a relational event, where he or she is aware of his or her audience and shaping what is said to create an impression or control the interaction. The story is a problem-solving event, through the 'necessity to configure events into a coherent whole' (Rennie, 1994a: 239). The story acts to 'emplot' emotions, often leading from a partial distancing from disturbing feelings into and through a more comprehensive re-experiencing of them.

On the face of it, the studies reviewed in this section have produced systems for analysing narrative process in psychotherapy that may appear quite different. However, it can be seen that there are two broad themes around which this work can be seen to converge. First, there is an interest in the sequencing or structure of stories told by clients. Second, there is an emphasis on the *way* that clients tell their stories. However, there are also some respects in which these studies make quite different assumptions about the key dimensions of therapeutic narratives. For example, only Rennie (1994a) uses the idea that the client is operating in parallel at different levels: telling the story and at the same time monitoring the telling. Only Russell et al. (1993) address the interaction of therapist and client modes of storytelling. Angus and Hardtke (1994) pay particular attention to the co-construction of narratives by client and therapist.

These research studies are important because they are beginning to provide a much richer picture of what happens when clients tell stories in therapy. Most of what has been written about narrative in constructivist therapy has been based on the clinical experience of practising therapists. However, although there is no doubt that what clinicians have to say is valid, it is also limited. For example, a therapist cannot have access to the experience of the client in the systematic manner achieved by Rennie. A therapist will emerge from a session with a partial memory of some of what went on, whereas the techniques used by Russell and by Angus and Hardtke carefully examine every utterance recorded in a therapy transcript.

Reading and writing as adjuncts to therapy

Behavioural and cognitive approaches to therapy have always employed a variety of 'homework' assignments to enable clients to extend and consolidate the learning that takes place in the actual therapy interview. As cognitive therapy has moved toward constructivism and an interest in narrative, many therapists have begun to invent narratively informed homework assignments. Although techniques such as keeping journals, writing letters and constructing autobiographies can be found in all modes of therapy, their widest used has been within constructivist approaches.

Therapy has in the main existed as an oral tradition. The greatest part of what goes on between therapist and client is talk. Nevertheless, there have always been therapists who have recognised the value of written communication, such as diaries and letters, or have encouraged their clients to read books that they considered would be helpful to them. These techniques can be regarded as broadly informed by an appreciation of the role of narrative in therapy, insofar as they enable clients to construct a narrative account of their troubles or use a narrative account created by someone else (for example, a novel) to provide some structure for their own life-story.

The work of Lange (1994, 1996) represents a particularly innovative approach to using client writing assignments, in this instance with clients experiencing debilitating grief and post-traumatic stress disorder. For example, one woman had lost a child and still, 25 years later, felt bitter about her husband's insensitivity to her during this period. Lange invited this client to 'write uninhibitedly about the situations that had hurt her'. This writing was ritualised, in that it was agreed that she would write at the same time, at the same table, for a fixed amount of time each day. These 'rotten fish' letters were not to be given to her husband. By the end of three weeks of such writing, the client reported that 'she had experienced the writing as if it was a pill that had softened her feelings dramatically and greatly reduced her pain'. The therapist then asked her to write a new letter to her husband, communicating her feelings in a 'worthy and dignified manner'.

The examples given by Lange represent a fairly structured form of therapeutic writing, using the letter format and at a particular time and place. Proponents of the therapeutic use of journals (such as Progoff, 1975; Rainer, 1980) suggest a variety of writing formats and structures. These strategies have been usefully summarised by Lukinsky (1990):

1 *Daily log*. Recording the day's events.
2 *Period log*. The subjective construction of the current period in the writer's life. Entries would begin by naming the period, and continue with 'It is a time when I . . .'
3 *Steppingstones*. Reviewing formative life experiences from the vantage point of the present.
4 *Dialogue*. Creating a dialogue with a person, event or object from the journal writer's life.
5 *Lists*. Clusters of ideas on a topic.
6 *Guided imagery*. Free writing stimulated by an image such as 'being on a journey'.
7 *Altered point of view*. Writing about oneself in the third person or about someone else in the first person.

Wiener and Rosenwald (1993) documented a wide range of techniques used by people who regularly wrote personal diaries. Other therapists have encouraged clients to engage in 'free' writing, choosing whatever means of self-expression they personally find facilitative and cathartic (McKinney, 1976).

Most of the work on writing carried out by therapy clients has been descriptive, drawing on clinical examples and case vignettes as evidence. However, James Pennebaker and his colleagues have carried out an extensive series of controlled research studies into the effects of writing about problems. The investigation by Pennebaker et al. (1988) can be taken as an example of the approach taken in this research programme. In this study, 50 healthy undergraduate volunteers were randomly assigned into two groups. Each group was instructed to write about either traumatic experiences or superficial topics for four consecutive days. The information given to the trauma group was as follows:

> During each of the four writing days, I want you to write about the most traumatic and upsetting experiences of your entire life. You can write on different topics each day or on the same topic for all four days. The important thing is that you write about your deepest thoughts and feelings. Ideally, whatever you write about should deal with an event or experience that you have not talked with others about in detail. (Pennebaker et al., 1988: 240)

Before beginning this writing task, and then again after the four days and at a six-week follow-up, participants' blood pressure, heart rate and skin conductance were measured. Blood samples were taken for analysis of immunological function, and health centre records were examined to record the number of visits made by each student in the five months prior to the study and the six-week period of the study itself. Questionnaires were administered to determine physical symptoms, mood and perceptions of the writing task.

The results of this study revealed that the students in the trauma group did indeed write about very personal and difficult experiences, such as loss and loneliness associated with leaving home, conflicts with members of the opposite sex, parental problems and bereavement. Compared to the control (writing about superficial topics) participants, the members of the trauma group reported significantly higher levels of physical symptoms and negative moods following each writing episode, indicating that the experience of writing was in itself distressing. However, those writing about trauma were found to have comparatively fewer health centre visits during the time of the study, and showed slight improvements in immune functioning. Those subjects in the trauma group who disclosed most in their stories, who wrote about topics that they acknowledged they had previously held back from other people, reported the greatest gains in health. Similar results were found in a replication carried out by Pennebaker et al. (1990), who were able to track the positive effects of writing over a one-year follow-up period. Spera et al. (1994) asked unemployed professionals to write about their thoughts and feelings surrounding their job loss, and found that those in an expressive writing group were twice as likely to find a new job within eight months than those in a control condition who had been instructed to write about their job plans but not to dwell on their feelings or opinions.

How can these findings be understood? Why does writing about difficult experiences produce physiological changes that contribute to gains in health and well-being? Pennebaker (1988, 1993a, 1993b; Harber and Pennebaker, 1992) has articulated a comprehensive model of the effects of disclosure of trauma that encompasses social, psychological and physiological dimensions of the process. Essentially, Pennebaker considers that there is a basic human tendency or need to disclose difficult experiences to other people, both in order that the teller of the story can achieve 'peace of mind', and so that the hearer and the community as a whole can be warned about possible dangers.

However, there are many factors within society that prevent people from 'putting stress into words', and, as a result, those who have experienced stressful or traumatic events are forced to find ways of inhibiting their memories of trauma and their need to disclose. This inhibition or 'mental control' has physical effects which in turn produce illness. The following list, drawing on Harber and Pennebaker (1992), illustrates the various stages in this process:

1   Inhibiting ongoing thoughts, feelings or behaviour is associated with physiological work. Short-term inhibition is manifested in increased autonomic nervous system activity. Long-term inhibition serves as a low-level cumulative biological stressor that can cause or exacerbate a variety of health problems, ranging from colds and flu to heart disease and cancer.
2   Active inhibition is associated with deleterious changes in information processing. In holding back significant thoughts and feelings associated with an event, individuals do not process the event fully, and are left with ruminations, dreams and other intrusive cognitive symptoms.
3   Confronting traumatic memories can help negate the effects of inhibition, by reducing the physiological work put into inhibition, and by enabling individuals to understand and assimilate the event.

This model of trauma disclosure describes a process that is applied most often when people *talk* about a difficult event, and indeed some of Pennebaker's research has examined the effects of talking about experiences such as surviving the Holocaust (Pennebaker et al., 1989; Shortt and Pennebaker, 1992) or coping with earthquake or war (Pennebaker and Harber, 1993). However, Pennebaker suggests that there are distinctive aspects of *writing* that operate to enhance the coping process. Many of his research participants commented that writing helped them to get events into a manageable perspective, and that this was facilitated by writing stories with clear beginnings, middles and ends. These stories externalised and gave structure to often chaotic and confused memories and feelings. Moreover, the discipline of constructing sentences forces the writer to dismantle the totality of the traumatic experience into its constituent 'bits'. Pennebaker uses the metaphor of the traumatic 'knot' to describe the way that images and fears can become tightly, and impenetrably, wound together. He observes that: 'by spinning out my tale into a coherent narrative string, I begin to unravel the traumatic knot' (Harber and Pennebaker, 1992: 378). Writing also promotes the assimilation of the 'knotted' section of thread into the general fabric of memory, by making links between the traumatic event and other everyday non-traumatic occurrences. Finally, writing can provide a safe place to express potentially shameful material. The writer has the choice over whether or not, at a later date, to let anyone else see what was written.

It is important, also, to take account of the type of writing that Pennebaker and his colleagues have found to be most therapeutic. The participants in his studies who have gained most from writing have been those who have written about difficult experiences, have examined events and themes that they had

previously held back from others, and who have written quickly and spontaneously. The *quality* of writing produced under these conditions is high, with
much fluidity and vividness, and a clear structure.

The unique value of the programme of research conducted by Pennebaker
and his colleagues is that it has presented 'hard' evidence concerning the
helpfulness of writing. In the past, therapists who suggested writing tasks to
clients, and those people who keep personal journals or diaries, have known,
intuitively, that what they were doing was valuable. Pennebaker has made the
process of therapeutic writing more explicit, and his research has legitimated
this kind of activity in ways that should encourage more counsellors and
psychotherapists to experiment with different forms of writing exercise as an
adjunct to conventional therapy.

Reading, or 'bibliotherapy', is another narrative-informed activity that has
often been used within therapy, or as an alternative to face-to-face psychotherapy. Rubin (1978) has collected together many of the important early
contributions to this field, dating back to 1927. Starker (1988) reported that
the majority of psychologists who responded to his survey acknowledged
that they encouraged some clients to read self-help books. Ogles et al. (1991)
compared the effectiveness of four different self-help books for people deal-
ing with the consequences of divorce or separation and found that, at least for
those who did not show severe problems at the outset, the levels of improvement on measures of depression and other symptoms before and after
'treatment' were similar to those attained by clients in conventional therapy.
The issue of *how* reading helps people with emotional problems has received
relatively little attention. Much of the literature on the use of reading in therapy has started from an assumption that clients employ self-help guides and
manuals to gain knowledge about their disorders and to acquire skills and
coping mechanisms that will enable them to deal with troubling feelings, relationships and situations (Glasgow and Rosen, 1978; Scogin et al., 1990).
However, when clients in a study carried out by by Cohen (1994) were asked
to describe their experiences of therapeutic reading their responses indicated
that they appeared to benefit most by entering into the story or stories
recounted in the book. They recognised themselves in the characters being
described, and felt validated, comforted and more hopeful as a result.

Using therapist-supplied stories

Up to now, the emphasis has been on stories produced by clients. Working
with narrative has involved helping the client to tell his or her story, listening
carefully to the narrative structure and timing of the story, and so on. There
are some therapists who go beyond this and recognise that the impact of the
story as a 'way of knowing' can extend to the therapist too. The interventions
made by the therapist can be cast in story form too. This can be done in a
relatively spontaneous manner, or it can represent a structured, intentional
therapeutic technique.

At the less formal, intuitive end of this dimension lie stories based on metaphors or images that seem suddenly to appear in the therapist's awareness. Much of the time, therapists may ignore or suppress this material, or be suspicious of its validity. These inklings can all too readily be condemned as indicative of 'counter-transference'. Yet, if brought into the open and shared with the client, such stories can have a powerful effect. An example of this kind of process is given by Bozarth (1984).

Such therapist-generated stories often appear to be able to bring together many of the strands in what is being experienced by the client. It is as if the story acts as a kind of metaphor for a situation in the client's life. This metaphoric aspect can be specifically highlighted when the therapist tells a story that is based on a fictional character.

These metaphoric and intuitive therapist stories resemble the appearance of anecdotes and jokes in ordinary everyday conversation: they are not planned, but suddenly 'come up'. Some therapists have attempted to go further and maximise the effectiveness of therapist stories by basing them on thought-out principles. The assumption is that therapeutic change can be facilitated by certain types of stories that are offered at certain times. These *intentional* therapist stories can be categorised into three types: guided fantasy, mythic stories and Ericksonian stories.

Guided fantasy is a therapeutic technique in which the therapist or group facilitator will invite the client to relax, and then will provide a basic story structure that the person then completes in his or her own imagination. Usually, the client will sit or lie with closed eyes and the therapist will read out instructions with pauses in between when the client fills in the details of the narrative. With this method, the therapist supplies the story *form*, while the client supplies the *content*. A typical guided fantasy (see Graham, 1992, 1995) would engage the client in envisioning himself or herself as undertaking a hazardous journey, overcoming obstacles, meeting a wise person, and returning with a gift or message. In such a scenario, the therapist intentionally engages the client in constructing a 'self-as-hero-on-journey-of-liberation' story, as a means of empowering the client and helping him or her to celebrate his or her own powers and capabilities.

The work of Gersie (Gersie, 1991; Gersie and King, 1990) involves the use of mythic stories to stimulate client exploration of meaning in relation to specific life issues. This approach is applied in a group setting. The group leader selects a mythic story that reflects an issue being confronted by members of the group, for example bereavement or loss. A group session is built around this story. For instance, the leader may begin the session by reading the story, then members will have an opportunity to express their reactions through drawing or writing, then may share their feelings with others in the group, and then may have time for silent reflection. Gersie places great emphasis on the structure of the group exercises that she has developed to accompany the telling of mythic stories. She also encourages the use of stories that are culturally unfamiliar to participants.

A third method of generating intentional therapist stories has evolved

within the field of Ericksonian hypnotherapy. The founder of this approach,
Milton Erickson, was a master storyteller (Rosen, 1982), who seemed to
operate in a somewhat intuitive, idiosyncratic fashion. His followers and students have attempted to analyse and codify the principles underlying his
storytelling techniques (see Lankton and Lankton, 1986). In this particular
use of therapist narrative, the goal of the therapist is to construct a story that
includes the core elements of the problem presented by the client, but re-told
in metaphoric form and with a more positive, optimistic ending, and employing repetition to reinforce key points and facilitate some degree of hypnotic
induction. Wallas (1986, 1991) provides examples of the use of this technique
with many different types of clients.

Conclusion

This brief account does not do justice to the richness of the constructivist
theoretical model, but can perhaps illustrate some of the principal features of
a cognitively informed narrative perspective on therapy. Like the psychodynamic models discussed in the previous chapter, constructivist narrative
therapy is built around the goal of story reconstruction, defined in terms of
the attainment by the client of a unitary and coherent life-story. In contrast to
psychodynamic theory, cognitive/constructivist theory is perhaps less prescriptive about the type of story the client may eventually arrive at, although
it should be noted that within cognitive therapy there are some strands of
practice (for example, Ellis's definitions of rationality/irrationality) that are
fairly explicit about the difference between 'good' and 'dysfunctional' stories.

    There is currently an explosion of interest and activity in the development
of constructivist approaches to therapy (Hoyt, 1996; Mahoney, 1995;
Neimeyer and Mahoney, 1995), much of it focused around the themes of
identifying client stories and working with metaphor and incongruity to shift
these stories. There can be no doubt that constructivist therapists have generated a wide range of powerful conceptual and practical tools. Nevertheless,
it is also important to be aware that constructivist approaches are firmly
based in an individualised image of the person. Constructivism inevitably
downplays the historical, social and emotional aspects of storytelling. For the
theorists and clinicans discussed in this chapter, a story told by a client in
therapy is fundamentally regarded either as a means by which experience
can be represented, or as a template or 'script' that guides behaviour. The
notion of 'schema' encompasses both of these meanings, and in either case a
schema is an entity that exists within the individual person, in his or her
head. However, there is another meaning of narrative, one that is difficult to
incorporate within a constructivist position. Stories exist within a culture,
between people, they are 'out there', to be entered and inhabited by persons.
This alternative way of understanding narrative is associated with a social
constructionist perspective, which is examined in the next chapter.

5

Narrative Therapy from a Social Constructionist Perspective

Foundationalist and constructivist psychologists and therapists have found increasing theoretical value in the concept of narrative, as has been seen in previous chapters. However, despite the undeniable utility of these approaches, a therapy that fully acknowledges the significance of storytelling must go beyond foundationalist and constructivist modes of thinking and address the social and cultural dimensions of narrative. It is only by adopting a social constructionist perspective that the intrinsically social nature of narrative can be grasped: stories are not merely cognitive or individual products, but are shared. The story is created between teller and audience.

Social constructionism is a philosophical approach that has developed over the last 20 years in the social sciences. The key ideas of social constructionism can be summed up as:

- A critical stance in relation to taken-for-granted assumptions about the social world, which are seen as reinforcing the interests of dominant social groups
- Rejection of traditional positivist approaches to knowledge as insufficiently reflexive
- Recognition that the goal of research and scholarship is not to produce knowledge that is fixed and universally valid, but to open up an appreciation of what is possible
- A belief that the way we understand the world is a product of a historical process of interaction and negotiation between groups of people
- A movement toward redefining psychological constructs such as 'mind', 'self' and 'emotion' as socially constructed processes, to be 'removed from the head and placed within the realm of social discourse' (Gergen, 1985: 271)

Although social constructionism has been most closely identified with the writings of Kenneth Gergen (1985, 1994), it can be taken to represent a broad movement within psychology and the social sciences centred around the idea that understanding can only be achieved as a result of careful analysis of the cultural and historical contexts of social life.

One of the recurring themes in the work of therapists influenced by social constructionist thinking has been a tendency to regard a concern for the client's process of narration as central to their work. Unlike the theorists reviewed in the previous two chapters, who used narrative as a method for gaining access to aspects of the person they assumed to be psychologically more foundational (such as unconscious dynamics or cognitive schema), constructionist therapists place the story at the centre of their endeavours. For these therapists, the person can be understood as a living 'text' (Gergen, 1988), inhabiting a 'storied world' (Sarbin, 1986).

It would be quite wrong to characterise social constructionist therapy as a coherent school or approach. There are two reasons for this. First, social constructionism can be viewed as part of a *postmodern* social and cultural movement that is attempting to move beyond modernism. At the time of writing, it is possible to identify only some of the general outline of what might replace modern Western industrial–capitalist culture and thinking. It is a time of transition. No one really knows where all this is heading. The constructionist approach to therapy is not yet fully formed. The second reason for not expecting a unified school of constructionist narrative therapy ever to emerge is that the idea of discrete schools or theories of therapy is itself a modernist notion. The pluralism and reflexivity of postmodern thought run counter to the formation of 'grand theory'. Instead, those influenced by postmodern ideas seek to develop 'local' knowledges, in which theory and practice are closely integrated. Polkinghorne suggests that what psychotherapists and counsellors do (and have always done) in their actual practice represents a 'forceful illustration of the implementation of a postmodern science' (1992: 147), even if the complexity and subtlety of this practice is not (yet) adequately reflected in psychological theory and research on therapy.

Constructionist therapies have, on the whole, been born out of frustration with existing models of therapy. The most important developments in social constructionist narrative therapy can be found in the work of writers who were started off (and to some extent remain) psychoanalytic or family/systemic in orientation. Other streams of postmodern narrative therapy have drawn upon philosophy, anthropology and social psychology. The aim of this chapter is to draw together some of the diverse strands of this emergent approach to therapy, in a way that will serve to make explicit some of its basic principles. Chapters 6 and 7 will examine the way that this approach operates in practice.

Donald Spence and the concept of 'narrative truth'

Donald Spence is a psychoanalyst who has actively deconstructed the basis of his own discipline. In a series of books and articles, Spence (1982a, 1982b, 1986, 1987, 1994) has focused mainly on the task of understanding what is happening when an analyst makes an interpretation, in particular when he or she makes an intepretation that attributes the origins of the client's problems to an early childhood experience. Spence points out that Freud regarded himself as engaged in a search for historical truth, for evidence of the actual events that now constitute memories buried in the patient's unconscious.

Freud sifted through the material offered by the client, as if he was an archae-
ologist digging deeper into the history of a civilisation. The archaeological
image or metaphor acted as a continuing source of inspiration for Freud. He
collected archaeological specimens, which were displayed in his consulting
room. He wrote that he sought to 'follow the example of those discoverers
whose good fortune it is to bring to light of day after their long burial the
priceless though mutilated relics of antiquity' (Freud, 1905 [1953]: 12). This is
an image that reveals a great deal about the place of psychoanalysis within the
modern world: the past, both individual and collective, is to be known not
through the medium of uncertain and often confusing and contradictory stories and myths, but is to become the object of a drive for scientific certainty
and progress.

Spence turns this image on its head by offering another metaphor, that of
the detective story. Freud, according to Spence (1987) portrayed himself as a
Sherlock Holmes figure. His famous cases, such as the analyses of Dora, the
Rat Man, the Wolf Man, can be viewed as examples of the Holmes genre
applied to therapy:

> The genre is familiar to us all. It features a master sleuth (therapist) who is con-
> fronted by a series of bizarre and disconnected events (symptoms) reported by a
> somewhat desperate and disorganized client (patient). The sleuth listens, watches,
> and ponders, never prejudging, never despairing, almost never surprised, always
> confident that when all the facts are in, the mystery will disappear and the truth will
> emerge. In the typical Sherlock Holmes adventure, the eccentric client makes a
> dramatic appearance, often arriving on a dark and stormy night, and presents an
> account which seems partly fantastic and somehow familiar. The events seem to
> have no logical connection with one another or with pieces of his past; frequently
> he seems close to despair and may have come to Holmes only as a last resort.
> Holmes, by contrast, listens calmly and dispassionately, serene in the knowledge
> that the patient sifting of all the evidence will always yield the singular solution.
> And it does. When the explanation is finally revealed, all the once baffling clues
> become obvious and integrated into a continuous account which leads inevitably to
> its conclusion; what was once disconnected and bizarre becomes understandable
> and almost commonplace. (Spence, 1987: 114)

The reader of a Holmes mystery, or a psychoanalytic case, is left not so much
with an appreciation of the experience or life-world of the client, as with an
admiration of the cleverness of the real hero, the therapist–investigator. The
ability to uncover the 'singular solution' is portrayed as the mark of a true
analytic sensibility.

Holmes/Freud has had an abiding appeal throughout the twentieth century.
The condition of life for most members of urban–industrial society during
this time has been that of increasing fragmentation and complexity, accompanied with resulting heightened levels of anxiety. It is attractive to imagine
that there can be a simple solution to the pervasive sense that something is
wrong. It is nice to think that there is someone, somewhere, who knows
enough to get to the bottom of it all.

But also, in coming to identify with Holmes/Freud, the reader (or analyst
in training) is offered a role, a style of engaging with other people's problems.
The therapist–detective is an authority, with impressive professional

credentials. He (usually he) does his work after the crime, and is able to be detached, separate. Spence draws out some of the implications of the famous image of Sherlock Holmes' magnifying glass: 'the observer is always separate from the object being studied . . . facts are knowable pieces of the reality "out there", distinct as to size, shape, and smell, guiding us inevitably in one direction or another' (1987: 118). Moreover, there is little or no requirement to consider alternative interpretations of the data, to enter into dialogue. The task is an intellectual puzzle. And finally, but perhaps most crucially, the hero is known and yet not known. Occasional glimpses of the investigator as person are allowed, but in a controlled way. The subjectivity of the hero is never openly explicated.

The value of the Sherlock Holmes metaphor is that it starkly illuminates the contours of a particular way of understanding therapy, and thereby makes it easier to see what the alternative might be. Virtually every aspect of Holmes/Freud is challenged by contemporary developments in therapy: the importance of the therapeutic alliance, the acceptance of counter-transference, the adoption of a generally more relational style. However, the one element of Holmes/Freud that has remained has been an insistence on the search for a factual, objective basis of the client's neurosis.

The distinction that Spence (1982a) has made between 'narrative truth' and 'historical truth' has made it possible to examine the implications of viewing therapy as an attempt to unearth the objective 'facts' of a person's early life. Historical truth represents an account of the 'way things were', based on an assumption that what the client tells the therapist about his or her life has a factual basis in what actually happened. Narrative truth, on the other hand, comprises an attempt to construct an account of events and emotional reactions to these events that is coherent and consistent:

> Narrative truth can be defined as the criterion we use to decide when a certain experience has been captured to our satisfaction; it depends on continuity and closure and the extent to which the fit of the pieces (of the story) takes on an aesthetic finality. Narrative truth is what we have in mind when we say that such and such is a good story, that *one* solution to a mystery must be true. Once a given construction has acquired narrative truth, it becomes just as real as any other kind of truth. (Spence, 1982a: 31)

Often in psychotherapy, the client's narrative may have a close correspondence with historical events. In other cases, it can be obvious that the 'story' has its basis more in current emotional or interpersonal circumstances than in observable past events. Spence argues that counsellors and psychotherapists must accept that they have no systematic way of knowing whether or not the client's story is grounded in actual historical events. In practice, therapy is in the business of enabling clients to achieve narrative truth, to create stories they can live by, and live with. People seek therapy because their life-stories are confused, incomplete, painful or chaotic. Through careful listening and sensitive interpretation of what is being said, the therapist facilitates the emergence of a more satisfying narrative, a 'good' story.

The distinction between narrative and historical truth introduced by

Spence has a number of radical implications. For example, the debate over the accuracy of 'recovered memories', which is discussed in Chapter 8, to a large extent hinges on the position one adopts over the truth status of the stories constructed by client and therapist during therapy. However, the most significant consequence of Spence's writings, and those of his fellow psychoanalyst Roy Schafer (1980, 1992), was the connection it enabled between the world of therapy and the work of writers such as Jerome Bruner, Theodore Sarbin and Kenneth Gergen, who were promoting the value of a narrative/cultural psychology (see Chapter 2). Spence's ideas, along with the root-and-branch reconceptualisation of psychology initiated by Bruner, Sarbin and Gergen, paved the way for the emergence of an approach to therapy that placed the concept of *narrative truth* at the heart of the therapeutic enterprise. The earliest version of this new approach came into being in the work of Michael White and David Epston.

Externalising problems: the contribution of Michael White and David Epston

A large part of the difference between mainstream/modern and postmodern approaches to therapy arises from the contrasting emphases placed on *internal* and *external* domains of human experience. Traditionally, the psychodynamic and humanistic therapies, informed by a notion of an 'autonomous, bounded self', have focused therapeutic attention on the inner life of the person. Postmodern therapies, on the other hand, have been based more on ideas of a relational self and as a result have paid more attention to what goes on between people rather than within them.

One of the main therapeutic strategies employed by White and Epston (1990) is a process they describe as 'externalising of the problem'. They regard the 'problem' that a client presents as a story that is collectively performed or lived out by that person and the other people (for example, family members) closely involved in his or her life. White and Epston argue that it is as though the person *becomes* his or her story, with his or her identity being defined through that particular narrative. In some cases the story will attribute innate, inherent, immutable characteristics to the person, such as 'schizophrenic'. It is in such circumstances that the therapist will strive to 'open space for persons to re-author or constitute themselves, each other and their relationships, according to alternative stories or knowledges' (White and Epston, 1990: 75).

The technique of externalisation used by White and Epston relies heavily on the use of certain types of questions on the part of the therapist. This technique is known as 'relative influence questioning', and comprises two sets of questions. First, participants are invited to 'map the influence of the problem in their lives and relationships'. Then, they are asked to 'map their own influence in the life of the problem' (1990: 42). This type of questioning can be illustrated through White and Epston's example of working with Nick, a six-year-old boy with a long history of encopresis, and his parents, Sue and Ron.

The 'problem' came to be referred to as 'Sneaky Poo'. Through relative influencing questioning, it was discovered that Sneaky Poo influenced the lives of Nick, Sue and Ron in a variety of ways: isolating Nick from his friends at school, forcing Sue to question her capacity to be a good parent, embarrassing Ron and stopping him from talking to his colleagues at work. The family were then asked about the influence that they each exerted on the problem. Some of the experiences that emerged were that Nicky remembered a number of times when he had not allowed Sneaky Poo to 'outsmart' him, and Sue recalled an occasion when she had put the stereo on rather than let Sneaky Poo make her miserable. Note that one of the key steps in externalising can often be to find an anthropomorphic label for the problem. In this case the problem became transformed from 'Nick-as-a-problem' to 'Sneaky Poo-as-a-problem'.

The next stage in this therapeutic process is to question participants about *how* they managed to be effective against the problem in these ways, and whether this success in the face of the problem gave them any ideas about how to influence it in future.

The concept of 'relative influence questioning' has its origins in family therapy, and there is perhaps a sense that the therapist can mechanistically or in a detached manner apply a set of questions (see White and Epston, 1990; or Parry and Doan, 1994: 84–97) that acts as a kind of formula that will produce a good therapeutic outcome. I believe that this may happen, particularly in situations where therapists are caught up in the pressure to deliver therapy in the shortest possible time. However, I would also suggest that behind the technical prescription represented by 'relative influence questioning' there can be glimpsed a rather more fundamental human process.

White and Epston view externalising as a first stage in 'opening a space' in which alternative stories can be told or heard. It is as though the individual or family are locked into one fixed, stuck way of narrating their experience. For the family introduced earlier, this might have been a story of 'when Nick soiled again yesterday we get so wound up, but we couldn't do anything about it – there must be something wrong with us.' Setting aside the specific intervention – relative influence questioning – used by White and Epston, it could be argued that what they have done is issue a general invitation to consider the possibility that there may be other ways of seeing the problem. This more general strategy happens in any form of therapy. Phenomenologically, the experience of the client is that it is as though a space does in fact open up in a hitherto locked-in personal world, and through this space can be glimpsed possibilities of other ways of being.

Jerome Bruner (1986: 143) observes that 'there are always feelings and lived experience not encompassed by the dominant story'. White and Epston refer to these 'previously neglected but vital aspects of lived experience' (1990: 41) as 'unique outcomes'. For them, the goal of relative influence questioning is to create the conditions for the emergence and exploration of unique outcomes. Many therapists working in different traditions will be aware that there are other ways of arriving at such outcomes. For example, the very act of listening can enable a speaker to externalise his or her story to the extent that the inconsistencies in it, the 'edge' of what is covered by the dominant story-line, become unavoidable. It may be that many of the clients seen by White and Epston needed special help to break out of their dominant stories, either because their stories were fixed in place by family structures, or because they had previously been serially involved with mental health professionals who had added the weight of diagnostic authority to the story. The key point here is that, although the process of externalising of the problem, leading to unique outcomes, can be achieved in the ways described by White and Epston, there are undoubtedly other methods of facilitating the same kind of result. Some of these strategies are described in Chapter 6.

Behind the work of White and Epston, and those closely influenced by their work (such as Monk et al., 1996; Parry and Doan, 1994), lies a basic shift in understandings of people and their problems. The concept of 'externalising' used by White and Epston can be viewed in metaphoric terms. The notion of the 'external' signifies a move away from an image of the person as somehow possessing an autonomous, inner self requiring continual exploration and attention, toward a sense of persons as engaged in action, immersed in a culture, as storied and story-making beings. The flavour of this approach is captured in the case of 'Rose' published by Epston et al. (1992). Rose was a young woman referred to David Epston because she had 'cracked up' at work whenever under any pressure. At the first therapy session, she reported: 'I don't have a base inside myself.' Epston responded by saying: 'There must be a story behind this. Do you feel like telling me about it?' At the end of this session, Epston sent Rose a lengthy letter, designed to offer an 'alternative' account of her life story. The letter began:

> Dear Rose,
> It was a very pleasing experience to meet up with you and hear some of your story, a story of both protest and survival against what you understood to be an attempt to destroy your life. And you furthered that protest yesterday by coming and telling me that story. (Epston et al., 1992: 103)

This, in practice, is the kind of way in which White and Epston seek to 'externalise' the dominant, oppressive narrative within which a client might be living. It is, as Payne (1996) has pointed out, an approach that in its warmth, humanity and concern for empowerment is in some ways surprisingly reminiscent of Carl Rogers.

The image of the person in postmodern narrative therapy

The notion of 'image of the person' comes from Shotter (1975), who used this phrase to characterise the philosophical assumptions or 'root metaphors' that underpin alternative ways of understanding what it means to be a person. Different approaches to psychology provide distinctive images of persons. For instance, behaviourism employs an image of the person as a mechanism, while neuropsychology, Piagetian developmental psychology and much humanistic psychology use an image of the person as an organism. Early cognitive psychology relies on an image of the person as an information processor or computer. Classical psychoanalysis employs an image of the person as combined mechanism (the 'hydraulic' model of libidinal energy) and organism (the 'id'). These images convert into images of therapy: a mechanism is 'fixed', an organism is 'healed', a computer is 're-programmed', a person 'grows'.

Those who have developed and espoused social constructionist approaches to therapy regard these images as inadequate and limiting. They are inadequate because they cannot capture or convey the experience of being a person in the late twentieth century, and because they ignore the immense diversity in conceptions of self across cultures. They are limiting because they are images that implicitly deny the capacity of the person to be aware, to challenge existing oppressive social structures, and to be creative in developing new ways of living together. Social constructionist therapies are based in an image of the person as a *social being*. Some of the key points of contrast between constructionist and other 'images of the person' operating within contemporary psychotherapy are summarised in Table 5.1. From a social constructionist perspective, *any* way of making sense of the self is socially constructed, and can be understood as deriving from a particular set of social, cultural and historical conditions. Baumeister (1987), Logan (1987), Taylor (1989) and others have traced the ways in which the concept of self first emerged and then changed across the course of Western history as a whole.

Table 5.1 *Interpretive frameworks for understanding human action*

Analogies drawn from	Social organisation constructed as	Problems constructed as	Solution constructed in terms of
Positivist physical science	Elaborate, machine, constituted by mechanics and hydraulics	Breakdown, reversal, insufficiency, damage	Isolating the cause, precise analysis, repair, reconstruct, correct
Biological sciences	Quasi-organism	Symptoms of underlying problem, functional	Identifying pathology, correct diagnosis, operating to excise pathology
Study of texts	Behavioural text	Performance of oppressive, dominant story or knowledge	Opening space for the authoring of alternative stories

Source: White and Epston, 1990

The conceptual uniqueness of social constructionist therapy is most apparent in its understanding of the notion of 'self'. The concept of self represents one of the defining characteristics of modern therapy. Psychodynamic therapy (as influenced by Kohut), humanistic therapy and cognitive–behavioural therapy (in ideas of self-efficacy and self-reinforcement) all rely heavily on an assumption of what Cushman (1995) has called a concept of a 'bounded, autonomous self'. In other words, each of these therapies in its own way sees the person as a discrete individual 'atom', with the heart of that atom being a 'self'. This image is nicely captured in Winnicott's idea of a 'true' self being hidden behind a more superficial 'false' self. Greenberg points out the extent to which the everyday practice of therapy is based upon the assumption of a discrete, unitary self:

> . . . it determines who seeks us out, and what they expect us to do. It determines our promises of confidentiality, our soundproofing, our individual offices with their securely closed doors. We 'close out' the world, the better to focus on the client, on who he or she 'really is' outside of the hurly-burly of the external world. . . . We convey the time worn notion that the problems are not 'out there', rather they are 'in here', in the therapy office, perhaps in the 'transference' that takes place there, and most of all in the psyche that neurotically contaminates the pristine present with its history of unresolved trauma. (Greenberg, 1994b: 274)

The kind of therapy that has grown to be an indispensable element of modern society has, for the most part, reinforced the tendencies in that society toward isolated individualism.

A social constructionist would understand, hear or read the concept of 'self' in a quite different manner. From this perspective, the modern 'self' is not an entity but is a construction. People in other cultures do not operate with such a sense of self (Landrine, 1992; Markus and Kitayama, 1991). The idea of the autonomous, bounded self can therefore be understood as part of the cultural system within which we live. We can then deconstruct the notion of 'self', we can examine the ways in which it is used, what it *does*. Cushman (and others) have argued that the modern self is consistent with conditions of modern society such as isolation, the replacement of community with individualism and privacy, and the rise of consumerism, advertising and the mass media. For Cushman, the modern notion of 'self' is a necessary element in modern mass capitalist society; it is needed as a means of constructing persons that fit within this kind of economic and political system.

In narrative constructionist therapies, the concept of the individual self is supplanted by that of the *person*. The sense of what is meant by this is perhaps expressed in the work of the Scottish philosopher John Macmurray, who argued that to talk about a 'person' necessarily meant a being who was at the same time an *active* agent, engaged in intentional activity, and also a *relational* being. For Macmurray, 'the idea of an isolated agent is self-contradictory. Any agent is necessarily in relation to the Other. . . . Persons are constituted by their mutual relations to one another' (1961: 24). There is not a 'self' that operates as a kind of guide and control to action. Instead, 'the Self has its being only in its agency . . . its reflective activities are but the negative aspects of this agency'(1961: 15). The words we use to describe ourselves and account for our actions (Macmurray's 'reflective activities'), words like 'self' or 'anger' or 'authenticity' do not properly refer to a *state* of the person, but are better understood as referring to *things we do*, with these things always happening within a social and cultural framework. To take a concrete example, a client in therapy may refer to his 'anger'. Most therapists would wish to explore the meaning of this anger within the context of the client's 'self'. A psychodynamic therapist might be interested in tracing back the anger to early experiences of rage and frustration in infancy. A humanistic therapist might explore the client's acceptance of his or her anger as a component of his or her self-concept. From a constructionist perspective, however, when people talk about something like 'being angry', they are almost always telling an 'anger story', which constructs the anger event through a set of intentions and social situations (Sarbin, 1989a,b; Lindsay-Hartz et al., 1995). The constructionist therapist would therefore seek to develop with the client an understanding of how 'anger' is constructed, what it means, and how its use locates the angry person within a tradition. The discussion of stories as means of 'emploting' emotion, in Chapter 2, suggests some ways in which this process can be achieved.

The image of the person as social being, rather than as mechanism or organism, draws the attention of the therapist to the social world that the person actually inhabits, rather than to hypothetical, theoretical constructs that will supposedly unlock the secrets of the individual psyche. The social world that a person lives in and through is experienced as a culture. Within everyday culture, people mainly communicate information about intentions, relationships and subjectivity to each other through stories. The image of the person implicit in therapy informed by social constructionism therefore inevitably ends up being a narrative therapy of some kind. It is through stories that we best express our sense of ourselves as active, relational beings. Spence sums up much of this in arguing that:

> . . . we are all the time constructing narratives about our past and our future; and that the core of our identity is really a narrative thread that gives meaning to our life, provided – and this is the big if – that it is never broken. Break the thread and you will see the opposite side of the story. Talk to patients in a fugue state, to patients with Korsakoff's syndrome or Alzheimer's disease, and you will sense the terror behind not knowing who you are, what happened yesterday, and what will happen tomorrow. Part of my sense of self depends on my being able to go backward and forward in time and weave a story about who I am, how I got that way, and where I am going, a story that is continuously nourishing and self-sustaining. Take that away from me and I am significantly less. (Spence, 1982b: 458)

Spence is using the example of patients with degenerative neurological diseases to illustrate the raw 'terror' of being unable to 'weave a story', the threat to person-ness associated with being unable to enter the narrative web.

Authors and voices

Running through the theory and practice of narrative-informed therapy, whether mainstream or postmodern, is the metaphor of person as 'author' of life-stories. The concepts of person as author, and therapy as 're-authoring', have been used in all three therapy traditions: classical, constructivist and social constructionist. It is now time to examine these ideas more critically from an explicit social constructionist point of view. I believe that there is a fundamental tension in the way that the idea of 'authoring' is employed in therapy. This key concept can be understood in terms of an image of a lone writer at a desk, individually creating a text. Alternatively, it can be used to refer to the experience of being immersed in a co-constructed 'storied world', and participating in a kind of endless human conversation involving the constant re-working and re-alignment of the stories that we 'inhabit'.

The image of the lone individual writer is drawn from the use of the term 'author' in literature. Literary models of authoring tend to highlight the existence of separate, boundaried stories with a beginning, middle and end, stories that are fixed and static, and which are clearly attributable to a single writer (who may acknowledge the partial assistance of an 'editor').

This sense that behind the stories a person tells there is a unitary 'author' or 'self' constitutes the common ground of both the 'exploratory' therapies (psychodynamic and humanistic) and the more recent constructivist therapies (see Chapters 3 and 4).

An alternative perspective is to take the view that stories are told *through* us. As MacIntyre puts it: 'we are never more (and sometimes less) that the co-authors of our own narratives' (1981: 213).

> . . . we enter human society . . . with one or more imputed characters – roles into which we have been drafted – and we have to learn what they are in order to be able to understand how others respond to us and how our responses to them are apt to be construed. (1981: 216)

Bruner makes a similar point in stating that:

> . . . when we enter human life, it is as if we walk on stage into a play whose enactment is already in progress – a play whose somewhat open plot determines what parts we may play and toward what denouements we may be heading. (1990: 34)

From the perspective of Alasdair MacIntyre and Jerome Bruner, a person is regarded as existing within a culture that comprises a stock of stories, and as engaged in negotiating the fit between his or her individual experience and the story-lines that are available. The task of therapy is, as a result, to open a 'space' in which the correspondence of person and story can be reviewed and re-adjusted. The emphasis lies not so much with excavating 'inner' meanings but in identifying and understanding the stories that are 'out there'. In MacIntyre's words, we 'have to learn what they are', we have to know how to find our way around the narrative resource of our culture.

White and Epston, following Foucault, point out that behind the notion of 'author' lies the functioning of power or 'authority'. There is implicit power in 'authoring', in having a voice. Being powerful requires a willingness of other people to listen, to hear, to be influenced by what that voice has to say. There are many people in the world who possess little power of this kind, who are effectively 'silenced'. Even those who may be supremely powerful in one sphere of life, such as chief executives, may carry intimate personal stories that are never heard. Whole communities of people, such as Holocaust survivors at the end of the Second World War, may have stories that few other people are willing to hear.

It is a mistake to assume that the notion of a person being able in some way to be the 'author' of his or her own story implies that there can ever be a final 'authoritative' rendering of the tale. The story told will depend on the circumstances, the audience, the state of mind of the teller. Once told, a story is reflected on and another version of it becomes possible. Each telling of a story implicitly refers back to all previous tellings. What this means is that being the 'author' of one's story is not the same as, for instance, witnessing an accident and writing a statement for the police. With a police witness statement the account is reified, fixed, there in 'black and white'. 'Authoring', in the sense meant by social constructionist therapists, is more like a conversation, a process of finding further horizons of meaning each time the tale is told. To 'author' is to participate in narration, to construct meaning through storytelling.

It is perhaps worth reflecting on the fact that the image of the individual author is very much a product of the modern world. Traditional stories – myths, Scripture, oral histories – always emerged from the tellings of many people. Before writing and printing became available, each time a story was told it would be modified by the audience's response to the way it was delivered by the teller. Similarly, in contemporary everyday life, the experience of telling a story to a group of friends is a shared activity. Other members of the group contribute questions, comments and observations. In the history of storytelling, formal 'authorship' has not been what has usually happened. Stories are *co-constructed*. Even when a teller is recounting a unique set of individual, personal events, he or she can only do so by drawing upon story structures and genres drawn from the narrative resources of a culture. Novelists and other writers are like this too. A novelist may like to think of himself or herself sitting alone in front of a word processor, but somewhere not too far in the background there is always a shelf of other peoples' books. And, in the end, the novelist's goal is to produce something that can take its rightful place on that shelf.

A social constructionist perspective reminds us that in therapy there are two people telling stories: therapist and client. Therapy 'talk' is a shared endeavour. Usually, in most therapies, the therapist's story is told in a funny kind of tangential manner, as if the therapist were reluctant fully to elaborate on his or her side of things. The therapist's narration of his or her experience of being in the therapy room, and being a member of society, is usually somewhat abstract, with an absence of the rich personal detail that the client's story provides. But it is there. Close inspection of what the *therapist* says during sessions reveals consistent narrative themes, or what Omer and Strenger (1992) have described as a 'metanarrative'.

Although every therapist has a story of the client whose tale profoundly affected his/her view of the world (see the dramatic example in Hobson, 1985), and many therapists are in the end ground down or 'burned out' through listening over and over again to the unremittingly grim tales told by their clients, the normal expected course of events is that it will be the thera-pist's story that will influence the client. Here again, a critical social constructionist approach encourages us to look at what is happening within a wider social context. Certainly, therapy clients may be expected to leave the therapy room with new or modified stories-about-self that they then tell to other participants in their social world. But much the same process occurs also for therapists. Part of being a therapist is to be able to tell therapy stories to a supervisor, to professional colleagues, in case presentations and pub-lished books and articles. Just as the encounter with the therapist gives the client stories to tell, so the encounter with the client provides a stock of stor-ies for the therapist.

The meaning of 'authoring' within therapy is complex and problematic. As far as I can see, the notion of 're-authoring' was first used by White and Epston, and perhaps fits most readily into this setting. White and Epston were influenced by Gergen's notion of the person as a 'text', and many of their clients had apparently previously been labelled by the 'authorities', an official, pathologising version of their life-story written down in medical or social work case files. White and Epston intentionally developed techniques using written communications (letters, certificates) to counteract the force of this dominant official narrative in the lives of their clients. The original, locally published edition of their book was titled '*Literary* means to thera-peutic ends'. The metaphor of the 'author' therefore permeates White and Epston's work, in ways that seem appropriate and creative. However, like any metaphor, the idea of 'therapy as re-authoring' highlights some important new meanings while hiding other possible meanings. In particular, authoring is a metaphor that can be seen to highlight notions of empowerment and change, while concealing from view the co-constructed nature of narration.

I think that there is perhaps another, maybe simpler image that can be used alongside the notion of 'authoring', which is the sense of therapy being about *telling*. The experience of telling, of giving *voice* to areas of experience that have been silenced, seems to me to be at the heart of any kind of therapy. The idea that the task of therapy is to open a space not for re-authoring, but for different voices to be heard, has been applied very effectively by Penn and Frankfurt (1994). In my own practice, I have found that the concept of 'voice' somehow brings together many different strands of what I would hope to be able to achieve with clients. Being able to give voice to experience is not merely a personal matter, not just a process of telling about secrets in the fam-ily or finding words for feelings. There is also a sense in which social groups, or people within social groups, need to voice their needs and concerns. An individual person can speak for, and from, a group of people or a tradition. Then, while the concept of 'author' implies a unitary self, a single conscious-ness generating a text, it seems commonplace to accept that a person will use many voices, depending on the circumstances. Also, there are the voices of two people in the therapy room; we are each of us engaged in our own type of telling. Finally, and in some ways most important of all, attention to the way of telling and the quality of voice is a reminder of how the the rhythm of the voice, the poetic and musical aspects of telling, draws people together in a way that the words alone can never do.

Counsellors and psychotherapists become quickly accustomed to the ways of the therapy room, and learn to look for underlying meaning and significance in the client's words. What can often be forgotten, from the therapist's chair, is just how important for clients is the *telling*. Howe (1993), in his review of studies into the clients' reports of their experience of therapy, summed up his conclusions by suggesting that there are three broad stages that clients pass through: being accepted, being heard, being understood. Returning to the examples of 'therapy' in other cultures discussed in Chapter 1, it can be seen that there exists a common pattern that can be described as a process of giving voice to troubles, having that voice accepted by a representative of the community (priest, shaman, therapist) – having it 'authorised' – then being able to use that voice in everyday discourse.

Shame

What stops us from telling our stories? Why do people need to enter therapy to tell or repair their stories? The structures and forms of life of the late twentieth century undoubtedly create many barriers: absence of public spaces, the passivity of consumerism, watching TV, the erosion of institutional forms of telling such as the confessional. But at the level of individual telling, possibly the biggest hurdle is that of overcoming the experience of *shame*. Thomas Scheff (a sociologist), drawing on the work of Helen Lewis (a psychoanalyst), suggests that one of the most overlooked emotional dynamics in contemporary society culture is that of 'by-passed shame'. In more collective cultures where 'honour' is a primary virtue, there exist shaming rituals and a greater openness to expressing and accepting the experience of shame. Shame in traditional cultures reflects the operation of a shared moral code that is maintained through public sanction. In modern society, by contrast, moral rules are internalised and guilt rather than shame functions as the signal that a thought or action is 'wrong'. In a Western culture characterised by individualism and a sense of a private, bounded self, shame is to be avoided or, if felt, minimised and suppressed. This is because the expression of shame signifies a failure of the individual's autonomy and boundaries. Lindsay-Hartz et al. (1995) describe shame as an experience of 'viewing ourselves through the eyes of another', of being 'exposed' and 'shrinking'. Shame is therefore the ultimate threat to the autonomous, bounded self: the 'other' is too close and too powerful (Greenberg, 1994a).

The account of shame provided by Lewis captures this sense of threat to the self:

> . . . shame is directly about the whole *self*. It is the vicarious experience of the other's scorn of the self, so that it is experienced in one's own and the other's eyes. The self in the moment of shame is felt to be in the 'eye of a storm' of disapproval. The metaphor, eye of a storm, is also literal. Eye contact between adults has been used as a measure of good communication . . . its absence usually signifies absence or

shame. . . . Shame is contagious. We can be embarrassed just by witnessing another person's shame. . . . While in a state of shame the self feels helpless, as if para-lyzed. . . . Most important of all, shame evokes a particular kind of anger – *humiliated* fury, which is simultaneously felt as inappropriate because it is only about the self, and unjust if it is meant for the beloved other. Most of us have the greatest difficulty finding an appropriate discharge or release for humiliated fury, so that it is easily succeeded by more shame. (1989: 40–1)

Shame is a relational emotion, evoked by other, highly valued, persons who are in close proximity. The state of paralysis induced by embarrassment or shame is difficult to assimilate or allow into a self that, in modern times, must be 'masterful' and in control.

Because the experience of shame so critically undermines the sense of self that is part of the 'project' of modernity, it has been given relatively little atten-tion in theories of psychology and psychotherapy. Lewis (1989) suggests that the more 'other-directed' or empathic style of women's ways of relating and feeling, combined with the tendency for psychoanalytic and other theorists to focus largely on *male* development and personality functioning, had the result in an absence of attention to shame in both theory and clinical practice. Scheff (1990) would add that the prevailing norms of social interaction in modern cultures (keep 'cool', maintain privacy, stay in control) contributed to a kind of mass denial of shame in everyday life that was mirrored in the neglect of patterns of shame in the emotional lives of therapy clients.

The gap between the apparently private discourse of therapy and events in the wider world can be bridged through Turner's (1982) concept of *social drama*. Turner argues that people seek to belong to groups that represent their core values, and which will provide them with love, contact and status. The groups may be family units, or be organised around work, political affiliation, leisure or friendship. To operate, such groups must exist in a state of relative equilibrium and consensus. However, from time to time a group member will publicly exhibit a *breach* of a group norm, an overt violation of one of the 'moral rules' of the group. There follows a growing *crisis* in the group, with members divided in ways that reflect fundamental moral dilemmas faced by the group. For example, a work team confronted by a managerial decision to introduce new technology may rapidly split into competing camps represent-ing the virtues of 'tradition' and 'innovation'. A family in which a teenager seeks to leave home may divide between those who value 'loyalty' and those who argue for 'autonomy'. In order to limit the impact of a breach in the group, mechanisms of *redress* are brought into action. The process of redress may include giving advice, arranging formal or informal arbitration, or the performance of a public ritual. The final phase of a social drama comprises either the *re-integration* of the previously disturbed and disrupted social group, or a *recognition of schism* with a consequent separation of the groups. Turner uses the concept of social drama as a general model of social conflict that accounts for a wide range of phenomena, from international situations in which the United Nations may be the mechanism of redress, through to local drama such as those addressed by the Ndembu healing ritual described in Chapter 1. In the modern world, social dramas are enacted constantly through the news media, in television soaps and in novels. However, in the modern world there are few credible public arenas for redress following social breach and crisis. It is possible to view therapy as a mechanism that has evolved in an increasingly individualised social world for seeking redress for 'local social breaches'.

One form of social drama has been described by the sociologist Harold Garfinkel (1957) in terms of the concept of 'degradation ceremony'. In this situation, the person who has engaged in a breach of an important social norm is denounced in the presence of at least one witness who is also a member of the group. The outcome of a successful degradation ceremony is to label the perpetrator of the breach as someone who is not now, and never really was, 'one of us'. Degradation ceremonies occur in all kinds of social groups, and represent a particular social drama 'script' that ends with the 'bad' person being allowed to remain in the group, but with low status or 'spoiled identity'. Bergner observes that many therapy clients have been degraded and humiliated at points in their life, and that for these people therapy can best be understood as a process of undoing degradation, with the task of the therapist being to: '*accredit* the client, that is, to bring about an enhancement of his or her status, and thus eligibility for community participation' (1987: 26). Bergner suggests different strategies by which a therapist can enable a client to undo the effects of degradation. In essence, these strategies involve reconstructing the story of the social drama in a way that allows the person to regain their sense of self-worth.

Perhaps one of the significant contributions of counselling and psychotherapy has been to constitute an arena within modern culture in which the person can safely enter into their feelings of shame. Carl Rogers pointed out the importance in therapy of communicating acceptance and respect to the client. According to Rogers, only in conditions of trust and safety will the person feel able to express feelings that are difficult for them to acknowledge. These conditions can be seen as designed to reduce the degree of shame experienced by the client telling his or her personal story. The expression, whether in therapy or elsewhere, of feelings such as loss, despair and anger may be painful and difficult. But it is the sense of shame that prevents the person from giving voice to these other emotions ('I am ashamed to admit just how hurt I was . . .' 'I am embarrassed that even after all these years I still get frightened when . . .'). In therapy, clients on the whole do not talk about shame – they enter into it. Shame is not part of the discourse, it is part of the performance. In describing the importance of 'tenderness' in therapists, Thorne (1985) is surely referring to the sense of tact and affirmation that can relieve the paralysis of shame.

Silencing and the uses of power: a narrative perspective on the origins of 'problems'

Why would anyone consult a therapist? How does a therapist make sense of the reasons a person gives for seeking help? The social constructionist position on these questions is crucial in defining the scope and limitations of a narrative approach to therapy. Mahrer (1989) has argued that any coherent model of therapy must contain an understanding of the causes of people's problems that is matched by the form of intervention that is offered. It is possible to identify three broad sets of needs that bring people to see a counsellor or psychotherapist: the search for personal growth and fulfilment ('I want more from life'), unresolved reactions to loss and trauma ('I can't get over this') and long-standing 'mental health' problems ('I never seem to be able to cope'). Despite the fact that narrative therapies of various kinds appear to have been used with all three of these client groups, relatively little attention has been given to formulating a narrative model of aetiology. Compared with most of the existing mainstream therapeutic approaches, social constructionist theory generates a much more culturally sensitive set of explanations for why people experience these difficulties in the first place.

It is perhaps important to note that 'problem' is a term that invites quotation marks in order to signify that 'problems' are socially constructed and defined. What is one person's 'problem' may be another person's 'solution'. Nevertheless, if reservations of this type over terminology can be put temporarily to one side, a narrative-informed examination of sources of 'problems' reveals that, although what troubles a person can be rooted in cultural, interpersonal or individual conditions (or a combination of all three), the common trouble that brings people to therapy is an incapacity to tell their story, a lack of opportunity, capacity or permission to narrativise important aspects of their experience in a satisfactory manner.

Two of the key figures in the development of narrative therapy, Michael White and David Epston, turn to the French social philosopher Michel Foucault for an account of the cultural origins of narrative troubles. Foucault argues that the knowledge that people have of their lives is part of the apparatus through which power and control are exerted in society. The 'knowledges' that people possess reflect dominant ideologies. Many of the cases described by White and Epston reflect the kind of oppressive cultural pressure or labelling to which Foucault referred, for example those whose life stories have been 'written' for them in the form of bulky case files that contain a narrative of pathology or 'deficit' (Gergen, 1990).

A particularly powerful example of the kind of cultural process that White and Epston are talking about can be found in the case of gender and autobiography. Gergen and Gergen (1993) studied the ways that men and women construct their life stories by analysing the structure of published autobiographies produced by men and women. They found that men's stories were more linear and achievement-oriented, rarely mentioning their families. Women's autobiographies, by contrast, made much more mention of events outside the writer's control, and placed great emphasis on family and other relationships. What this research suggests is that men and women learn to tell different types of stories. Yet, in submitting their actual experience of life to the shape demanded by the culturally sanctioned 'story-line', a man or woman will inevitably be forced to omit important intentions and feelings.

After all, women are achievement-oriented as well as relational, and men have family ties running alongside their career trajectories. So, from White and Epston's point of view, there will always be a hidden or untold story, a 'unique outcome', running alongside the version that is publicly recounted.

The Foucauldian analysis presented by White and Epston is compelling, but is perhaps incomplete in itself. The examples they give appear to assume that a person inhabits a single monolithic culture, whereas many people experience themselves as caught between different cultural systems, and are pulled in different directions by the contrasting stories that are told in each setting. For example, Tseng and Hsu (1972) have studied traditional Chinese children's stories, and found that a common theme in these tales is that of the child making a sacrifice to rescue a parent, usually its mother. This is quite the opposite of most Western fairy tales, which usually end with the parent making sacrifices to ensure the well-being of the child (for instance, Little Red Riding Hood). A person exposed to both these contrasting sets of cultural stories may well need to find some means of integrating these narratives, of arriving at a story that somehow reconciles these opposing accounts of the relationship between parent and child.

The notion of someone caught between Chinese and Western cultural narratives dramatises this sort of situation by offering an extreme example. The problem of finding how to integrate rival narratives happens in more mundane ways, all the time. Couples bring into a marriage contrasting stories of how to make love, spend money, bring up children. A student finds herself at university with a 'how-to-study' story that is at odds with the one held by her tutor. Young people enter adulthood with a guiding narrative of getting a job and a flat of their own, to be faced by the necessity of constructing a new self-narrative around the realities of being unemployed and homeless.

The culture we live in supplies us with stories that do not fit experience, and experience that does not live up the story. It may also fail to supply us with appropriate arenas for narrating whatever story it is we have to tell. The common theme across all of these circumstances is the experience of silence, of living with a story that has not or cannot be told. And, taking into account the fact that storytelling is a performance, an event that requires an audience, very often the existence of a personal 'problem' can best be described as a response to *silencing*, the unwillingness of others to hear the story that in some sense 'needs' to be told.

The concept of 'silencing' appears to have been first used in the field of therapy with survivors of child sexual abuse (Lister, 1982). It is well known that many perpetrators of sexual abuse threaten their victims with physical violence, emotional blackmail or psychological mystification to prevent them telling anyone else about what has happened. Fear of the consequences of disclosure operates to keep the secret of the abuse. However, abuse survivors frequently report that their attempts to disclose are met with denial on the part of other family members or potential professional helpers such as their teachers or priest. As a result, the enforced silence initiated by the perpetrator is amplified by a cultural silencing arising from the unwillingness of third parties to face up to a situation that may frighten or disgust them, or which they may not believe. Self-help books typically encourage survivors of abuse to 'break the silence' (Bass and Davis, 1988) and regard the act of disclosure as itself a healing act. Lister (1982: 875) observes that in such circumstances, clients may 'feel as though they are risking their lives to tell their stories'.

A similar process can be observed in the case of survivors of the Nazi Holocaust. The murder of Jews and others by the Nazis was a tragedy and atrocity on an unimaginable scale. The struggle to comprehend the meaning of these events is a continuing challenge for anyone who values the human capacity for love and community. The emotional as well as physical needs of the survivors of that horror were immense. And yet one of the most amazing aspects of the Holocaust is that, at the end of the Second World War, the people who had lived through this experience found themselves silenced:

> ... after liberation, as during the war, the survivors were victims of a pervasive societal reaction comprised of indifference, avoidance, repression, and denial of their experiences. Shunned, abandoned and betrayed by society, the survivor could share the most horrifying and painful period of their lives and their immense losses only with their children, with fellow survivors, or even worse, with no one. The most pervasive consequence of the conspiracy of silence for survivors and their children has been a profound sense of isolation, loneliness and alienation that exacerbated their mistrust of humanity and made their task of mourning and integration impossible. (Danieli, 1988a: 220)

As Danieli illustrates in her research, the 'conspiracy of silence' extended even to the psychotherapists to whom survivors turned for help. She found that, for example, some therapists would defend against the wish of their clients to talk about events in the camps by interpreting these accounts as manifestation of early childhood 'anal fixations' or 'pregenital sadism'.

Those sceptical of the significance or pervasiveness of silencing might argue that the Holocaust, or even incest and child sexual abuse, are extreme and unusual situations, and that it is a mistake to generalise from these instances, to read too much into them. Perhaps, they might suggest, silencing is a societal or cultural reaction to ultimate horror, and less awful problem stories can usually find an audience. In fact, research into other types of difficult events seems to confirm the existence of silencing as a pervasive cultural phenomenon. Pennebaker and Harber (1993) carried out a series of large-scale surveys of local residents in the year following the Loma Prieta earthquake in the San Francisco Bay Area in October 1989. The earthquake, which was the largest in the locality since the great 1906 San Francisco earthquake, killed over 60 people and caused substantial destruction. In the survey, informants were asked about how many times they had talked about and thought about the earthquake in the preceding 24 hours. One of the main findings of this study was that people tended to stop talking about the event around two weeks after the earthquake. People reported at this point that they continued to think about the earthquake, and wanted to talk about it, but did not want to hear other people talk about it. During this phase (two to six weeks post-earthquake), levels of illness, quake-related dreams and interpersonal conflict all showed a significant increase. Pennebaker (1993b) describes a variety of 'mechanisms of social constraint' which inhibit talk about problems beyond an initial short-lived 'emergency' phase, for example the stress of hearing about trauma, and the difficulty in knowing how to offer appropriate assistance.

The concept of silencing is consistent with the findings of other research studies. Brown and Harris (1978) established that women were more likely to become depressed in circumstances of social isolation, unemployment, living in a high-rise block, their mother dying while they were a child or adolescent, and having no one close to them with whom they could talk intimately. These women were effectively silenced by their social environment. The research literature on the effects of self-disclosure and social support similarly confirm the value of being able to talk.

Replacing the language of deficit

> The mental health professions operate largely so as to objectify a language of mental deficit. In spite of their humane intentions, by constructing a reality of mental deficit the professions contribute to hierarchies of privilege, reducing natural interdependencies within the culture, and lend themselves to self-enfeeblement. This infirming of the culture is progressive, such that when common actions are translated into a professionalized language of mental deficit, and this language is disseminated, the culture comes to construct itself in these terms. (Gergen, 1990: 353)

Approaches to therapy that are informed by social constructionist thinking do not regard narrative in therapy, the stories clients tell, as merely events within a therapy hour. Each client story is an individual version or rendering of a broader cultural narrative. When a client in therapy recounts a story, he or she is selecting from among the many story forms available in the culture. The client speaks 'from' a tradition. If it is acknowledged that an experience can be 'narrativised' in many different ways, that in principle the same event or experience can generate a multiplicity of accounts, then the factors that influence which story form is used in which circumstances become key issues for therapy. Gergen (1990) argues that the setting or cultural milieu of therapy invokes the telling of 'deficit' stories: 'common actions are translated into a professionalized language of mental deficit'.

If therapy is to be emancipatory and empowering, then clearly it is not at all helpful for therapists to conspire in constructing realities of mental deficit. An important implication of social constructionist, narrative approach to therapy is the invitation to the therapist to consider ways of avoiding framing the therapeutic encounter as a meeting of unequals grounded in the inadequacy of the client. Gergen (1996) suggests that the deficiencies of the client are a response to the projected superiority of the therapist. He argues that the procedures of therapy:

> . . . furnish the client a lesson in inferiority. The client is indirectly informed that he or she is ignorant, insensitive, or emotionally incapable of comprehending reality. In contrast, the therapist is positioned as the all-knowing and wise, a model to which the client might aspire. The situation is all the more lamentable owing to the

fact that in occupying the superior role, the therapist fails to reveal its weaknesses. Almost nowhere are the fragile foundations of the therapist's account made known; almost nowhere do the therapist's personal doubts, foibles, and failings come to light. And the client is thus confronted with a vision of human possibility that is as unattainable as the heroism of cinematic mythology . . . each form of modernist therapy carries with it an image of the 'fully functioning' or 'good' individual; like a fashion plate, this image serves as a guiding model for the therapeutic outcome. (Gergen, 1996: 210)

Gergen proposes that therapists should seek to dismantle this hierarchical relationship, and accept that their theories are not inherently superior to those of the client. Therapist and client can then act as collaborators, as 'co-constructors of meaning'.

The means of achieving this kind of equality of authority between client and therapist is for the therapist to adopt what Anderson and Goolishian (1992) have called a 'not-knowing' stance toward the client. The notion of 'not-knowing' derives directly from hermeneutic and postmodern modes of understanding. For example, Cheney writes that:

. . . in the light of postmodern deconstruction of modernist totalizing and foundationalist discourse, can we any longer make sense of the idea of privileged discourse, discourse which can lay claim to having access to the way things are? The dominant postmodern view is that this is not possible. (1989: 117)

The implication for therapy here is that the therapist's theory or formulation, as an instance of discourse that makes a special claim to 'have access to the way things are' is no more than one voice in a conversation. It is hard, in a postmodern world, to sustain the illusion that any one perspective enjoys the status of an overarching, all-seeing, all-knowing 'God's-eye' view of things.

The principle of 'not-knowing' is also implicit in hermeneutic, interpretive approaches to knowing:

A person trying to understand a text is prepared for it to tell him something. That is why a hermeneutically trained mind must be, from the start, sensitive to the text's quality of newness. But this kind of sensitivity involves neither 'neutrality' in the matter of the object nor the extinction of one's self, but the conscious assimilation of one's own bias, so that the text may present itself in all its newness and thus be able to assert its own truth against one's foremeanings. (Gadamer, 1975: 238)

Anderson and Goolishian (1992) regard 'not-knowing' as an application of hermeneutic principles to therapy. They write that 'the excitement of the therapist is in learning the uniqueness of each individual client's narrative truth' (1992: 30), and argue that it is a mistake for therapists to search for patterns in the client's narrative that may validate the therapist's theory but 'invalidate the uniqueness of the clients' stories and thus their very identity' (1992: 30).

Hoffman (1992) described her experience in working with therapists employing a 'not-knowing' approach. She observed that:

. . . their questions or comments are marked by tentativeness, hesitancy and by long periods of silence. Often, the voice of the interviewer sinks so low that it is difficult to hear. They tend to begin their sentences with 'Could it be that?' or 'What if?' (Hoffman, 1992: 18)

The effect of this mode of relating to clients seemed to Hoffman to be a 'deliberate immolation of the professional self' that in turn appeared to 'encourage both participation and invention' on the part of clients.

For Gergen, the ultimate goal of a social constructionist narrative therapy is not to 'replace one story with another', but to 'enable clients to participate in the continuous process of creating and transforming meaning' (1996: 215). In other words, to join in with, to make their contribution to the collaborative discourse, or conversation, that constitutes a tradition and a culture. Therapy from this perspective is not about arriving at a final, definitive, fixed understanding of 'self', but of keeping understanding *on the way* (Anderson and Goolishian, 1992). The role of the therapist in this work is that of a 'conversational artist – an architect of the dialogical process – whose expertise is in the arena of creating a space for and facilitating a dialogical conversation' (Anderson and Goolishian, 1992: 27).

At a time in history when to be a 'therapist' involves belonging to a system that promotes a 'language of mental deficit', the strategy of 'not-knowing' offers one way of beginning to create a space for conversations that do not perpetuate the myth of client inadequacy and therapist superiority. But of course this strategy threatens the fundamental basis of professional status. If the defining characteristic of a profession is the ownership and use of a distinct body of knowledge, then how can someone be a professional and yet at the same time 'not know'? The resolution of this paradox represents a major challenge to those who would wish to establish a social constructionist therapy.

The therapeutic relationship in postmodern narrative therapy

Different approaches to therapy have tended to be associated with different ideas about the client–therapist relationship. The various images of the therapeutic relationship are reviewed by Clarkson (1995). These different therapist relationship styles can be understood as reflecting different roles or tasks the therapist can carry out in relation to the client-as-storyteller. The therapist can be *audience*, in the sense of being there to listen, giving the other an opportunity to tell. The therapist can go further and be a *witness*, someone with a culturally sanctioned capacity to affirm the validity or reality of the client's experience. The therapist can be a *director*, assisting the client to find the most effective ways of telling the story. The therapist may be an *editor*, deleting and moving about parts of the narrative until it makes most sense. The therapist may be *interpreter* of the client's story, translating it into another (usually psychological) 'language' or conceptual system. Finally, the therapist can be *co-author*, engaging in a mutual process of storytelling. These are just some of the metaphors for the therapist role that are generated by a narrative therapy perspective.

These models of therapeutic relationship provide only one perspective on the relationship that exists between a professional helper, a psychotherapist or counsellor, and a person (the client) who comes for some kind of 'help'. In fact, the perspective is that of the professional. Existing images of the thera-peutic relationship reflect the categories and ideas used by therapists. From a social constructionist point of view, there is no need to privilege the therapist's understanding of the therapeutic relationship. If the social reality of the ther-apeutic encounter is indeed 'co-constructed' by client and therapist together, then the client's understanding of that relationship is equally as important as that of the therapist. Indeed, given that the therapist is the more powerful par-ticipant in the relationship, and therefore more likely to have access to, or apply, stories of domination and control (White and Epston, 1990), it seems probable that at this point in the history of therapy, there is more to be gained by exploring the nature of the therapeutic relationship from the side of the *client*. As Gergen (1996: 214) puts it, 'the modernist view of the therapist as superior knower' makes little sense from a constructionist perspective.

Implicit in the preceding discussion has been a sense of the goals of social constructionist narrative therapy. Clearly, a postmodern narrative therapist does not have an agenda that involves 'curing' or 'fixing' the client or patient. It is important to keep hold of the idea that, for many people, the mere oppor-tunity to tell their story, and to have that story valued and received, is an immensely affirming experience. There are other people who feel themselves to have a life narrative that is perfectly acceptable to them, but which is in need of maintenance and repair. For these people, a legitimate goal of therapy is to review the functioning of the 'stories they live by', leading to some minor adjustments and realignment. There are other people who are trapped in telling life-stories that are destructive of self and others. For these people, there is often a wish to create a story that is radically new and different.

Conclusion: the shape and structure of a postmodern narrative therapy

The general sense of the new form of practice that is gradually emerging from the alliance between postmodern thought and narrative theory is cap-tured well by Mair, when he writes that:

> Every act of saying, every telling of a tale, is an act of war. We have to fight for our existence, for our place in the sun. . . . We do not exist in a static and placidly endur-ing world that we can describe at our leisure with words that quietly picture what is there before us. . . . We tell stories to our children and create story worlds in which to dwell. The kinds of stories we tell sometimes see us through and often fail when things don't turn out the way we have been led to suppose. When a story and the associated story world fail then we may be in difficulties. Our essential stories are not just casual entertainment. It is as children ourselves that we speak and listen. We are thrust into the darkness of the universe. We try to create worlds to live within and to spin our stories through time so that we and our world are constantly being recreated, retold, revised. We are creating ourselves and being created in our stories. (1989a: 279–80)

As a psychotherapist, Mair perhaps expresses more than any other writer the pain of living in a world in which the tradition of caring and respect have been eroded by the marketplace, and of leading what he describes as the 'double

life' of the therapist: 'you have to live in the public world of ordinary convention and also in the underworld of secrecy and dread' (1989a: 281).
Therapy in the age of uncertainty often resembles an act of war, finding ways
to make some difference to clients and services fighting for their existence.

As Gergen puts it, 'narratives gain their utility primarily within social
interchange' (1996: 217). Stories are 'situated actions'. Stories sustain relationships, provide coherence to groups and institutions, make social life
intelligible. Therapy provides an arena for storytelling and re-authoring, for
reflecting on stories being lived. But how does this happen? The next chapter
looks at the process.

6

The Process of Narrative Therapy: Strategies for the Retrieval of Meaning

> The storyteller takes what he tells from experience – his own or that reported by others. And he in turn makes it the experience of those who are listening to his tale.
>
> (Benjamin, 1969: 87)

Within the recent research and theoretical literature in psychotherapy, use has increasingly been made of a distinction between *process* and *outcome*. The outcome of a therapy session, complete course of therapy, or even of a single therapist intervention, is taken to mean the benefit to the client of these events. The process of therapy, by contrast, refers to what actually goes on in therapy, the actual behaviour, action and interaction of therapist and client. 'Process' is what produces 'outcome'. A large array of process elements have been identified by therapy theorists and researchers (see Orlinsky et al., 1994). There have been criticisms of the process–outcome distinction in therapy, on the grounds that what might be defined as an 'outcome' can also be a 'process' in its own right. For example, a process intervention such as making an interpretation may lead to client insight (an outcome). However, the experience of a moment of insight is in itself a cognitive, affective and interpersonal process.

Another meaning of 'process' in therapy, one that is less mechanistic, refers to the *experience* that both client and therapist have that one thing flows into another, that feelings, thoughts, the relationship itself all change over time. From this perspective, to study or make sense of the process of therapy is to develop ways of conceptualising this experiential flow. It is this second definition of process that will be employed in this chapter. The value of knowing about this type of process is that to do so enables therapy participants to anticipate what is happening or what might happen, and intentionally to shape their actions according to what they want to happen. For instance, one of the most widely studied process concepts is 'empathy'. A therapist who understands the process of empathic engagement with the world of another will know that if he or she is taking a history and is intent on gathering factual information about childhood illness and loss, closed questions are more productive than empathic reflection. On the other hand, if the client is wishing to explore the meaning and emotional significance of these childhood events, empathic reflection would be appropriate and closed questions would be likely to bring this kind of process to a halt.

One of the major difficulties in making sense of the process of therapy is that everything that occurs in therapy is interlinked with everything else. It can be hard to know how best to divide up what is a unitary experience. Any system of categorisation or analysis can be seen to be to some degree arbitrary and false. Nevertheless, there seems to be some consensus (see, for example, Elliott, 1991) that a comprehensive understanding of therapy process involves consideration of four distinct time-frames.

1 *Speaking turn* (interaction unit): a response by one speaker, surrounded by utterances of the other speaker.
2 *Episode* (topic/task unit): a series of speaking turns organised by a common task or topic.
3 *Session* (occasion unit): a time-limited situation in which client and therapist meet to work on therapeutic tasks.
4 *Treatment* (relationship unit): the entire course of treatment relation.

First, there are 'microprocesses' associated with momentary therapist or client experiences and actions. An interpretation by a therapist would be an example of a microprocess. Second, there are sequences of interaction between client and therapist that can be identified as distinct 'events' within a therapy session. Telling a story could be viewed as an event. Third, it is possible to observe longer sequences or 'cycles' that link together several events, for example over the whole of a therapy session. Finally, there are longer-term, global processes that may span the whole of a therapy encounter.

Narrative theory opens up many new ways of understanding therapy process. However, the application of narrative concepts to the understanding of therapy process is only possible by adopting a view of storytelling as a *performance*. There can be no story without a narrator and a listener. In her review of theory and research into personal narratives, Langellier argues that it is inadequate to regard a story as merely a linguistic text: 'a story implies storytelling' (1989: 249). It is important to understand how the story is told, the reaction of the audience, and other contextual factors. A storytelling performance can be regarded as a conversational interaction, in which an emerging narrative account is co-constructed by storyteller and audience, or collaboratively constructed by a group. For Langellier, however, the meaning of the performance of a story goes beyond the immediate interaction between teller(s) and audience. She suggests that 'telling personal narratives *does something* in the social world' (1989: 261). And beyond even the social impact of storytelling, there is a political dimension. It is possible to see that some stories are legitimate and others are not. There are circumstances where it can be risky to tell a personal narrative. The credibility of a story may depend on issues of power, control and authority.

These various facets of storytelling as an interpersonal, social and political performance have been widely studied within the fields of sociolinguistics and communication studies (see Finnegan, 1992; Langellier, 1989). Unfortunately, little has been written on the application of these perspectives to the understanding of storytelling performances in therapy. This chapter therefore represents an initial, somewhat tentative exploration of this area, drawing mainly on existing concepts of therapy process.

The social and political context of the therapy narrative

The location of psychotherapy as a cultural practice has been extensively discussed in Chapter 1. It is apparent that the therapy room represents a relatively unique storytelling arena. The client is encouraged to tell whatever *personal* story he or she chooses. Turner (1982) describes the cultural space inhabited by therapy, along with other more traditional forms of healing, as *liminal*, as on the edge of the culture or society in which the person lives. Often, stories told in therapy are the ones that cannot be told in everyday life. The notion of 'silencing' as an experience and social condition that leads many people into therapy was discussed in the previous chapter. The implication of that for therapy practice is that it is necessary to create a 'cultural island' or 'transitional space' (to borrow metaphors from other therapeutic discourses) that will enable the client or patient to reflect on the events of his or her life in an environment that is safe enough to permit the examination of painful feelings and experiences.

As many writers have pointed out, therapy takes place within a frame. However, from a social constructionist perspective it is necessary to take a critical, questioning look at the nature of that frame, and the messages it sends. In most mainstream approaches, the therapist, as audience, seldom reciprocates by offering his or her own personal story, and attempts rigorously to adopt a neutral stance toward whatever the client or patient has to say. At the same time, the therapist is perceived by the client as a 'member of society in good standing', a person whose approval would normally be sought and positively valued. Therapy is typically conducted under conditions of privacy and confidentiality. Therapists informed by social constructionist and postmodern thinking question many of the assumptions underpinning the conventional therapeutic frame. For example, the client will almost certainly be influenced by the values and ideology of the therapist, so perhaps it is better to make the therapist's views clear from the start. Also, the creation of a confidential, private space can have the result of eliminating or neutralising the social or political dimensions of the client's story.

The process of narrative therapy as a whole

Implicit in the discussion of narrative therapy in the previous chapter was the idea that the client and therapist engaging in this work make progress through a series of distinct stages or phases of activity. The first stage is the telling of the client's story. The second stage involves an emergence of alternative versions of this story. As the person becomes aware that there are more ways to tell the story, as the initial, 'stuck' narrative is deconstructed, he or she comes to adopt a story that is more satisfying, meaningful or tolerable than the original. Finally, this new story is tried out, is told to others outside the therapy room, and becomes a feature of the real interpersonal world of the person.

The four stages – telling, deconstructing, adopting and proclaiming – represent a vastly over-idealised picture of what happens in therapy. It is rarely, if ever, as neat as this. However, the value of having a model of the *whole* process of narrative therapy, from beginning to end, is that it provides a context for making sense of the operation of the smaller scale within-session or even moment-by-moment processes that constitute the whole.

The process within a session

Focusing on the action that takes place over the course of a session of therapy brings to the foreground the importance and centrality of the stories told by the client. Within a session, a client will typically recount a series of identifiable 'stories', and between these stories are episodes of discourse that are clearly *not* storytelling. A session, therefore, can be seen as comprising a cyclical moving into and out of story mode. It is as though the intention of the client to express to the therapist what 'the problem' is inexorably leads him or her toward recounting a story that exemplifies 'the problem'. The story is the best way the client can find to communicate fully the intricacy of what has been happening in his or her life. Then, once the story is told, there is a period of reflection, of explaining (by both participants) what the story might mean, of clarifying some of the ambiguities in the story, linking it with other stories previously told. This reflection is likely to be associated with moments of insight; the breakthroughs and new understandings achieved by the client usually occur at the stage of unpacking the meaning of a story, rather than during the telling. But, usually, the search for meaning leaves some aspects of the 'problem' still not quite understood, and the growing pressure to communicate these unresolved experiences leads into another story.

This notion of a cyclical process that moves into and out of stories over the course of a therapy session has been adapted from the work of both Gendlin (1969) and Bucci (1993, 1995). From a person-centred perspective, Gendlin has described the role of an inner, bodily 'felt sense' in the creation of meaning in therapy. For Gendlin, the implicit meaning of any situation, relationship, dilemma or other human activity is located in the set of feelings experienced by the person in connection with that activity. In order to make these meanings explicit, for example to become consciously aware of what a situation means, or to convey this meaning to another, the 'felt sense' must be symbolised. Most often, symbolisation occurs through words and images, although it can also take place through bodily movement and music. The result of accurate symbolisation of a felt sense is an experience of 'rightness' ('yes, that is what it is all about . . .'), and to open up for expression those areas of feeling still unsymbolised that were until that moment concealed by what had been until that moment the main thread of feeling and meaning. The cycle of stories in a therapy session describes a similar process, except that from a narrative perspective the symbolisation of felt meaning is understood to take place mainly through the telling of a story. And of course a story is a form of communication that provides a structure in which many aspects of a felt sense are expressed together.

The process model developed by Wilma Bucci is informed by an integration of psychoanalytic and cognitive psychological theory. For Bucci, clients' stories are a bridge between emotional, imagery-rich processing and reflective, cognitive processing of information. Implicit in her model is a sense that the skill or artistry of the therapist involves guiding the client through these phases in the most effective way. A narrative perspective on how a therapist might shape or structure a session to allow the story to be best told and the meaning in it to be most fully retrieved is offered by Omer (1993a). He proposes that it can be helpful to think about a therapy session, or a course of treatment, as a drama, with a beginning, middle and end. The impact of the new understanding and insights generated during this drama depends in part on the level of emotional intensity that is achieved. Omer suggests that therapists can, unwittingly, structure therapy sessions in ways that heighten the emotional intensity and impact of their messages. For example, some sessions proceed through a gradual rise in intensity, and arrive at a climax near the end of a session (or the end of a series of sessions). In other therapeutic situations, for example in crisis work, the intensity is at its peak at the beginning, gradually diminishing through the session. Techniques such as Gestalt two-chair work create emotional intensity through a dialectical process. The key point is that skilled therapists learn to use these forms and sequences to facilitate both the telling of powerful stories and the retrieval of meanings that are memorable.

The adoption by most therapists of the Western medical notion of the fixed-length appointment with the 'doctor' limits the scope for dramatic, emotionally cathartic storytelling. Wilson (1988) has described a 'transethnic' approach to treating post-traumatic stress disorder in Vietnam Veterans. This approach draws on traditional Native American healing and purification rituals used to reintegrate into the community warriors who have returned home from battle. In particular, sweat lodge purification ceremonies of the Lakota Sioux have been employed. In this ritual, between seven and 20 men gather in a dome-shaped tent or 'sweat lodge', in the centre of which is a pit filled with rocks that have been heated in a fire outside the tent. Participants sit cross-legged in a tightly packed circle around the rock pit. The heat is intense and there is no light apart from the glow of the rocks. In this setting, the medicine man or shaman takes the group through a set of rituals that requires each of the men to share his own individual prayer, telling of his personal concerns and needs. This situation induces claustrophobia, pain, an urge to escape, a feeling of extreme self-awareness alongside an awareness of the presence and voices of others. It is a powerful emotional experience.

Gendlin, Bucci and other writers on psychotherapy have identified a process in which the client is observed to alternate between spontaneous, almost unreflective telling or disclosure, characterised by the presence of feeling or emotion, and phases of more cognitively controlled contemplation or analysis. The purification ritual described by Wilson (1988) can be viewed in similar terms. These processes can be placed in a more general framework by returning to the philosophical ideas of Macmurray introduced in Chapter 5. Macmurray proposes that the idea of a person implies action in relation to other persons. Action and relationship are the primary attributes of a person. The notion of an individual self that is a static entity emerges from intellectual reflection on experience, but can never in itself fully capture what it is to be a person. Applying Macmurray's philosophy to the process of therapy, it is as though the active, intentional, relational person is communicated through stories that are told and stories that are enacted during the therapy hour. The ability of the client and therapist to make some sense out of these stories is necessary, but this cognitive 'sense-making' is not sufficient in itself, since it is only in action in relation to others that the person is realised.

In Chapter 2, the nature of storytelling and narrative as a 'way of knowing' was explored. The story as a linguistic form has the potential to convey intention and purpose, causality, the teller's 'landscape of subjectivity', social context and relationships, the contrast between the normal and the exceptional, events that happened, and the moral import of these events. There is, or can be, an immense amount of meaning conveyed by a good story. In Macmurray's terms, there is the possibility that what it means to be a person can be conveyed through narrative. But, in telling stories we are 'telling more than we know'. A story can be heard or read in different ways. The story carries meaning that the reader or hearer must work to unpack. In everyday life, the stories we tell each other are unpacked to a very limited extent. In literary criticism, by contrast, generations of scholars may succeed in generating fresh understandings of the meanings contained within a novel or poem. In therapy, similarly, the therapist and client work together to make sense of the stories told by the client. The central task of therapy, then, is that of *retrieval of meaning*. There is always more meaning to a story than is ever recovered by therapist and client. The client may rush on and want to tell another story, and so brush over much of the meaning conveyed in a story they have told. Alternatively, the story overtly told by the client may be a shell within which there is another, covert version of the story to be told. But mainly, it is unlikely that the therapist will be sensitive to all aspects of what a story might mean.

In any of these circumstances, the chances are that the client will tell the story again, or offer a slightly different rendering of it, until the point gets across (or the client gives up). Each re-telling of a story potentially allows several therapeutic processes to operate. First, every time a story is re-told gives both therapist and client another opportunity to hear and understand what it means. Second, as Pennebaker (1993b) has demonstrated in a series of studies, if a person expresses negative or difficult emotions (such as anger, shame, guilt, despair) in the stories he or she tells, these feelings become less troubling to the person (this phenomenon is discussed more fully in Chapter 4). Third, the telling of a story always contains within it some notion of why the story is 'worth telling'; it communicates the teller's sense of what Bruner has called 'departures from the ordinary'. And, as it opens up this tension, a story will also attempt to resolve it: each story is an exercise in problem-solving.

Narrative microprocesses

The moment-by-moment microprocesses that occur in therapy can be viewed from the perspective of the therapist or that of the client. Client and therapist microprocesses have tended to be understood in terms of taxonomies or lists of what each participant *does* during the moment-by-moment process of therapy. The lists of therapist and client responses produced by Hill and her colleagues are typical of this approach. These responses can be re-framed from a narrative approach. The verbal responses of the therapist can be categorised as:

- *Approval.* Provides emotional support, approval, reassurance, or reinforcement. *Accepting or validating the client's story*
- *Information.* Supplies information in the form of data, facts or resources. It may be related to the therapy process, the therapist's behaviour, or therapy arrangements (time, fee, place)
- *Direct guidance.* These are directions or advice that the therapist suggests for the client either for what to do in the session or outside the session. *Structuring the process of storytelling*
- *Closed question.* Gathers data or specific information. The client responses are limited and specific. *Filling-in the story*
- *Open question.* Probes for or requests clarification or exploration by the client. *From a narrative perspective, open questioning can be used to invite the telling of a story, or to explore the meaning of elements of a story*
- *Paraphrase.* Mirrors or summarises what the client has been communicating either verbally or nonverbally. Does not 'go beyond' what the client has said or add a new perspective or understanding to the client's statements or provide any explanation for the client's behaviour. Includes restatement of content, reflection of feelings, nonverbal referent, and summary. *Therapists using a narrative approach may wish to communicate to the client that they have 'heard' the story, or may attempt to focus attention on a particular aspect of a story*
- *Interpretation.* Goes beyond what the client has overtly recognised and provides reasons, alternative meanings, or new frameworks for feelings, behaviours, or personality. It may establish connections between seemingly isolated statements or events; interpret defences, feelings, resistance, or transference; or indicate themes, patterns or causal relationships in behaviour and personality, relating present events to past events. *This response includes a wide range of narrative-informed interventions, centred on the general goal of re-telling the story in different ways.*

- *Confrontation*. Points out a discrepancy or contradiction but does not provide a reason for such a discrepancy. The discrepancy may be between words and behaviours, between two things a client has said, or between the client's and therapist's perceptions. *In narrative therapy, the client is encouraged to resolve the tension or incongruity between opposing versions of a story.*
- *Self-disclosure*. Shares feelings or personal experiences. *The therapist gives an account of his or her own story, either in terms of relevant episodes from a personal life-story, or framed in terms of a therapeutic metanarrative, or drawn from myth and other cultural sources.* (Hill, 1989, italicised sections added)

The verbal responses of the client can be categorised in these terms:

- *Simple response*. A short, limited phrase that may indicate agreement, acknowledgement or approval of what the therapist has said, indicate disapproval or disagreement, or respond briefly to a therapist's question with specific information or facts
- *Request*. An attempt to obtain information or advice or to place the burden of responsibility for solution of the problem on the therapist
- *Description*. Discusses history, events or incidents related to the problem in a storytelling or narrative style. The person seems more interested in decribing *what* has happened than in communicating affective responses, understanding or resolving the problem. *From a narrative perspective, this kind of basic storytelling is the fundamental cornerstone of therapy*
- *Experiencing*. Affectively explores feelings, behaviours or reactions about self or problems, but does not convey an understanding of causality. *The feeling or emotional component of narratives*
- *Exploration of client–therapist relationship*. Indicates feelings, reactions, attitudes or behaviour related to the therapist or the therapeutic situation. *The construction of a shared story of 'what happens in therapy'*
- *Insight*. Indicates that the client understands or is able to see themes, patterns or causal relationships in his or her behaviour or personality, or in another's behaviour or personality. Often has an 'a-ha' quality. *The process of reflection on the meanings implicit in a story or series of stories*
- *Discussion of plans*. Refers to action-oriented plans, decisions, future goals and possible outcomes of plans. Client displays a problem-solving attitude. *The part of therapy that involves testing out new stories on others*
- *Silence*. Pause of 4–5 seconds between therapist and client statements, or immediately after a client's simple response
- *Other*. Statements unrelated to the client's problem, such as small talk or comments about the weather or events. (Hill, 1986, italicised sections added)

Rather than merely list therapist and client behaviours, it can be more useful to look at therapist *intentions* – in particular those that specifically aim to facilitate narrative events and processes in therapy. These therapist activities can be divided into four broad categories: *construction, deconstruction, reconstruction* and *rehearsal*. These therapist activities or intentions correspond to the four stages of narrative therapy (telling, deconstructing, adopting and proclaiming) introduced above.

The task of telling a story

There are many things that therapists do to help clients to tell their story. The use of open-ended questions, listening skills and appropriate posture are just some of the ways in which clients can be encouraged to narrate significant life experiences. Some therapists will use an assessment interview to piece together the client's life-history or whole life-story. There are several other means of bringing out a story. Reflecting back what has been understood is a way of reassuring the person that the bit of the story they have already told has been understood and makes sense. The client can be invited to 'say more'. He or she can be asked about what preceded a piece of action or what followed it. These are simple conversational strategies that are available to functioning members of a cultural group.

There are other, more 'technical' methods of helping a story to be told, for example through writing exercises (including projective techniques), dramatic enactment, guided fantasy, reading, use of toys and other play materials, and the use of music. In psychoanalysis, the reporting of dreams and free association are techniques that allow the client to create stories.

Whatever type of response the therapist is using to assist or enable a client to tell a story, the role of the therapist is not neutral. One way or another, the story that emerges is a co-construction of client and therapist together. In the Hill (1989) list of therapist responses (see above), the therapist activity of reflection can be understood as constituting a subtle yet powerful process of narrative co-construction. When a client talks about an event, when he or she begins to tell a story, the areas of content and feeling reflected back by the therapist serve to draw attention to those particular elements of the story. At times, the therapist can be seen to act as a 'chorus' (McLeod and Balamoutsou, 1996), holding and offering back aspects of the story that have special resonance.

Spence (1982a) points out that in psychoanalysis clients are instructed to 'free associate', to give voice to whatever images, thoughts and fantasies arise in their consciousness. While clients in other types of therapies may not be explicitly told to engage in this kind of activity, there are certainly times when their speech is disjointed and lacking in coherence. This is perhaps especially likely to happen at moments in therapy when the client is 'lost for words', is groping to find words to express a new or unfamiliar idea. Spence suggests that at these times the therapist, far from engaging in 'free-floating attention', is forced to work hard to make sense of what is being said:

> . . . to register the utterance with some kind of understanding, we must supply a wide range of background assumptions and listen in an active, constructive manner, making assumptions about incomplete sentences, filling out ambiguous references, and otherwise supplying what the patient leaves out. (Spence, 1982a: 29)

To talk of telling a story is misleading; people tell different stories in different contexts. We are all of us capable of speaking with different 'voices', and one of the functions of therapists is to facilitate this multiplicity and generativity of self-expression. Among the therapists who have given most emphasis to this aspect of storytelling are Penn and Frankfurt (1994). A central aim of their approach is to counterbalance the influence of self-defeating mono-logues (such as 'You're hopeless, you've failed, you're incompetent') through the 'discovery or invention of our other voices – more positive, confident, even ecstatic' (Penn and Frankfurt, 1994: 218). One method of achieving this goal, they have found, is to use forms of writing such as journals, letters, personal biographies, dreams, poetry and dialogues. Clients use writing to 'sound out' alternative voices originally discovered in conversation with their therapist. Over time, this body of writing becomes a 'participant text', maintaining the ongoing existence of these multiple voices and meanings.

Another aspect of the storytelling process in therapy concerns the extent of emotion and feeling with which a story is recounted. At times, clients may be so immersed in re-experiencing feelings such as fear or loss that the narrative thread of their story is temporarily hidden. On another occasion, a client may tell a story in a detached, 'objective', over-linear fashion. The question of expression of emotion has received a lot of attention in the psychotherapy literature, through work such as that of Klein et al. (1986) on experiencing level, and Rice and Kerr's (1986) studies of the significance of voice quality. Scheff (1977, 1981) draws on theories of dramatic criticism in his usage of the idea of emotional *distance*. An *underdistanced* story or drama evokes raw emotion in the audience, while an *overdistanced* performance fails to engage the audience. In between these extremes are dramas or stories that display an amount of distance that is neither overwhelming nor over-abstracted. Scheff suggests that one of the key roles of the therapist is to monitor and if necessary control or modulate the emotional distancing of the client so that he or she is able to express 'repressed' feeling, but is at the same time able to process these feelings, is able to be both participant and observer. There are many techniques in the therapeutic repertoire that can be viewed in this light. For example, the enactive strategies used in Gestalt two-chair work, or in psychodrama, are methods of reducing emotional distance. The client-centred method of reflecting feeling attempts to do the same kind of thing in a more gradual fashion. By contrast, relaxation training or cognitive re-framing may be used to help a client too bound up in feeling to find perspective on events. From a narrative therapy position, many ways of telling more or less emotion-bound stories can be imagined: whispering, shouting, writing a letter, writing a journal, telling in the first person, telling in the third person, telling with eye contact, telling into space.

Finally, it is important to acknowledge that telling a story in therapy is not by any means a simple act. As discussed in Chapter 2, there is a lot happening when someone engages in narrative. From the point of view of the client, for example, the moment-by-moment narrativisation of experience that takes place in therapy can be seen as made up of several different types of activity. Some of these processes were reported in the post-session client recall interviews conducted by Rennie (1992, 1994a). The person in the role of client is aware of telling stories and (even at the same time) reflecting on the meaning and significance of these stories (client reflexivity). Clients may choose to hold back parts of a story. While telling a story clients may have a sense of needing to keep going until the end, which Rennie has categorised as being 'on a track'. They are also aware of the therapist as audience to their story, and may select a particular way of telling the narrative in order to create a favourable impression. The story may lead into new areas of feeling and emotion, or be a vehicle for expressing emotion (catharsis).

There are other client narrative actions that did not emerge from the post-session interviews carried out by Rennie, but which can be identified through analysis of transcripts of therapy sessions. Clients mark the beginning and end of stories through pauses, voice quality and phrases such as 'an example of this sort of problem was when . . .' or 'that kind of sums it up'. Clients locate specific stories within a broader life-narrative through time and place markers such as 'about two months ago . . .' or 'it was when I was living in London . . .'. Also, analysis of therapy discourse reveals many ways that clients control their emotional distance in relation to stories that are being recounted. Some stories may be told through the filter of objectifying linguistic strategies such as 'it' or 'you', past tense, or an absence of experiential detail and colour. Other stories that are much more emotionally immediate or present will include vivid descriptions of place, direct speech and use of present tense.

Listening for stories

From a therapist's point of view, perhaps the most significant difference between narrative therapy and other types of therapy is that a narrative approach involves *listening for stories*. While many psychodynamic or constructivist therapists have been influenced by narrative ideas, their purpose in working with stories is to gain access to what lies behind the story, for example unconscious processes or cognitive schemas. Narrative therapists, on the other hand, are interested in the story for itself. The work of Edelson (1993) gives a sense of what this means in practice. The list below gives a summary of the guidelines Edelson supplies to therapists in training, to sensitise them to the rhythm and impact of narrative, and to help them to tune in to the actual stories told by their clients.

- When you are doing psychotherapy, and want to get your bearings, call to mind childhood experiences of wanting to be told a story, how you got your mother to tell you a story, memories of how you listened and responded to stories, what you liked and didn't like, what you wanted and especially enjoyed, what made you restless or turned you off, and what went on between you and the storyteller

- Call to mind sitting with a friend at lunch, talking about what's been happening in your life, and your friend's life, asking and answering, 'What have you been doing? How has the week gone?' What kinds of things would each of you say and ask as the other told about various happenings? What did each of you do to arouse the interest of the other? How did each of you know that the other was not interested? How did that affect what was told?
- Call to mind watching a movie. Reflect on how a movie went about affecting you. What made you feel that it was a great, a good, a lousy movie?
- Don't make an effort to figure things out. Instead, perk up when an image of any kind, a daydream, or some story you know pops into your head
- Eschew the vague and general, and pursue the particular
- The client reports a series of events. You make a story out of these events. Show how they might be causally connected to each other. Where there appears to be a gap, where you cannot provide one of the causal links from what the client has reported, inquire about the event that is missing
- Where the client has dropped a narrative line, ask, 'What happened next?'
- Tell the client a story that answers these questions: Why is the client telling this story now? In response to what event? To accomplish what purpose, to deal with what feeling, to arouse what feeling in me?

The task of deconstructing a story

One of the big differences between therapeutic storytelling and everyday storytelling is that, in the latter, people can often tell and re-tell the same story in the same way for years at a time, while in therapy the expectation is that the story will change. Both therapist and client, therefore, engage together in the work of deconstructing the stories that are told, with the goal of finding better tales to tell. White describes this process in the following way:

> Deconstruction has to do with procedures that subvert taken-for-granted realities and practices; those so-called 'truths' that are split off from the conditions and the context of their production, those disembodied ways of speaking that hide their biases and prejudices, and those familiar practices of self and of relationship that are subjugating of persons' lives. Many of the methods of deconstruction render strange these familiar and everyday taken-for-granted realities and practices by objectifying them. In this sense, the methods of deconstruction are methods that 'exoticise the domestic'. (White, 1992: 121)

For the therapist, the task of deconstruction requires being able to 'render strange' the 'familiar', with the aim of reversing the split-off and disembodied ways of talking about self exhibited by the client during a therapy session. There seem to be different ways that therapists go about this task. Some therapists consistently endeavour to assimilate the client's story into a therapeutic metanarrative that has greater explanatory power. This strategy has its origins in psychoanalytic interpretation and cognitive re-framing. Other therapists draw the client's attention to the way he or she constructs his or her story, and through this either invite the client to consider other ways of telling, or may even supply a model or example of how else the story might be told. This approach has traditionally been associated with the humanistic, experiential therapies. Still other therapists ask questions that lead the client to discover inconsistencies in his or her story or stories. This final method has been particularly developed by therapists working in the family therapy tradition. It is quite likely that all therapists engage in all these strategies to some degree, while 'specialising' in one or another according to personal predilection, training and professional affiliation.

The strategy of attempting to show the client how his or her story can be assimilated into a much broader, grander narrative scheme is summed up by Schafer:

> People going through psychoanalysis – (analysands) – tell the analyst about themselves and others in the past and present. In making interpretations, the analyst retells these stories. In the retelling, certain features are accentuated while others are placed in parentheses: certain features are related to others in new ways or for the first time; some features are developed further, perhaps at great length. This retelling is done along psychoanalytic lines. . . . The analyst's tellings progressively influence the what and how of stories told by analysands. . . . The end product of this interweaving of texts is a radically new, jointly authored work. (1980: 35–6)

One feature of the client's stories that would certainly be developed 'at great length' in psychoanalysis would be the story in which the therapist played a role: the transference story. The therapist activity that drives along this process is interpretation. From the point of view of the client, it is as though every tale he or she tells is consistently and rigorously re-told by the therapist in the language and according to the world-view of psychoanalysis.

There appears to be a tendency in recent writings on narrative therapy to emphasise the centrality of the therapist's metanarrative or 'macronarrative'. However, it is also necessary to understand that, while the coherence and explanatory power of a therapeutic 'grand narrative' such as psychoanalytic theory may have a part to play in helping some clients to 're-author' their life-story in a consistent fashion, most of the re-telling of stories that occurs in therapy is much more ordinary, guided by alternative narratives drawn from everyday life rather than from theoretical systems. For example, Sheinberg (1992) writes about the dilemmas of working with families in which incest has taken place, and the value of enabling the story of the problem to be told from a 'care' perspective as well as from the point of view of 'justice'. She suggests that although male perpetrators of sexual abuse may fairly readily admit that what they did was 'wrong', they rarely seem to be able to empathise with the experience of the victim. For these men, telling the story from a 'care' perspective can have a major impact.

Another type of alternative story that can be found in the everyday ways that people talk about their lives is what White and Epston (1990) and deShazer (1985), among others, have characterised as 'solution' stories. There is an assumption that people go to see therapists to talk about their *problems*. However, embedded in everyday discourse, or available to awareness if asked to think about it, are stories of occasions when the person has encountered a problem but has dealt with it effectively: solution stories. Therapists such as White and Epston and deShazer base their approach very much on a thorough search for solutions, followed up by an attempt to learn from these events – what did the person do that 'worked'? How can he or she achieve the same outcome the next time the problem arises?

The basic therapeutic strategy for 'subverting taken-for-granted realities and practices' is to discover different ways of telling the story, different versions of a story. One way of doing this is to find or create alternative stories that, as it were, sit alongside the dominant 'problem' story in the person's narrative repertoire and thereby invite further attention and re-formulation as the person struggles to deal with the dissonance between the different versions. The other main deconstructive strategy is to disrupt the telling of the dominant story, to make it untellable in its original form.

Sluzki (1992) describes a set of what he calls 'transformative micro-practices', intended to 'destabilise' the client's story. He regards stories as structured in terms of six key dimensions: time, space, causality, interaction, values and mode of telling. Therapist interventions informed by this model operate to draw the client's attention to the way he or she has constructed his or her story along one or other of these dimensions, and so to open up possibilities for other versions of the story to emerge. Examples of the kinds of question a therapist might ask in relation to these dimensions are given in Table 6.1.

Table 6.1   *Transformative micro-practices: invitations to narrative change*

Example of a client narrative: 'This has been bothering me for the last ten years. It all started when I lost my place at college after failing some exams. It just made me so anxious in any situation where I felt I was being assessed, like in a job interview. And every time I failed to get a job, my mother used to get really angry with me. She keeps saying how stupid I am, but I know she only gets so upset because she cares so much about me.'

Narrative dimension	Examples of questions that invite a narrative shift
Time	'Why do you consult me *now*?'
Space	'In what circumstances/situations is the problem more/less noticeable?'
Causality	'What was going on *before* this problem emerged?'
Interaction	'Throughout these confrontations with your mother, who was the grown-up and who the child? . . . who was supposed to look after whom?'
Values	'How do *you* act toward someone you care about?'
Mode of telling	'Would you describe for me what actually happens when you are in a job interview, as if I were witnessing it?'

Source: Sluzki (1992)

While Sluzki's model usefully delineates the kinds of narrative 'disruptions' a therapist might employ, and has value in stimulating practitioners to reflect on the kinds of deconstructive routines they either do or do not employ, it is likely that, much of the time, therapists and other helpful people engage in this kind of activity in a fairly spontaneous and intuitive manner. A powerful example of this type of deconstruction can be discovered in the 'communications' model of psychotherapy developed by Young and Beier (1982). These therapists argue that self-defeating and 'subjugating' life-stories are perpetuated through interactions in which the other person responds to the client in predictable ways. For instance, a client who behaves in a caustic or critical manner will evoke negative reactions from other people, which in turn will reinforce his or her definition of self (or story about self) as unlikeable and unworthy. If, however, the therapist declines to respond in the predicted manner, opportunities may be opened up for the client to see, as if for the first time, just how strange are the taken-for-granted strategies they employ to objectify themselves. In the following excerpt from a therapy session, the client is a student seeing a counsellor at a university counselling centre, and has two weeks remaining of a time-limited therapy contract:

> *Client*: Well, you know we have only two weeks left in the semester, and I, uh, well, just don't see the point in continuing. I'm sure it's just a waste of time now – since I'll be leaving soon. Maybe we should just stop now.
>
> *Therapist*: [with exaggeration and a smile] Thank goodness you said something. All I think about is how I could spend my extra hour on Thursday if only you weren't around.
>
> *Client*: [Laughs] I guess I didn't mean it quite that way. I guess I felt sort of sad about stopping and did not want to prolong the agony. (Young and Beier, 1982: 271)

This brief interaction is one of the ways in which a story can be deconstructed. The opening statement by the client can be understood as a fragment of a story he tells himself about being inadequate ('a waste of your time'). The therapist declines to give the expected reassurance, and in the ensuing moment of uncertainty the client offers another quite different story-line about himself. Now he describes himself as sad and in 'agony' over the ending. This example also illustrates the important role of *humour* in subverting, destabilising and deconstructing the taken-for-granted reality perpetuated through oft-told stories. Warm humour creates a space in which joker and hearer can, as it were, stand aside from the topic of the joke and see it in a fresh light.

A common theme running through this discussion of narrative deconstruction has been that of sensitivity to the nuances of language, to the multiple meanings conveyed by the way a story is constructed (see Chapter 2). Van Langenhove and Harré (1993) draw attention to the use of the term 'I' in autobiographical stories, the issue of the *positioning* of the self in the narrative. They point to the profound difference between an autobiographical account in which a person recounts that 'Sharon said to me, "You cannot work here any more"', and the same information conveyed as 'Sharon said that I could not work there any more'. In the first example, the speaker dramatises the account in a vivid and personal way that invites the hearer to participate in the drama. In the second version, by contrast, the speaker offers a more distanced 'reporting' of what happened, with correspondingly less opportunity for the hearer to engage, deconstructively or otherwise, in the story being performed.

Perhaps the crucial aspect in any of the deconstructive manoeuvres described above – the thing that in the end makes them therapeutic, is that they open up the *possibility* that there could be another story that could be told in relation to a set of problems. People seek out the services of therapists because they are *stuck*, because they keep feeling the same awful feelings, thinking the same terrible thoughts, behaving in the same self-destructive ways. One of the interesting findings to come out of therapy research is that clients often attribute great value to their therapist's *mistakes* (Strupp et al., 1964). A therapist can utterly misunderstand the client, offer an interpretation that is quite confused, and yet, if there is a sufficiently good relationship between them, the client will report that what was said turned out to be helpful. This type of therapist error can be seen as constituting an opening up of the *possibility* of an alternative version to the story. The version offered by the therapist, his or her interpretation or re-telling, may in itself be implausible, but it can serve as a very effective signal, all the more convincing for its clumsiness and misplaced sincerity, that there could, perhaps, be another way of thinking, feeling or behaving, another way of narrating the events being described. The client brushes aside the narrative proferred by the therapist, but is then left with the question: 'Well, that didn't fit, but how else can I account for what happened?'

The point here is that, from a social constructionist perspective, there is not and can never be a final version of a story, a definitive 'true' telling. Constructing a life-narrative is, to borrow MacIntyre's (1981) image, an endless *quest*. Therapy cannot provide a definitive, once-and-for-all storyline. All it can strive to do is to support the person in his or her endeavour to discover the 'possibilities of choice' (Bruner, 1993).

Narrative events

The main type of narrative process event that can be observed in a therapy session is simply that of telling a story. Often, a client may have a pressing need just to share something that has happened. However, there are different ways in which therapist and client can work together to tell and then retrieve meaning from stories. The telling, the associated leading-up-to-the-telling and the reflecting-on-the-telling often form an identifiable unit or segment of a therapy session. Elliott has argued that change in therapy is often mediated through significant events occurring within the therapy hour, and that it is valuable to study the structure of these events. It is possible, therefore, to regard one aspect of therapy process as consisting of events, sequences of interaction that address a specific topic over a period of several minutes.

Perhaps the most compelling account of the variety of helpful events that can occur in therapy sessions is contained in the Greenberg et al. (1993) manual of experiential psychotherapy. One of the important features of this model is that it has been developed out of an interplay between clinical practice and research. In this form of therapy, the key task of the therapist is to detect the expression of signs or 'markers' on the part of the client that he or she is ready to, or needing to, engage in a particular type of emotional processing. Table 6.2 presents a summary of the six types of therapeutic event found in the research carried out by this team. Each of these event structures can also be understood in narrative terms. For instance, the event described by Greenberg et al. as *systematic evocative unfolding at a marker of a problematic reaction point* comprises situations where the client reports an incident in which he or she found him- or herself reacting in an unexpected, unreasonable or otherwise problematic manner. The marker for this type of event has three main features:

> (1) The client recounts a particular instance of a reaction in a particular situation. (2) The reaction that is felt as problematic is the client's own, not that of someone else. (3) There is some indication that the client views his or her reaction as problematic, not simply as an unfortunate consequence of someone else's behaviour. (Greenberg et al., 1993: 144)

From a narrative perspective, this marker can be seen as comprising a story: the client tells a story to convey to the hearer his or her puzzlement as to how he or she acted in a specific situation.

Table 6.2　*Types of therapeutic events*

Events identified by Greenberg et al. (1993)	Narrative dimensions of these events
1　Systematic evocative unfolding at a marker of a problematic reaction point	Re-telling, deconstructing and completing the story
2　Experiential focusing for an unclear felt sense	Finding the words to tell a story; finding the most important story to tell at that moment
3　Two-chair dialogue at a self-evaluative split	Giving expression to different 'voices'; differentiating between versions of the story told from the point of view of the dominant cultural narrative and from a subjugated, personal voice
4　Two-chair enactment for self-interruptive split	Recognition that a dominant narrative is embodied (i.e. expressed through gesture, posture and action)
5　Empty-chair work and unfinished business	Telling a previously hidden emotion story; constructing a more satisfying or coherent emotion story about a relationship with a significant other (e.g. 'my anger is disappointment at the loss of love')
6　Empathic affirmation at a marker of intense vulnerability	Being enabled to tell, probably for the first time, the story of an extremely painful event

The next stage in the Greenberg et al. model of the problematic reaction event involves the therapist inviting the client to explore his or her reaction by re-entering the scene and re-experiencing it in a 'live and vivid but slowed-down fashion, with an exploratory stance' (1993: 148). Again, from a narrative perspective this therapeutic strategy can be viewed as representing a less distanced re-telling of the story. It is also an opportunity for therapist and client to function together in a 'slowed-down' way, on a co-constructed version of the story, since it is clear from the case material that Greenberg et al. offer that the therapist makes a major contribution to the 'exploration' that occurs. Within a narrative model, the therapist is applying the kinds of *deconstructive* strategies decribed earlier in this chapter, with the goal of opening the story up to some kind of re-authoring.

It is significant that Greenberg et al. observe that the end-point of this thera-peutic process is that the client comes to recognise the problematic reaction as 'an example of a broader aspect of [his or her] own mode of functioning' (1993: 148). In narrative terms, the client is able to bring the whole story to a satisfactory closure, with the *evaluation* element of the narrative being fol-lowed by *resolution* and *coda* (Labov and Waletzky, 1967). The role of the therapist has been to assist the client to tell a complete story, and in so doing to relate the narrative of a particular 'departure from the ordinary' (J.S. Bruner, 1986) to the overarching life-story that he or she lives within, or is striving to reconstruct. The brief case examples offered by Greenberg et al. capture this sense of both narrative completion and the making of a link (or, in Greenberg et al.'s terms, a *meaning bridge*) from a story of an actual occur-rence to the wider story of the good life.

The point here is, even though the process-experiential approach developed by Greenberg et al. does not explicitly use concepts of 'narrative' and 'story', their event-focused style of therapy can be seen in narrative terms as a set of strategies for, first of all, heightening the emotional and interpersonal impact of the stories told by the client, and, second, retrieving and reflecting on the meanings conveyed by these stories in service of the goal of re-examining, or re-authoring a broader life-story. In the list of therapy events described in Table 6.2 it is apparent that Greenberg and his colleagues make frequent use of what Vogel (1994) calls 'perspective by incongruity': creating moments in which the client cannot help but confront the existence of opposing narrative versions of reality.

There are other kinds of narrative event that can be observed in the work of practitioners of other orientations to therapy. For example, using dream material in therapy introduces a distinctive type of narrative event in that the story told by the client is recounted in a form that can invert the cause-and-effect sequences found in normal, 'real' life and normal, 'factual' stories. Practitioners of Ericksonian hypnotherapy, or Gersie's story-telling therapy, create therapeutic events that are structured around the therapist telling a metaphoric/symbolic story. Therapists trained in Cognitive–Analytic Therapy (CAT) or in White and Epston's narrative therapy, may construct events char-acterised by the therapist's *written* re-framing of the client's story. Parry and Doan (1994) describe a category of narrative therapeutic event based on client *rehearsal* of the new story he or she is planning to tell to significant others.

Some of the most elaborate and intriguing narrative events are to be found in behavioural approaches to therapy. Behaviour-oriented therapists are interested in bringing about change in what clients *do*, in their actual behaviour. On the face of it, this strategy might appear to leave little room for a narrative perspective. Using a technique such as systematic desensitisation, for example, a behavioural therapist would aim to replace an anxiety or fear response to a given stimulus with a relaxation or coping response. The therapist would teach relaxation skills to the client, then help him or her practise these skills in different fear-evoking situations. From a narrative perspective, this sort of procedure can be understood as giving the client the basis for telling a different story. Before systematic desensitisation, a client may have many versions of a story of 'when I am asked to speak in public, I just have a panic attack'. After behaviour therapy, the client will have at least two new stories to tell. One will be about 'when that therapist came to the meeting with me, I was able to make my presentation without any bother', and 'this is how I learned to get over my panic attacks'. Systematic desensitisation can therefore be interpreted, from a narrative point of view, as a storytelling event where the author has to do some personal research in order to gather material to be able to tell the story convincingly. Just as George Orwell spent time washing dishes in order to be able to write authentically about working-class life, so a fearful person may choose to do brave things in order to be able to tell believable coping stories.

Thinking about therapy at the level of in-session events opens up, from a narrative-informed point of view, the implication that there may be many more types of therapeutic storytelling event than have yet been discovered or invented. Different world cultures have their own characteristic ways of telling stories. Narrative genres and forms of oral performance represent alternative modes of storytelling. All of this is potentially a huge resource for therapists.

Conclusion: story, author, process

In therapy the narrativisation of experience in the form of a story 'makes it the experience of those who are listening to the tale'(Benjamin, 1969: 87). All of the narrative processes discussed in this chapter lead in the direction of the construction of 'better' stories, which vividly and compellingly communicate to the therapist a sense of the world of the client, and therefore make possible what Widdershoven (1993) has called an *edifying dialogue*. It remains difficult to describe the process of therapy in other than psychological terms. The account of narrative therapy process given here is without doubt over-psychologised, reflecting the overwhelming tendency within the psychotherapy and counselling literature to seek to explain therapy as a branch of science. Further interdisciplinary studies of therapy will surely bring to light the many cultural dimensions of the experience of therapy. For example, many clients report to their therapists that they have read a novel or seen a film that has had an impact on them. It is unusual for a therapist to give any special significance to such reports. However, from a narrative point of view it can be seen that if users of therapy are engaged in a process of authoring and re-authoring, they are likely to be searching around in their cultural backyard for stories and myths that will help them to bring more sense and meaning to their own personal narrative. Also, the story structures that exist within a cultural milieu are likely to influence and shape the therapy process in ways that at the moment we can only begin to grasp. For example, Edelson (1993), a psychoanalytic psychotherapist committed to the 'narrative turn' is clear that the client stories he hears are structured (in his mind) along the lines of Hollywood melodrama. He admits: 'I do sound more like a moviegoer than a cognitive scientist when I am doing and teaching psychotherapy' (Edelson, 1993: 312). His writings illustrate the value of making sense of therapy from this culturally constructed perspective.

But what happens if Edelson's client or patient is employing fairy-story genre to frame his or her experience, or tells the story of his or her life as if it were a television soap? Or a detective story? The use of such cultural resources clearly happens within the process of therapy, but is as yet little understood. In the next chapter, some case material is presented that illustrates the operation of such cultural processes in therapy.

7

Postmodern Narrative Therapy:
A Case Example

The aim of this chapter is to use a single case to explore some of the ways in which different aspects of narrative therapy might be applied in practice. The case chosen for discussion is taken from the novel *Therapy* written by David Lodge and published in 1995. This novel focuses on a two-year period in the life of a man receiving cognitive-behavioural therapy for depression.

There are several reasons for using a novel as case material, rather than seeking access to data from a 'genuine' therapy case. First, there is no danger of threatening the confidentiality of what a 'real' client may have disclosed to a 'real' therapist. Case studies in counselling and psychotherapy are often either bland, in concealing the actual life of the client behind a heavy overlay of theory, measurement and interpretation, or can be personally revealing to an uncomfortable extent. While clients may give their counsellor or therapist permission to publish case material, they may not fully appreciate the degree to which they are exposing themselves in print. Sometimes, too, the willingness of a client to agree to such a venture may reflect an imbalance of power: my therapist has given me so much, how could I refuse this request?

Another factor in favour of using a novel as case material is that the basic text is clearly in the public domain, readily accessible to anyone interested in developing an alternative reading of the case. As Spence (1986) has pointed out, most of the cases used in the therapy literature are grounded in samples of therapy interaction or dialogue that have been thoroughly 'smoothed' to achieve a neat correspondence between the quotes or other 'raw' material that is cited and the interpretations of that data that are then based on it. Spence (1986) has argued that this approach has the effect of placing severe limits on the ability of those reading case studies to judge whether the interpretation of the case is justifiable, accurate or comprehensive. Part of the problem here is the sheer amount of data that is required to give a full account of a case.

The final reason for taking a novel as the basis for a clinical case analysis is that there can be no doubt over whether the events that are described in the book are factually true: they are not. What David Lodge has done in this novel is to construct a representation of the experience of therapy. I have no knowledge of the extent to which *Therapy* may or may not draw upon events from David Lodge's personal involvement in therapy. However, he was Professor of Modern English Literature at the University of Birmingham. He is therefore middle-class, professional, educated, economically secure and, as a result, a member of the social group most likely to use the services of a therapist. In terms of reflecting the understanding of therapy prevalent in that social milieu, Lodge would appear to be a reliable and credible informant. The extent to which his account of therapy is itself credible can be judged by anyone who has read the novel. The novel has been widely read, and reviewers do not appear to have commented negatively on the general credibility of his account of the experience of psychotherapy.

It is certainly unwise to overgeneralise from a single case. Other stories of therapy might express quite different themes. The attraction of the individual case has always been that it can provide a richly detailed exemplar of 'what is possible'. And in this respect the therapy described in *Therapy* cannot be held to be typical of all cases seen by counsellors and psychotherapists. Like Lodge's other novels, *Therapy* is written in a mainly comic genre. It is funny. It contains many observations of everyday life in the Britain of the 1980s. It is just this ordinariness that makes it an appropriate choice for a case study. The characters and events are recognisable.

The client

Laurence (Tubby) Passmore is 58 years old, married to Sally, a college lecturer in linguistics. They have two children, Jane and Adam, both grown up and living away from home. Tubby's mother died four years ago, his father seven. His brother, Ken, lives in Australia. Tubby is a writer for a popular television sit-com, *The Family Next Door*, which features the conflicts between two families, one middle class and one working class, who live next door to each other. Tubby is well-paid and successful, with a house in an exclusive area of 'Brummidge' (which British readers will readily identify as Birmingham) and a flat in London. He enjoys a strong, supportive, sexual relationship with his wife, and has a close but non-sexual friendship with Amy, whom he meets when in London on business. Tubby has two problems. He suffers from intermittent pains in his knee. And he is depressed. Tubby Passmore is a user of therapy, and is discriminating in the choices he makes about which kind of therapist he wishes to consult:

> I have a lot of therapy. On Mondays I see Roland for Physiotherapy, on Tuesdays I see Alexandra for Cognitive Behaviour Therapy, and on Fridays I have either aromatherapy or acupuncture. Wednesdays and Thursdays I'm usually in London, but then I see Amy, which is a sort of therapy too, I suppose. (pp. 14–15)

Tubby is aware that other types of psychotherapy are available. For example, he knows that Amy sees a psychoanalyst five times a week, but he considers this to be indulgent and ineffective.

He is depressed: 'I have depression, anxiety, panic attacks, night sweats, insomnia' (p. 4); 'I can't decide. I can't make a decision about anything these days' (p. 14). But this state of mind makes no sense to him. He reflects that:

> I can remember a time when I was happy. Reasonably content anyway. Or at least, a time when I didn't think I was *un*happy, which is perhaps the same thing as being

happy. But somewhere, sometime, I lost it, the knack of just living, without being anxious and depressed. How? I Don't Know. (p. 16)

The pain in Tubby's knee makes more sense, at least initially. He consults an orthopaedic surgeon, who carries out an arthroscopy, a procedure in which a small camera is inserted under local anaesthetic, to guide the microsurgical excision of bits of cartilage, bone and tissue. This operation is not effective, and the consultant arrives at a diagnosis of 'Internal Derangement of the Knee' (IDK). Tubby's physiotherapist, however, tells him that IDK is medical jargon, or a doctor's joke, which means 'I don't know'. This idea sticks in Tubby's mind, and the association between pain (physical or emotional) and 'not knowing' stimulates his struggle to know, his search for meaning within the life situation in which he finds himself. His psychotherapist, Alexandra, regards his depression and self-doubt as attributable to negative self-talk. As a homework exercise, she asks him to write a self-description. He finds this useful, and starts to keep a journal. The novel comprises this personal journal.

Tubby's knee pain and his emotional pain gradually merge. For example, after a setback over a last-minute cut in a script:

I feel self-esteem leaking out of me like water from an old bucket. I despise myself both for my weakness in accepting the cut and for my vacillation over whether to do anything about it. My knee has begun to throb, like a rheumatic joint sensitive to the approach of bad weather. I sense a storm of depression flickering on the horizon, and a tidal wave of despair gathering itself to swamp me. (p. 60)

Tubby's life-narrative

The journal/novel, as an account of a journey through therapy (or therapies), encompasses a number of different story-lines. One of the central stories is Tubby's life-story. He was born into a working-class family. One younger brother. His father was a tram driver. As a boy, Tubby won entry to a grammar school, but did not do well:

I believe now that I would have been happier, and therefore have learned more, at some less prestigious and pretentious establishment. I had the innate intelligence, but not the social and cultural back-up, to benefit from the education on offer. . . . I never fitted in and never did well academically, languishing at the bottom of my class for most of my school career . . . the only success I enjoyed at school was as a comic actor in the annual play. (pp. 222–3)

After school, Tubby found a job in the office of a West End theatrical impresario. Following this, he did his National Service, where 'the only escape . . . from terminal boredom was through acting in and writing scripts for revues, pantomimes, drag shows and other home-made entertainments on the base' (p. 258). After National Service, he formed a small travelling theatre company, touring schools, 'doing stripped-down versions of Shakespeare for secondary schools and dramatized fairy-tales for juniors' (p. 194). It is on a visit to a junior school in Leeds that he meets Sally, a few years younger than he is, there as a student on teaching practice.

Sally's father was a minister in an inner-city Leeds parish, earnest, well-meaning, disapproving. Tubby found their family life bizzare:

> . . . as archaic as the *Forsyte saga* . . . sitting down *en famille* two or three times a day, with grace before and after meals, cloth napkins which you had to replace in your own special napkin-ring at the end of each meal so as to save laundry, and proper cutlery, however worn and tarnished, soup spoons for soup and fish knives and forks for fish. (p. 197)

Tubby's later success, as a scriptwriter creating stories that touched on, but made light of, the conflicts between working-class and middle-class norms and attitudes, can be seen as an expression of one of the core themes in his own life. Tubby was, from his school years, culturally caught between these contrasting class worlds. His way of coping was to perform, to make others laugh, to be the observer outside the action, the writer who was later to watch the audience watching the production of his show. At school and during National Service he got through by starring in comic roles. He charmed Sally, too, by making her laugh, in spite of their differences and his 'scruffy dark sweaters with holes in them, and greasy hair' (p. 195).

Behind this account of his life lies Tubby's sense of the 'good life', the overarching, mythic macronarrative in which his life-story is embedded. The one passage in the text that vividly conveys Tubby's sense of the 'good' is his account of his reaction to learning the news of Bobby Moore's death. Tubby recalls an England humiliated at football by South American and European sides, being led by Bobby Moore, 'calm, confident, poised': 'he would bring the ball out of defence and into attack, head up, back straight, like a captain leading a cavalry charge' (p. 90). He also recalls his memories of watching the 1966 World Cup Final on television as a communal occasion:

> . . . when the ball went in the net you could hear the cheering coming out of the neighbours' open windows; and when it was all over people went into their back gardens, or out into the street, grinning all over their faces, to babble about it to other people they'd never said more than 'good morning' to in their lives before. (p. 91)

The good life depicted here gives a feeling of a narrative unity that has been lost, a time of straightforward moral values and pride in national identity that has been supplanted by a world of *Reservoir Dogs* and adultery in the Royal Family.

The therapy

Another central story-line concerns Tubby's narrative about what happens to him in his psychotherapy. He has apparently tried therapy on two occasions five years previously: a few sessions of couple counselling with a marriage counsellor, followed by around six months of individual therapy for depression. His therapist, Dr Alexandra Marples, was recommended by his GP on the basis that 'she's very practical. Doesn't waste time poking around in your unconscious' (p. 16). Tubby was 'relieved to hear that'. He is sceptical about the supposed benefits of psychoanalysis: 'analysis has a way of unravelling the self: the longer you pull on the thread, the more flaws you find' (p. 31).

Tubby explains his preferred approach, cognitive behavioural therapy, in the following terms:

> . . . say you were sexually assaulted as a child in a train when it went through a tunnel or something like that, by a man who was sitting next to you – say he interfered with you while it was dark in the compartment because of the tunnel and you were terrified and ashamed and didn't dare accuse the man when the train came out of the tunnel and never even told your parents or anyone about it afterwards but suppressed the memory entirely . . . a cognitive behavioural therapist would probably give you a programme for conditioning yourself to travelling by public transport, like going round the Inner Circle on the Tube, travelling for just one stop the first time, then two, then three, and so on, in the off-peak time for starters, then in the rush hour, rewarding yourself each time you increased the length of your journey with some kind of treat, a drink or a meal or a new tie, or whatever turns you on – and you're so pleased with your achievement and these little presents to yourself that you forget to be frightened and finally waken up to the fact that there isn't anything to be frightened *of*. That's the theory, anyway. (pp. 15–16)

Clearly, Tubby has picked up the cognitive–behavioural metanarrative, the therapist's story of how therapeutic change occurs.

In practice, Alexandra appears to use a combination of behavioural and cognitive interventions. She teaches Tubby to control his anxiety through relaxation and breathing exercises, and also employs a number of cognitive techniques designed to challenge his negative self-talk. For example, he reports that 'she's always picking me up on negative words I use about myself, words such as *pathological* . . . privileged wanker' (p.17). She asks him to carry out writing homework tasks: a self-description, a list of the good and bad things about his life. She suggests that he sets impossibly high standards for himself, and suffers from lack of self-esteem. She advises against using Prozac. Finally, at the point of Tubby's deepest crisis, when Sally has told him that the marriage is over, she suggests that he 'writes down exactly what I thought other people were saying and thinking about me' (p. 212) .This final homework assignment ends up as a journal written from the perspective of the other key people in Tubby's life.

The process of change

Tubby's life-story, and his account of the process of his therapy form the backdrop or context for the most important aspect of the novel/case: what it says about how Tubby eventually overcomes his depression (and his sore knee). *Therapy* offers Tubby a happy ending, of sorts, and the tale of how he arrives at this resolution of his problems represents the message, or 'moral' of the story. Tubby Passmore, like many other people who are depressed, is indefatigable in his efforts to do something about his predicament. He tries, with the help of his therapist, a range of 'experiments in living', some of which are unsuccessful and others more productive. The sense is of a person who is actively trying out alternative life-stories in order to find the one that fits, that can be lived in, that can form the basis for a satisfying life.

The point of crisis for Tubby, the moment when a vague disenchantment with the world becomes something more acute and immediate, comes when he imagines that his wife is having an affair with her tennis coach. At this point, Tubby's response is to attempt to restore his world to its former state. He challenges the coach, even to the point of breaking into his house. The next strategy Tubby adopts in order to re-create a familiar world is to find another sexual partner. In different ways, he tries out three potential lovers. The first is Amy, his long-time friend and confidante. The second is Louise, a Hollywood film executive who had made a pass at him some years previously. The third is Samantha, a young and highly attractive member of the production staff on *The Family Next Door*. All three of these attempted liaisons end in comical failure. They can perhaps be regarded as fairly standard approaches to the crisis of middle years taken by men in Western society: sexual intimacy as the solution to isolation, lack of meaning and alienation. In this phase of his reaction to the news that Sally has ended the marriage, Tubby acts as if to repair his story, to re-create a re-jigged life story in which he can continue to live in a similar manner. His wish is to continue the plot, with different actors playing the same old characters.

However, while Tubby is pursuing these unsuccessful affairs, he also finds himself being drawn in other directions that are quite new and unfamiliar. He comes across Kierkegaard, and becomes fascinated by the thought that it might be possible to understand what he is feeling. Even though he finds it hard to make sense of Kierkegaard's writing, there is something there that seems to reach out to him. He finds himself, his own experience, in Kierkegaard. He also finds himself thinking more and more about Maureen, his childhood sweetheart. He wonders what has happened to her. 'What kind of a person is she now?' He remembers Maureen's habit of 'looking admiringly at me': 'nobody ever did it since, not Sally, not Amy, not Louise or any of the other women who've occasionally made a pass at me' (p. 37).

To compensate for his sense of being an educational failure, Tubby often looks up unfamiliar words in dictionaries. Amy uses the word 'angst' in conversation with him. In checking the meaning of this term in a dictionary, he follows up further references to existentialism, and then to Kierkegaard. He describes his experience of first reading about Kierkegaard in a biographical dictionary:

> . . . his life sounded as dull as it was short. But the article listed some of his books at the end. I can't describe how I felt as I read the titles. If the hairs on the back of my neck were shorter, they would have lifted. *Fear and Trembling*, *The Sickness Unto Death*, *The Concept of Dread* – they didn't sound like titles of philosophy books, they seemed to name my condition like arrows thudding into a target. (pp. 64–5)

Tubby reads his way through most of Kierkegaard's writings, as well as becoming fascinated by the failed engagement between Kierkegaard and a young woman called Regine. At first, the books were 'dead boring and very difficult to follow' (p. 8), but gradually Tubby discovers in this work a set of concepts and explanations that enable him to begin to make some sense of 'not knowing':

Reading Kierkegaard is like flying through heavy cloud. Every now and again there's a break and you get a brief, brilliantly lit view of the ground, and then you're back in the swirling grey mist again, with not a fucking clue where you are. (p. 109)

The more that Tubby reads Kierkegaard, the more he remembers Maureen. Tubby's search for Maureen becomes a means of finding meaning in his life. Through this quest he becomes able to integrate more than ever before his story of who he was as a child, who he is now, and who he wishes to be in the future. The story of his relationship with Maureen, and its ending, emerges as pivotal in his construction of a different type of life-narrative.

Maureen Kavanagh had been Tubby's first girlfriend. They went to different schools, and met each other in the mornings while waiting for the bus or tram to school. Maureen came from a strict Catholic family, and their friendship was closely controlled by her mother, and centred on Church activities. Tubby returns to the Church, and discovers that Maureen had married Bede, the middle-class boy who had been his rival for Maureen's affections. He traces their current address, and goes to visit them. On arriving at their house, he is told by Bede that, following an illness and the death of their son, Maureen has chosen to go on a pilgrimage, a thousand-mile walk to Santiago de Compostela in Spain.

In his big new car, symbol of modernity, Tubby sets off to make contact with Maureen on the road to Santiago. He is now on his own, free of any contact with his old life. His meeting with her, and his eventual participation in the pilgrimage, become his epiphany, his moment when things change.

Narrative process in Tubby Passmore's therapy

What can we learn from this novel/case about the nature of counselling and psychotherapy in a postmodern world? What does *Therapy* tell us about therapy? First, the client is in many respects a characteristically postmodern person. He is employed in the information/entertainment industry, even if his actual business involves re-working traditional family structures. He is a 'professional', but not in one of the old professions. He is reflexive; there is a sense of Tubby observing himself and being aware of other possible readings of his action. His network of relationships is fragmented and global: he can be different 'selves' to people in different places. He is sensitive to risk, to the dangers of the world. He is a discerning consumer. In many ways, he appears to be a person with surface but without depth. He does not construct his story around the metaphor of a journey into an inner self or unconscious. His story is one of quest, but his journey is to a series of places: reference books, libraries, Kierkegaard's grave, Spain.

Tubby is an active consumer of therapy. He has a good working knowledge of the therapies that are available, and what each of them has to offer. And, although he carries out most of the suggestions or tasks suggested by his therapists, there is no sense that he is a 'patient' passively taking a prescription. He is not 'in the hands of' Alexandra, his psychotherapist, but is actively using her to meet his needs as he sees them. This point is reinforced through contrast with Amy, who is portrayed as engaged in interminable analysis and dependent on her analyst. Tubby does not find this possibility at all appealing. For him, therapy is a means to an end. While it can be seen that some of Alexandra's therapeutic interventions (for example, inviting him to keep a journal) were extremely helpful to Tubby, it is also clear that he has developed these ideas, has built on them in ways that she could not have anticipated. For example, when asked to write about how he might be perceived by other people in his life, Tubby was able to dramatise his story in a way that went beyond the expectations of his therapist. What had been for her an exercise in confronting negative self-statements and cognitions became for him an invitation to embark on a thorough and highly revealing exploration of the futility and lack of meaning in his current life-narrative. And the act of writing about how other people saw him required Tubby to retreat from the world for a period of time, to withdraw into the sanctuary of his flat in London and actively to avoid contact with the people through which his old, unworkable narrative had been sustained.

It may well be that most, or even all, clients approach therapy in this way, adapting and assimilating therapist interventions or suggestions in ways that the therapist may hardly recognise. It could be that this aspect of therapy has been concealed by the absence of open and detailed client reports on their experience of therapy, or even by the fact that, when such reports are elicited, they are collected by representatives of the profession, whose presence may silence the active voice of the client. Indeed, the very term 'client' hints at a sense of being a recipient, a 'person-with-a-problem', rather than an active, choosing, intentional agent.

Another significant aspect of the case concerns the extent to which Tubby's life-story contained within it not only a full account of the *problems* that he was experiencing, but also incorporated the basic elements of the *solution* to these problems. Much of Tubby's journal, particularly at the start, consists of descriptions of his anxieties over his relationship with his wife, his career, his attractiveness to others, his painful knee. There are many self-deprecating stories, which convey a sense of Tubby as someone lacking worth. What White and Epston (1990) might call 'unique outcomes' or 'solution' stories seem to flit in and out of this 'problem-saturated' discourse. For example, Maureen and Kierkegaard, the figures around which a new life-narrative begins to be constructed, initially appear almost as random intrusions into Tubby's consciousness. Somehow, these images are meaningful, are clues to where to go next.

The ways that the Maureen and Kiekegaard stories develop into significant themes in Tubby's life are consistent with the notion of the person engaging in a search for meaning. Initially, both Maureen and Kierkegaard are, somehow, important, but quite why or how these images or icons are meaningful is not at all clear. It is as though the meaningfulness of these parts of Tubby's life is very much implicit. There is, perhaps, a human capacity to respond to stories in this way, to know that there is more there than can be told all at once. There are some stories we are drawn to, that we want to follow through to the end and other stories that do not engage us at all. Tubby writes about Maureen that 'she's been flitting in and out of my consciousness ever since I started this journal, like a figure glimpsed indistinctly at the edge of a distant wood, moving between the trees, gliding in and out of the shadows' (p. 221). Tubby is slowly able to *retrieve* the meaning for him of the story of his adolescent relationship with Maureen, and then to *construct* a new story in a form that incorporates this set of meanings. He 're-stories' or perhaps 'restores' Maureen to a place in his life-narrative.

The narrative of *Therapy* returns again and again to the central importance of physical, bodily experiencing. Tubby reflects that in his early life, sport acted as his therapy. In the crisis of mid-life that forms the centrepiece of the case, the pain in his knee serves as the focus for his discontent. His knee prevents him from participating in sport. His knee leads to visits to various therapists. He discovers a strange and ambiguous significance in his pain: 'I don't know'. And it is through being willing to take the risk of intentionally exposing himself to this pain that he eventually arrives at his breakthrough. In taking to the road with Maureen he clearly risks exacerbating his knee problem. But in fact the opposite happens, and the knee stops troubling him. In most types of therapy, the therapist's or client's account of bodily experiencing takes the form of reporting/expressing feeling and emotion, or the interpretation of gesture and posture. Usually, in therapy, the client and therapist are sitting in chairs. They are not really engaging with the world in a physical sense. Lodge seems to be saying that for Tubby Passmore 'therapy' was not merely sessions with Alexandra but comprised a whole set of activities during a period of his life. From this wider perspective it might be said that his epiphany was not a cognitive event, a moment of insight (although it was that too), but was a physical event: walking on the road to Santiago.

Finally, one of the key messages of *Therapy* is that the construction of meaning in a life is not merely a matter of making psychological links, such as understanding the connection between childhood experience and adult emotions and actions, or seeing the ways that 'irrational', self-defeating or self-critical thoughts maintain feelings of depression. Arriving at this type of individual narrative coherence is undoubtedly helpful to Tubby Passmore, but what is more important is to find ways of engaging with some of the more all-encompassing stories of his culture, to find his place in the bigger 'canopy of meaning' represented by religion. It is as though, in Lynch's (1996) words, he becomes able 'to move out into the stories of a culture'. What turn out to be the most important aspects of Tubby's therapy are his engagement with two quite different types of narrative cultural resource: existentialist philosophy, as expressed through the story of Kierkegaard's life, and the experience of pilgrimage. These narrative strands are all brought together in a scene in Spain where Tubby encounters a BBC film crew making a documentary on modern pilgrimages. He is interviewed on camera, and tells them that it is possible to understand pilgrimage in terms of Kierkegaard's theory of stages of personal development – aesthetic, ethical, religious. Having completed the interview, the producer asks Tubby to sign a release form. It is only at this point that he realises who Tubby is, and re-frames the whole interview as a piss-take. To add a final layer of meaning to this story, the author, Lodge, chooses to tell us right at the start of the book that all characters and events are 'entirely fictitious' with the 'possible exception' of this documentary producer.

Therapy is a story about a man's struggle to make the best of a life that appeared to be slipping away from him. Toward the end of the book, Lodge provides a set of images that act as metaphors through which the sense of fundamental change in Tubby Passmore's life can be felt by the reader. Just before they leave Spain, Tubby and Maureen visit Finisterre, the 'end of the earth'. On his return to London, Tubby discovers that his flat has been stripped bare by thieves. But perhaps the most powerful metaphor arises from a dilemma that weaves its way through the plot: the key character in *The Family Next Door*, the Shakespearian actress Debbie Radcliffe, has decided to leave the show, to concentrate on stage work. How can they write her out of the plot without losing their audience? In the end, the character dies in a road crash and immediately comes back as a ghost who can speak to and be seen by her husband but by no one else. Here, Lodge/Passmore is telling us, is what can happen when a person is successful in changing the life-story that they tell to the world. For other people, it is for the most part only the new story, the revised plot-line, that they see. But the old story remains a presence, a voice that can warn and advise.

Conclusions: reflecting on *Therapy*

Can the story of Tubby Passmore's knee be read as a case of a 'postmodern' narrative therapy? Here is a person who is thoroughly a member of the modern world: disembedded, reflexive, a believer in progress and expertise. He is someone who has lost or renounced the traditions and rituals around which his parents or grandparents organised their lives. However, in the process of creating meaning in his life, he participates in one of the oldest rituals of the traditional Christian world, the pilgrimage to Santiago de Compostela, and finds in the writings of Kierkegaard another way of seeing his life. But he cannot belong wholly within these worlds. He arrives at his own way of combining elements of modernity and tradition. Tubby observes that he is now able to be 'present to myself'. He is in alignment with the stories within which he lives. The stories somehow 'fit' better. In the events of this period of his life he has undergone a kind of personal *rite de passage*, through which his previous life-narrative, as husband-of-Sally, can be subsumed into an account that embraces not only that set of experiences but has been extended to encompass his earlier and current relationship with Maureen and his engagement with a set of knowledges represented by existential philosophy. And this new narrative carries with it a sense of a future that was not there before. In contrast to his static, self-obsessed state at the start of *Therapy*, by the end Tubby is moving into a future of possibility, of meaning, of purpose.

The story of Tubby Passmore brings together a number of key themes in narrative constructionist therapy. The person-in-therapy is active, a reflexive, intentional agent, constructing an identity from the cultural resources available to him. He is a being embedded in society and culture. His sense of who he is is derived from a set of relationships and roles, and a cultural as well as a personal history. His experience of being a person does not involve to any significant extent an encounter with a deep 'inner self'. Instead, he experiences core existential dilemmas in and through his relationships with others and in his embodied relationship with a physical world of place and pain. The therapist is clearly an important and influential figure in his life. The main function of the therapist appears to be that of enabling the person-in-therapy to accept the disintegration and loss of one life-narrative while engaging in a search for another narrative into which it can be subsumed. However, this new narrative or life-story is not in itself provided by the therapist. It is a story-line that is 'out there', in the culture, and it brings with it different ways of acting in the world and different types of relationships with others.

8

Reinventing Therapy

In this book, it has been argued that there exists an emerging new approach to therapy theory and practice, an approach based on an appreciation of the centrality of narrative in human communication and society. I have attempted to map out some of the ideas and examples that constitute a narrative therapy based in postmodern, constructionist thinking. This final chapter examines some of the implications of the 'narrative turn' in therapy. While psychodynamic and cognitive/constructivist therapists have contributed a great deal to our understanding of the role of narrative in therapy, their approaches nevertheless remain bound to a modernist conception of a therapy designed to sustain the individual, autonomous, bounded self. It is my belief that a constructionist narrative therapy, as described in the previous three chapters, entails a different stance toward therapy, a stance that foregrounds a sense of persons as social beings, living in and through a culture and its stories. This difference has implications for a number of domains of therapeutic endeavour: training, research, ethics and, ultimately, the very nature of psychotherapeutic helping.

Training for narrative therapy

Currently, there is a fair degree of consensus over the necessary components of training in counselling and psychotherapy (see Dryden and Thorne., 1991; Dryden, et al., 1995). It is generally accepted that those who become therapists should acquire an appropriate base of theoretical knowledge, develop a variety of interpersonal skills, and become familiar with a range of professional issues concerning ethics, confidentiality and professional boundaries. Most trainee counsellors and psychotherapists are also required to become aware of the importance of cultural dimensions of their work, and to appreciate the contribution of research. Finally, all of these aspects of the curriculum are, hopefully, integrated within the person of the therapist through personal therapy or experiential groupwork of some kind. Training programmes in counselling and psychotherapy are increasingly based in universities, and resemble programmes designed to train doctors, nurses and social workers and other human service professionals, insofar as there is an intended interplay between experiential learning (often in the form of a placement or internship) and academic study. Most trainee counsellors and psychotherapists are recruited from a background of a first degree in psychology or enter the therapy profession following prior experience in a human service occupation such as nursing, medicine, social work or teaching.

What difference might a narrative approach make to therapy training? If the intention of narrative therapy is to enable persons to reflect on the stories they tell, then it is clearly necessary for the therapist to be attuned to narrative, the ways that the therapist's clients construct and relate their tales. Some writers on narrative in therapy have drawn attention to the multiplicity of ways that meaning is shaped and formed in the precise telling of a story (Bamberg, 1991; Russell and van den Broek, 1992). Most therapists are aware of the emotional significance of linguistic features such as active/passive voice or denial of subjective intention in phrases such as 'I must . . .'. By drawing upon the insights of narrative linguistic theorists such as Gee (1986, 1991) or Langellier (1989), it is possible to hear more of the meaning embedded within a client's story. Bamberg calls for an appreciation of the potential of narrative theory as a means of enhancing the effectiveness of 'clinical listening'.

Turning to the role of therapist as active co-constructor of the client's story, Omer (1993a) suggests that it is essential for practitioners to see their work as a craft that calls upon an understanding of drama, creative writing and rhetoric. Omer emphasises the value of consciously using not only individual therapist statements but also the whole of the flow and rhythm of a therapy session to achieve the maximum impact. For example, he proposes that it can be useful to envisage a therapy session as an entity: 'the formal organization of a session . . . may be as important as that of a story or musical piece' (Omer, 1993a: 64). Some sessions gain impact through climactic endings, some through climactic beginnings. Some sessions are structured around dialectic forms, for example through the employment of a Gestalt two-chair technique. At a more molecular, moment-by-moment level, specific statements made by therapists need to be formulated with regard to their 'poetic' quality. Omer observes that:

> . . . the first lesson in psychotherapeutic style [is] similar to a first lesson in good writing: keep it short, simple and concrete; avoid jargon and euphemisms; make it personal; use the active voice. (1993a: 60)

Other components of therapeutic style include an ability to use metaphor and imagery, the effective use of physical props, and a capacity to modulate voice quality in terms of pace, pitch and tenderness. Omer has suggested that 'if we are to take seriously the decline of positivism in psychotherapy, questions of style must rise in importance relative to questions of theory' (1996: 331). Omer (1996) offers compelling descriptions of the differences in style that can be observed in well-known and successful therapists operating within the same theoretical domain. The implication is that, in order to have maximum impact on their clients, each therapist needs to develop a therapeutic style that allows them to express their own personal qualities, values and cultural identity.

Therapists who are listening for stories need to be aware of the stock of stories culturally available to their clients. Often, a client may mention a film or novel with which their therapist is unfamiliar, which has no meaning for the therapist. Clients and therapists who are members of different cultural or ethnic groups may have minimal overlap of narrative resources. In such situations, a story that has meaning for a client may represent a powerful means of entering his or her world. Too few therapists invite their clients to recount the religious or fictional stories that have meaning for them, or take the trouble to read these stories at first hand.

If it is desirable for narrative therapists to possess sensitivity to stories, it makes sense to recruit them on the basis of previous experience and interest in this domain. Clearly, some people who have been trained in linguistics, literary criticism, drama studies or anthropology will have an extremely well-developed ear for narrative. However, many other people who have not received this kind of formal training may nevertheless have cultivated narrative competence through personal reading, writing, participation in storytelling or watching television.

Medical education is of necessity highly technical, and there is a widely recognised danger that medical students may lose their ability to relate to patients as people. In some medical schools, students are given the opportunity to study and discuss selected literature as a means of gaining an appreciation of what their patients might be experiencing. This is an idea that could readily be applied in psychotherapy training, as a means of facilitating awareness of story-lines and genres. Knights (1995) offers an excellent introduction to this field.

Miller Mair (1989b, 1990b) has called for the reconstruction of psychology as a 'discipline of discourse', which would involve, among much else, a return to the 'ancient discipline' of rhetoric, which he defines as the study of:

> . . . the ways in which we speak, and especially . . . the crucial importance of imaginative, inventive speech by means of which new 'places' for thinking are created, like clearings in the forest which then allow for further cultivation and habitation. (Mair, 1990b: 8)

In a real sense, Mair is referring to the same set of issues discussed by Omer (1987, 1993b) in the context of therapeutic 'impact': how can the therapist best contribute to the construction of a healing psychological conversation? Like Mair, both Glaser (1980) and Frank (1987) advocate further exploration of the relevance for psychotherapy of theories of rhetoric.

It can be seen that the adoption of a narrative perspective on therapy begins to open up an array of possibilities for training. Perhaps the most significant of these pathways concerns the invitation to therapists to reflect on the stories that they themselves inhabit, and to share what they discover with colleagues and even with clients. There is nothing more certain than that such self-exploration leads to an appreciation of the local and culturally co-constructed nature of the stories we live and work by. As a result, the adherence, by therapists and their trainers, to supposedly scientifically based universally valid metanarratives (that is, theories of therapy), can be seen to be little more than the imposition in the therapy sphere of one of the central values of modernity.

Research and the construction of knowledge

A narrative perspective also leads in the direction of a different agenda for research into counselling and psychotherapy. Most, or perhaps all, of the existing studies of the role of narrative in therapy have been cited in earlier chapters, and it should be apparent that there are many gaps in current knowledge. It may be more accurate to say that there is more gap than there is knowledge. The comprehensive and authoritative review of research in psychotherapy edited by Bergin and Garfield (1994) contains *no* references to narrative or story in its index. On the whole, research that has considered narrative process in therapy has included it as a by-product of inquiry into other aspects of therapy. For example, Luborsky's studies of client narratives have been part of a broader programme of research into the psychoanalytic concepts of transference and interpretation. Rennie's work on storytelling has been embedded in a larger study of the client's experience of the therapy hour. It is probably only in the studies carried out by Angus, Russell, McAdams, and within my own group, that narrative has been the main focus of the research.

The role of narrative in therapy and the process of narrative-informed therapy are examples of areas in which research can make a significant impact on practice, if for no other reason than that there is so much to be learned. Among the many questions that arise are:

- Are there distinctively different processes of story co-construction in different therapeutic orientations?
- What are the patterns or processes of story repair or reconstruction that occur in 'successful' therapy?
- What is happening with the story when the therapy is 'stuck' or at an impasse?
- What is the relationship between 'problem' stories told in the therapy room, and those told in other settings, for example in conversations with friends?
- To what extent is 'improvement' in therapy clients expressed in the ways that they tell their stories, or in the type of stories they tell? Can stories be used as outcome measures?
- How effective is the introduction of narrative techniques in therapy, assessed in terms of scores on depression or anxiety scales?
- Do therapists trained in narrative approaches become more effective?
- What are the differences in therapeutic storytelling associated with membership of different cultural and ethnic groups?

Research into these (and other) questions will need to draw on concepts and methods not only from psychology but also from disciplines such as philosophy, linguistics, social anthropology, literary criticism and cultural studies. It is in these disciplines that therapy researchers will find an immense resource in terms of understanding of narrative. It is inevitable, too, that studies of narrative in therapy will demand the use of interpretive, hermeneutic methods that respect the integrity of the story as a unit of meaning in a context (Riessman, 1993).

A narrative perspective leads in the direction of a different approach to research into counselling and psychotherapy. Most contemporary research into therapy employs a model of inquiry taken from mainstream psychology, placing heavy emphasis on quantification and 'objective' measurement, operational definition of 'variables', and the use of experimental research designs implemented by detached observers. If the 'scientific' knowledge base of therapy can be defined in terms of what is published in journals such as *Psychotherapy Research*, *Journal of Consulting and Clinical Psychology*, *Journal of Counseling Psychology*, or reported in the proceedings of the *Society for Psychotherapy Research*, it is obvious that the field is almost wholly committed to, or in the grip of, what J.S. Bruner (1986) would consider as a 'paradigmatic' way of knowing. Only very recently has 'qualitative', interpretive research achieved sufficient legitimacy to be acceptable (see McLeod, 1996), but even here the type of qualitative work that is done is such that the narrative accounts of research informants are usually converted through data-reduction procedures into abstracted, schematic, paradigmatic knowledge (see Polkinghorne, 1988; Rennie and Toukmanian, 1992).

The act of researching looks different from a constructionist perspective. Rennie (1994b) has drawn attention to the relevance for psychotherapy research of a 'human science' tradition that stretches back to Dilthey, and which takes as its goal the elucidation of meaning. Gergen (1985) characterises constructionist research as destabilising and questioning the assumptions underpinning social definitions and performances. In a similar vein, Rorty (1980) has argued that one of the legitimate goals of systematic inquiry can be to sustain conversation and debate, rather than to attempt to function as a 'mirror to nature', as a source of foundational, universal truth. It is clear that in 'research' conceived in these terms, the 'researcher' can no longer be regarded as a neutral or even invisible presence. Indeed, the intentions and experiences of the inquirer, the quality of his or her engagement in the task of constructing knowledge, become central to the process of the investigation. The research act cannot but participate in the reflexivity and irony that are so constitutive of late/postmodern life (Giddens, 1991).

To date, there has been very little research into counselling and psychotherapy that is explicitly constructionist. The work of Cushman (1995), Davis (1986), Ehrenhaus (1993), Gergen (1990), Greenberg (1994a), Lewis et al. (1992), Lindsay-Hartz et al. (1995) and McLeod and Balamoutsou (1996) provides some examples of the kind of study that can be carried out from within this philosophical perspective. There exist few studies within the psychotherapy literature that specifically examine narrative processes, but there is a growing literature on narrative analyses of social and psychological topics that has been brought together in recent years in the *Journal of Narrative and Life History*, and in the *Narrative Study of Lives* series edited by Lieblich and Josselson (Josselson and Lieblich, 1993, 1995; Lieblich and Josselson, 1994). In addition, there is a substantial literature concerned with narrative analysis of experience and discourse around health and illness, much of it influenced by the seminal work of Kleinman (a psychiatrist) and Mishler (a sociologist) (see, for example, Hyden, 1995; Kleinman, 1988; Mishler, 1986; Monks, 1995; Stacey, 1996). There is, therefore, no shortage of research models and approaches that narratively inclined psychotherapy researchers might follow.

One of the issues that requires further consideration from those researching narrative in psychotherapy is the question of the relationship between oral and literary modes of expression. The culture that we live in is so print-dominated that there is an inevitable tendency to regard the stories that people tell in therapy as being similar to *written* stories such as novels. This approach to making sense of therapy stories is in danger of seriously missing the point. Therapy is a form of conversation, and the therapeutic relationship can be seen as creating the equivalent of an oral microculture between therapist and client (or between the members of a therapy group). Ong (1982) has identified many of the ways in which written and oral forms of communication can have different psychological effects. It is important, in research, to find methods for preserving the spoken, co-constructed, conversational nature of the stories told by clients and therapists. One technique that can achieve this goal is to represent the text of a therapy session in stanza form (Gee, 1986, 1991; Richardson, 1992). Poetry is a form of writing that has grown directly from oral performance, and the structure and rhythm of the *stanza* form goes at least some way toward capturing the lived experience of hearing a story. Below, in stanza form, is a story told by a therapy client, Carl, at the beginning of a session. This story has already been used in Chapter 2 (see page 37), displayed in standard prose text. The stanza version is more sensitive to the feeling being conveyed by the storyteller, and to the different voices existing within his experiential world.

'I Feel She Forces Me'

Two weeks ago
One of my friends called me from Holland

> I am going back to Holland again
> In the middle of September
> And we decided
> To rent this flat together
> And share this flat together.

When I was in Holland
I was talking to her
And mentioning to her
'Where can I find some work?'
'I don't know where I can find work.'

> I'm not quite sure where I can find work
> And what I can do.

Then she mentioned
She knows a person
Who was a teacher in a school.

I am a teacher.
Well, I was a teacher.

I can ring this person
And I can ask her
If I could have
Some hours of teaching.

And I said
I can do that

Then I came back here
And a couple of weeks ago
She called me and asked me
'Did you ring this person?'
And I said 'no'

And I have this feeling

        Why can't she not let it happen in my way?
        To let it happen for myself?
        Why does she force me to do that.

I couldn't say to her: 'I really appreciate your concern
    but frankly I don't think I will do that'

Because I have this fear
That she might reject me.

So I didn't tell her that.

I feel she forces me.

Different modes of practice

The social constructionist movement has been built on a willingness to examine and question the assumptions and the processes of social construction
that underpin its own practice. The writings of Kovel (1981), Cushman
(1995), Gergen (1990), Greenberg (1994a), Lynch (1997), Parker et al. (1995)
and Sass (1987, 1990) represent examples of this 'deconstructionist' impulse
applied to the field of psychotherapy and 'mental health'. In some of this
work, there is almost a sense that, when viewed from a social constructionist
perspective, psychotherapy as a discipline is in danger of collapsing under the
weight of its contradictions. Gergen observes that:

> If there is no 'illness' in nature, then what counts as 'cure'? Yet, questioning at this
> level sends ripples of anguish across the profession. For if the concept of cure is sac-
> rificed, so is the function of therapy placed in question. If there are no problems, in
> reality, and no solutions, then how is help to be justified? Why should people seek
> therapeutic help, why should one enter the profession, and why should people be
> charged for the services? (1996: 214)

The central issue concerns the cultural positioning of therapy. As discussed
in Chapter 1, counselling and psychotherapy are woven into the fabric of
twentieth-century society through the espousal of some of the key themes of

modern life: the replacement of faith by science, the power of the medical profession, engagement with the demands of the marketplace, intellectual colonialism, an individualist conception of the person, and the denial of morality. Social constructionism brings all of these positions into critical focus, and makes it difficult to sustain a therapy culturally configured along such lines.

It is not surprising, then, that therapists using narrative concepts and methods have started to develop new forms of practice that depart from the well-established traditions of the ongoing weekly fifty-minute individual appointment. One of the most straightfoward ways of deconstructing this tradition is to begin to ask how many sessions there need to be, or how long a session should last. Rosenbaum (1994), for example, reports on the effectiveness of single-session therapy in a psychiatric out-patient clinic, with the session running for up to two hours. He found that 58 per cent of clients felt that one session was sufficient, with 88 per cent rating their presenting problem as much improved or improved when followed up three months later. Other therapists (such as Epston et al., 1992; Holland, 1979; Zhu and Pierce, 1995) negotiate the gap between sessions to reflect the needs of the client, rather than assuming that weekly sessions will be appropriate for every client. Not all of these therapists operate within an explicit narrative constructionist framework, but their practice illustrates the way that, in a postmodern era, it is increasingly accepted that the client is an informed consumer who will choose the type and duration of therapy that he or she perceives as being suitable for them, rather than the 'treatment' that is deemed appropriate by professional experts. Indeed, the White and Epston school of narrative therapy invites clients to become 'consultants', who return at the end of therapy to advise the therapeutic team on how best to help people achieve change.

As discussed in Chapters 4 and 5, the practice of narrative therapy can include different forms of writing tasks. Birren and Birren (1996) describe the use of 'guided autobiography' groups as a mode of promoting personal insight that not only fully exploits the therapeutic impact of writing, but which also manages to avoid the sometimes negative implications of being labelled 'therapy'. A growing number of therapists have sought to counteract the universalist and colonialist tendencies of Western approaches to therapy by deliberately working alongside healers and shamans from other cultures, or incorporating their ideas and techniques in their practice (for an introduction to some of these developments, see Gersie, 1991; Lee and Armstrong, 1995; Walter, 1996). Rappaport and Simkins (1991) discuss the use of life-enhancing narratives at the level of small, supportive communities.

Perhaps one of the most exciting aspects of narrative therapy is the huge creative potential that it opens up. When therapy stops being a science-based 'treatment' and becomes a way of assisting people to examine the authority of the stories through which they live, many possibilities for new forms of therapeutic practice start to emerge. There is a huge cultural resource, which counselling and psychotherapy have scarcely explored, of discourses, rituals and practices that have evolved to define and sustain the 'good life'.

Up to this point, this chapter has considered some of the more practical implications of a narrative therapy, in terms of therapist training, modes of organising therapy, and the research agenda. We now turn to some of the difficult conceptual issues that are implied by the reinvention of therapy.

The 'truth' of survivor stories

Counselling and psychotherapy can often involve a lengthy and arduous examination and exploration of every aspect of a life. From a narrative point of view, one of the key tasks in therapy is to achieve a sufficient sense of coherence across and through the different stories that can be told about that life. Therapy may entail a narrativisation of areas of life experience that perhaps have never been articulated before. The therapist may be the first to hear certain very painful or shameful stories. None of this is surprising or even particularly noteworthy – listening sensitively to a client's stories is a core therapeutic skill.

What has become highly controversial in recent years is the question of the *truth value* of client stories. This debate has focused on two related clinical entities: *recovered memories* of sexual abuse in childhood, and *multiple personality disorder*. The factor linking these two phenomena is the mechanism of *repression*: people who have been abused in childhood react to the overwhelming fear and terror associated with these events by splitting off their memories of what happened, with the resulting danger that these 'dissociated' parts of the self may develop into discrete sub-personalities or 'sub-selves'. The particularly contentious part of this theory concerns the recovery by clients during therapy of previously forgotten or repressed incidents of abuse in childhood, and then the decision of some of these clients to denounce the parent–perpetrator and in some cases even to seek redress through the courts. Within the psychological and therapeutic professions, the many-sided debate over what is sometimes called 'false memory syndrome' elicits very strong feelings. There has also been a substantial amount of media, legal and general public interest in the issue. The large and complex literature arising from this debate has been reviewed by Ganaway (1989) and Enns et al. (1995), among others.

At the heart of the argument over whether memories of distant events can indeed be buried for many years and then re-surface, or whether these supposed memories are in fact 'planted' by over-zealous therapists, is the problem of the truth value of stories. Almost every time anyone tells a story, whether in therapy or elsewhere, they are giving an account of an event in the past. Although it is possible to tell present-tense and future-tense stories, these are rare: most stories draw on memories of some prior occasion. The story is a vehicle for communicating a memory.

The debate over false memories represents a significant challenge for any approach to therapy that aims to give special attention to the stories told by clients. A sceptic might argue, reasonably enough, that it is foolish to practise therapy in a way that may encourage a client to become enmeshed in potentially false and groundless 'fantasies' about the events of his or her life. Much better, the sceptic might add, to stay with clinical methods that allow the therapist a vantage point from which to make judgements about the veridicality of the client's narrative. For example, a psychoanalytic approach to therapy permits the interpretation of the story in terms of unconscious phantasy and the operation of mechanisms of psychological defence. A behavioural or neo-behavioural approach demands evidence of observable behaviour – the story is used merely as a guide in the search to identify behavioural routines. The false memory issue provides a sharp reminder of the potential danger of narrative-focused therapy: what if the narrative is wrong, a malicious fiction, a pack of lies?

The distinction made by Spence (1982a), concerning the difference between narrative and historical truth, does nothing to reassure the sceptic. Indeed, Spence's writings have been considered by some to be partially responsible for the seeming explosion of false memories. It has been argued that therapists interested only in narrative truth can completely lose sight of the 'reality' basis of what the client is reporting, and fail to check whether the events being recounted 'actually' took place.

It seems to me that the current fascination with 'false memories', and the level of emotion raised by the topic, can only mean that the subject has somehow come to act as a catalyst or lightning rod for a number of the tensions that exist within contemporary psychotherapy: the status of experimental research vs. clinical evidence; therapy as emancipatory vs. therapy as a means of social control; self-help vs. professionalised help; the validity of directive vs. non-directive therapeutic techniques; individualised vs. collectivist images of the person; the politics of gender. I make no claim to be able to sort out this tangle of issues. However, I would like to make some limited and somewhat cautious observations from a narrative social constructionist point of view.

First, the lengthy discussion of the nature of storytelling offered in Chapter 2 gave an outline of the multiple functions of the story in human discourse. In no sense can a story be seen as merely an 'objective' report of 'what happened'. Even the simplest story conveys information about subjective intentions and motives, feeling states, social and cultural context, and moral evaluations. Furthermore, there is an inevitable ambiguity in the telling of any story. A story comprises one possible structuring of a set of events. Retellings of the story at different times and in different settings can produce versions of the tale that vary in significant ways. A therapist drawing upon narrative theory will be aware of these factors, and as a result will be careful about attributing factual status to *any* story told in therapy.

A second important aspect of narrative therapy that is relevant to this issue is the presumption that the therapy narrative is *co-constructed*. Whatever stories arise in the therapy hour are the product of client and therapist working together. The therapist's 'metanarrative' (Omer and Strenger, 1992) or macronarrative of the 'good life' inform and mould the therapist's contribution to the story performance that constitutes a therapy hour. There is no sense at all in believing that the client is sole author of the stories he or she tells in therapy. Just as the stories that are brought into therapy are saturated in the dominant or subjugating narratives of the culture, so too are the stories that appear to originate in sessions. The tale the client tells is the one he or she chooses to tell his or her therapist, given what the therapist is willing or able to hear. The situation of the therapy session is so powerful that any story told there is virtually always a 'therapy story'.

A third key factor in understanding the truth value of stories told in therapy lies in the realisation that stories look forward as well as backward. A story is a speech *act*, not merely a record or chronicle of past events. As Gergen puts it, a story is not just a lens through which reality is perceived, nor is it merely a guide to action. Instead, it represents a 'situated action, a performance' (1996: 217). A story always has an effect on the teller or the listener, and in this way shapes the future. Implicit in this idea is the notion that the storyteller is an active agent, capable of intending certain outcomes through the narration of a story. For example, a client seeking approval from his or her therapist will tell stories that match what he or she knows of the therapist's preferences. A psychoanalytic patient tells dream-world stories. In person-centred counselling the client tells stories of self. In solution-focused therapy the client tells stories of successful achievements. The point here is that to understand the meaning of a story told in therapy, it is necessary to take into account the role of the story in actively constructing a world in the here-and-now and in the future.

A final consideration in making sense of therapy stories is that therapy is embedded in a cultural context, and that the stories that are told there are drawn from a stock of potential plot-lines and genres that are available within that culture. In recent years there has been an explosion in the media coverage given to therapeutic stories. The culture of modernity has from the start been characterised by a widespread publication and dissemination of self-help and self-improvement manuals. Early self-help best-sellers included the writings of Mary Baker Eddy, Dale Carnegie and Norman Vincent Peale (see Mahoney, 1995). More recently, detailed accounts of trauma, abuse, relationship difficulties and other psychological troubles are portrayed in popular magazines, television programmes and 'recovery' books (Greenberg, 1994a) that are consumed by millions of people. By telling a personal problem story in a particular way, perhaps influenced by what they have come across in the media, an individual is not just making a personal statement but is at the same time identifying himself or herself as part of a broader cultural process or movement.

These four elements of a narrative approach to therapy – the ambiguity of stories, co-construction of the therapy narrative, the story as a purposeful act, and the existence of a cultural stock of stories – provide the possibility of arriving at some fresh understandings of the question of 'false' memories and multiple personality. The writings of Keen (1995), Sarbin (1995a, 1995b) and Spence (1994) set out the basic principles of a narrative perpective on the issues under discussion. Essentially, this perpective involves looking at the way that stories told in therapy are socially contructed. As Sarbin (1995a) argues, until recently therapists could operate on the basis that what they were attempting to do was to help the client 'reconstruct a failing self-narrative', without worrying too much about the historical truth of the new story that emerged. Over the last decade, however, a new social phenomenon, that of victims seeking legal redress from perpetrators of crimes against them, has led to a situation where therapists are increasingly caught between the contradictory demands of narrative truth and of historical truth. Sarbin (1995b) points out that another aspect of the social construction of this debate is associated with the fact that the supporters of, on the one hand, multiple personality disorder theory, and on the other hand 'false memory syndrome', have formed distinct sub-cultures to pursue their own particular moral agendas. Spence (1994) focuses on the ambiguity inherent in narrative accounts, and suggests that therapists and other professionals working with survivors of abuse should be more willing to entertain the possibility that there are some instances where abuse stories are operating as metaphors for something else. Spence suggests that clients struggling to recover memories of awful events from long ago will typically communicate in a 'child's voice', marked by uncertainty, confusion, doubting, shifting point of view, and general lack of coherence. By contrast, a 'voice-over' story told by an 'omniscient narrator' is, for Spence, an indicator that the story is a 'metaphor for something else', a way of conveying unhappiness over a current problem or relationship. And it is just this sensitive ear for differences in story construction and performance that a narrative-informed therapist needs to develop.

Behind the specific arguments put forward by Sarbin and Spence, which identify particular cultural processes associated with the 'false memory' debate, there lies a much broader set of cultural issues associated with the social construction of cruelty, humiliation, shame and anger. The contours of this set of issues are mapped out very effectively by Alcoff and Gray (1991). These writers point out that, although the principle of 'breaking the silence' is an accepted component of many therapeutic and self-help approaches to helping survivors of abuse, the value of 'speaking out' depends on the circumstances in which personal disclosure takes place. Drawing on the work of Foucault, they argue that, ever since the invention of the confessional, and continuing through the evolution of psychotherapy, there has existed a set of cultural practices by which 'the speaker discloses her innermost experiences to an expert mediator who then reinterprets these experiences back to her using the dominant discourse's codes of "normality"' (1991: 260). The result of this process is that the interior life of the speaker is 'made to conform to prevailing dogmas'. Alcoff and Gray follow this theme through a set of examples of women college students who had been victims of 'date rape' and had subsequently been invited to appear on television programmes. On the face of it, this invitation might be seen to represent an opportunity to 'speak out' on a grand scale, before an audience of millions. In fact, the format of the programme effectively reinterpreted the students' testimony in terms of prevailing dogmas: the entire show was characterised by an objectification of survivors, a reaction to survivors' accounts that mixed pity and scepticism, and a 'deflection away from men's responsibility for rape' (p. 276). Alcoff and Gray go on to document the efforts of women students in their college to gain a hearing for their anger over rape in ways that did not lead to objectification and further experiences of humiliation. These students invented a technique of 'anonymous accusation', and began listing the names of rapists on the walls of women's bathrooms. The college administrators attempted to contain this emancipatory discourse by instructing cleaners to erase the lists as soon as they appeared, writing to the men listed, offering to help them file complaints (1991: 286–7).

The observations offered by Alcoff and Gray are consistent with the experience of many people who have been humiliated and cruelly treated in our society: they are not believed. The dominant narrative allows little space for such unpleasant stories. It is instructive to place Alcoff and Gray's work alongside recent publications by Mulhern (1994) and Spanos et al. (1994). These writers review and discuss the existence of reports by psychiatric patients and therapy clients of organised occult and extraterrestrial abuse. Mulhern opens her paper with the following statement:

> . . . during the past decade in North America, a growing number of mental health professionals have reported that between 25% and 50% of their patients in treatment for multiple personality disorder (MPD) have recovered early childhood traumatic memories of ritual torture, incestuous rape, sexual debauchery, sacrificial murder, infanticide, and cannibalism perpetrated by members of clandestine satanic cults. (1994: 265)

To this list of terrors, Spanos et al. add a catalogue of reports of UFO abductions and past-life identities. Both Mulhern and Spanos et al. come to the conclusion that there is no corroborative factual evidence to support these claims, which constitute 'fantasy constructions' (Spanos et al.) or a 'social delusion' (Mulhern).

Mulhern and Spanos et al. make a convincing case for the view that satanic abuse and being taken away in the night in silver spaceships do not actually take place in the way in which clients and patients report these events. But they do not address the question of quite *why* a person might elect to construct such a story. From the point of view of Alcoff and Gray, on the other hand, it is possible to imagine that there are some people who may be driven to create 'fantastic' stories simply in order to be heard. The history of the psychological therapies, from the time of Freud's abandonment of the 'seduction theory' (Masson, 1988) until very recently supplies little evidence that a woman with a story of intrusive assault on the part of an apparently loving father or family friend would be believed, or even that such a person would be allowed to tell her story. And, in fact, there is reason to believe that it may be just as hard, or harder, for sexually exploited men to receive a hearing (Etherington, 1995).

This discussion is in part concerned with the *rhetorical* dimension of narrative: how does a story need to be told to be plausible, to have an impact? As Mair has argued, the 'science' of psychology and psychotherapy has long neglected the question of rhetoric. I would like to examine the rhetoric of therapeutic narration of trauma by shifting from the domain of sexual abuse to that of the Holocaust. Although the Holocaust represents a uniquely extreme and awful set of events, I believe that it can be regarded as one of the defining episodes in modernity, and that the struggle of survivors of Nazi genocide to tell their story reveals a great deal about the essential dynamics of survivor discourse.

Danieli, in reviewing the post-war evasion of the experiences of Holocaust survivors, describes a long-term *conspiracy of silence* between survivors and society: 'after liberation, as during the war, the survivors were victims of a pervasive societal reaction comprised of indifference, avoidance, repression, and denial of their experiences' (1988a: 220). Danieli studied the reactions of psychotherapists to Holocaust survivor clients. Therapists often reported feeling overwhelmed and disbelieving when confronted by their clients' stories: 'many used distancing . . . they listened to the stories as if they were "science fiction stories" or "as if it happened 5,000 years ago"' (1988a: 224). Some psychotherapists defended themselves through use of theoretical jargon: one therapist 'nam[ed] the following Holocaust-derived dream imagery reported by a survivor's offspring as "pregenital sadism". The dream contained pits full of hundreds of corpses . . . mutilated bodies against barbed wire . . . a baby blown to pieces while thrown up in the air . . . a skeleton crying for food' (1988a: 225).

Berating the therapists behind these quotes as insensitive or uncaring does little to advance our understanding of the dynamics of survivor discourse. The therapist formulating a diagnosis of 'pregenital sadism' in response to images of Auschwitz has been placed in that position, has been given the power to think these thoughts, by a long process of social construction. It is characteristic of modern culture to individualise tragedy, to set up situations where the individual survivor contains the meaning of such events within his or her personal story, and where the burden of hearing such stories is given to one person sitting in an office. It is characteristic of modern culture to inscribe the 'interior life' of the person into the 'prevailing dogmas' of scientific psychological theory (Alcoff and Gray, 1991). And there is little space in the dominant social narrative of progress, development and improvement for stories of loss.

A 'conspiracy of silence' implies two sides – one not hearing, one not saying. The not saying can perhaps be understood as arising from the difficulty in putting some experiences into words. Some experiences, for some people, are 'indescribable', with the result that silence is better than misrepresentation or the risk of being misunderstood. Abramovitch (1986) offers an account of an interview with a survivor of Mengele's medical experiments at Auschwitz. This man had kept his silence for 40 years, even with his family. He chose to be interviewed in his parked car, doors closed and windows rolled up. Abramovitch writes that 'over and over again he seemed to come up against the limits of language, the inadequacy of words to describe what he had gone through, saying, "There are no words to describe my suffering"' (1986: 204).

Survivors who were children at the time of the Holocaust may possess only fragments of stories about their parents and extended families. Here, the silence arises from the absence of a narrative, and the absence of anyone with whom to share the story. Hogman (1985) and Mazor et al. (1990) interviewed a number of child survivors, many of whom had lost their parents. Although there were different patterns of coping, it was clear that at the point when they were interviewed, the majority of these people were actively engaged in reconstructing a narrative of their early life, for example through historical research, collecting photographs and other relics, and talking with people who had information about their parents or their early lives. A few used writing – the creation of fiction and poetry – as a means of constructing stories to live in. It was significant that many of them had become more involved in this process of personal reconstruction as time went on – immediately after the war their energies had been devoted to immigration, developing a career, getting married. However, in later life they appeared to need more and more to retrieve and recover memories and stories of childhood.

One of the distinctive aspects of Holocaust survivor discourse has been the collection of testimony, for the purpose of establishing a historical archive and record for future generations. Starting with the work of the Yad Vashem Holocaust memorial and archive centre in Jerusalem, there are now testimony projects active in many countries. Survivors participating in testimony-giving are invited to tell the story of their Holocaust experiences in chronological order, and although an archivist is present and may ask questions to clarify points, he or she does not interpret the story or offer any other type of therapeutic response. Paradoxically, most testimony-givers find the experience 'therapeutic', and report that there is great meaning in being able to leave this legacy for their children (Krell, 1985a).

Some of the main themes emerging from research studies into the experiences of Holocaust survivors telling their stories can be summarised:

1   The task of putting the 'indescribable' into words represents a huge challenge to the human spirit, calling on all of the creative capacities of the person.
2   There are powerful cultural forces acting to close down the possibility of telling such stories.
3   For survivors, there are times when it is necessary to get on with life, rather than remember.
4   Many survivors find meaning in using the telling of their story to contribute to the social good; there exists a variety of ways in which 'testimony' can be carried out, some of which are culturally and politically oriented.

Ehrenhaus (1993) identifies similar themes in his study of survivors/veterans of the Vietnam War.

If reality is *socially* constructed, then what is believable, or what can be talked about, depends on the maintenance of a community, or what

MacIntyre would call a 'tradition' that can sustain the telling of an ongoing narrative. People who have experienced cruel and humiliating acts against them find that there is little place for their account within the dominant narrative of modern society, and they seek out opportunities to align their personal story with that of a community. The role of counsellors and psychotherapists in this process can be viewed in either of two ways. A therapist can work with a client or patient to assist him or her in finding the discourse 'out there' with which the client feels most comfortably aligned. Alternatively, the therapist can act as a recruiting agent for one particular cultural narrative. Many therapists have adopted the latter approach. For example, in the field of therapy with survivors of child sexual abuse, some, as documented by Masson (1988), have reflected the patriarchal consensus line that such things do not happen or are not important. More recently, therapists adhering to Bass and Davis (1988) have actively promoted a view that a great deal of psychological distress is attributable to hidden sexual abuse. It is clear that therapists operating from either of these 'recruiting agent' positions are in danger of the kind of involvement with the justice system that brings meaningful therapy to an end, because the particular moral stances they represent are being fought out in bigger social arenas, including the courts. I think that what a social constructionist perspective has to offer here is a framework for exploring and making sense of the 'truth' of survivor stories, or of any other client narratives, in their wider social, historical and cultural context, and not just in terms of the psychology of memory.

The stories told by survivors are moral tales, ways of communicating what is right and wrong. However, *any* therapy that takes stories seriously will necessarily open up a space for moral discourse. Stories are structured around an 'evaluation' of what has happened. A story is not merely a chronicle of events. A story is an account of events set against a landscape of moral values. Narrative therapy involves the rediscovery of the 'moral'.

Therapy, place and the meaning of narrative unity

Keith Basso is a social anthropologist who has spent many years studying the Western Apache, a Native American community in east-central Arizona (Basso, 1984). One of his particular interests has been to explore the relationships between this people, their stories and their landscape. Basso cites a statement from one of his research informants:

> I think of that mountain called 'white rocks lie above in a compact cluster' as if it were my maternal grandmother. I recall stories of how it once was at that mountain. The stories told to me were like arrows. Elsewhere, hearing that mountain's name, I see it. Its name is like a picture. Stories go to work on you like arrows. Stories make you live right. Stories make you replace yourself. (Mr Benson Lewis, aged 64, 1979) (1984: 21)

This statement sums up much about the meaning of place for Western Apache people, specifically the linkage between places, stories and 'living right'.

Within Western Apache culture, place-names usually take the form of complete sentences, for instance 'water flows downward on top of a series of flat rocks', or 'muddy water lies in a concave depression'. These place-names are used in ordinary everyday discourse to refer to actual locations. However, they also play an important part in what Basso calls 'historical tales'. These are accounts of events that took place 'long ago', and are used to communicate moral messages about appropriate conduct for members of the group. The linguistic structure of a 'historical tale' requires that, in contrast to other forms of Apache storytelling, it must always start and finish with a place name. By this means there is a strong connection between features of the land, and the set of moral rules that guide behaviour in the community.

An example of a Western Apache historical tale is this:

It happened at 'men stand above here and there'.

Long ago, a man killed a cow off the reservation. The cow belonged to a Whiteman. The man was arrested by a policeman living at Cibecue at 'men stand above here and there'. The policeman was an Apache. The policeman took the man to the head Army officer at Fort Apache. There, at Fort Apache, the head Army officer questioned him. 'What do you want?' he said. The policeman said, 'I need cartridges and food.' The policeman said nothing about the man who had killed the Whiteman's cow. That night some people spoke to the policeman. 'It is best to report on him,' they said to him. The next day the policeman returned to the head Army officer. 'Now what do you want?' he said. The policeman said, 'Yesterday I was going to say Hello and Good-bye but I forgot to do it.' Again he said nothing about the man he arrested. Someone was working with words on his mind. The policeman returned with the man to Cibecue. He released him at 'men stand above here and there'.

It happened at 'men stand above here and there.' (Basso, 1984: 38)

This story describes what happens to an Apache who behaves too much like a white man. To an Apache audience, it is perfectly acceptable that, at a time of oppression and famine, a white man's cow should have been killed for food. What is not acceptable is that another Apache should have arrested him and considered handing him over to authority. In the story, it is implied that witchcraft was used on the policeman: 'I was going to say Hello and Good-bye but I forgot.' Basso's informants summed up this story as 'a harsh indictment of persons who join with outsiders against members of their own community' (1984: 39).

The way that such a story may be employed by members of the Western Apache is demonstrated through an observation of an incident at a girls' puberty ceremony. The convention is that girls taking part in this ceremony should wear their hair loose. One girl, who had been attending a white school, turned up for the occasion wearing pink plastic hair curlers (at that time considered fashionable among her school peer group). Although there was considerable covert disapproval, no one spoke to her at the ceremony about her attire. However, at a family birthday party two weeks later, without any warning her grandmother narrated a version of the tale of the policeman who behaved too much like a white man. Basso reports:

Shortly after the story was finished, the young woman stood up, turned away wordlessly, and walked off in the direction of her home. Uncertain of what had happened, I asked her grandmother why she had departed. Had the young woman suddenly become ill? 'No,' her grandmother replied. 'I shot her with an arrow.' (1984: 40)

Basso concludes this example by recounting that some two years after the incident occurred, he found himself in the company of this young woman, and asked her what she remembered of these events. She confirmed that the telling of the policeman story had affected her deeply, and that every time she passed by or thought about 'men stand above here and there' she was reminded of what was for her an important learning experience.

There are at least two aspects of these Western Apache stories that have meaning for narrative therapy. First, they provide a clear example of the way in which telling a story is a social act. The Apache use a hunting metaphor to describe their use of historical tales. The effect of the story on its target is like 'being shot by an arrow'. The land 'is always stalking people'. The other striking aspect of Apache stories is that they operate in a cultural environment where everyone knows the same stories, has access to a shared narrative resource. But the stories are not 'just' in people's heads, they are somehow located in the landscape. The stories that carry this culture's moral sensitivity are bound up with the physical world in which members of the culture move and act. As Cheney (1989) puts it, the language of stories is 'contextualised', is tied to place.

The narrative significance of place can be further elaborated by considering the writings of the philosopher Alasdair MacIntyre, who is well known for his analysis of the inadequacy of much contemporary debate on moral issues. Specifically, he argues that it is not possible to identify abstract moral principles that can serve as a guide to right action and the 'good life'. Instead, it is necessary to understand that moral decisions take place in the context of what he calls a 'tradition'. This tradition comprises the body of knowledge accumulated by members of a social group, and it is communicated mainly through stories. MacIntyre does not mean to imply that a tradition is a static, unchanging set of moral tales. On the contrary, a live tradition needs to be viewed as a 'continuous argument': 'traditions, when vital, embody continuities of conflict' (1981: 222). He writes that:

> ... when an institution – a university, say, or a farm, or a hospital – is the bearer of a tradition of practice or practices, its common life will be partly, but in a centrally important way, constituted by a continuous argument as to what a university is and ought to be or what good farming is or what good medicine is. (1981: 222)

MacIntyre introduced the notion of 'narrative unity' as a means of making sense of the challenge faced by individuals in making their own life choices. He suggests that we are all engaged in a *quest* for narrative unity, we are attempting to create and maintain a coherence in the stories we tell about our lives. But, in envisaging this process as a quest, MacIntyre argues that, while we may have a sense that there is a 'good life' that can be discovered and lived, we have perhaps only the most general notion of what this might look like:

. . . the medieval conception of a quest is not at all that of a search for something already adequately characterised, as miners search for gold or geologists for oil. It is in the course of the quest and only through encountering and coping with the various particular harms, dangers, temptations and distractions which provide the quest with its episodes and incidents that the goal of the quest is finally to be understood. A quest is always an education both as to the character of that which is sought and in self-knowledge. (1981: 219)

But, for MacIntyre, the quest is always in relation to a tradition:

I can only answer the question 'What am I to do?' if I can answer the prior question 'Of what story or stories do I find myself a part?' We enter human society . . . with one or more imputed characters – roles into which we have been drafted – and we have to learn what they are in order to be able to understand how others respond to us and how our responses to them are apt to be construed. (1981: 216)

So, the task of constructing narrative unity is not achievable at a purely individual level: 'the narrative of any one life is part of an interlocking set of narratives'.

It is no accident that MacIntyre draws on the *medieval* conception of the quest, since in many ways his overall aim is to transcend modernist thinking by pointing out the continuing relevance of earlier, 'traditional' modes of thought. The notion of narrative unity put forward by MacIntyre can be usefully compared with the discussion of the same topic provided by Polkinghorne (1991). In this paper, Polkinghorne regards 'life-story' as essentially a more satisfactory reworking of the notion of 'self-concept'. A 'life-story' or 'self-narrative' is 'an alternative way to conceptualize the self', one which 'brings to light the temporal and developmental dimension of human existence'. Polkinghorne is here (although not in some of his more recent writing) reflecting many of the assumptions that characterise the work of mainstream, modernist therapists reviewed in Chapters 3 and 4. The goal of therapy is defined as constructing a 'personal' narrative that 'coheres the client's past and future'. The therapist 'is engaged in helping clients clear the decks of dysfunctional plots' (1991: 150). This is therapy very much rooted in an image of the person as an individual, autonomous self.

Lassiter (1987) describes the immense psychological distress brought about by the relocation by the United States government of more than 10,000 Navajo (Dineh) Native Americans under the authority of the 1974 Navajo–Hopi Land Settlement Act, a piece of legislation widely attributed to have been passed to meet the demands of the coal and uranium mining companies. What happened to these people can be seen as a microcosm of what has taken place for untold millions as a result of the advance of modern industrial society. Who is there left whose family has not experienced dislocation some time in the last three generations for economic reasons or because of war? However, in this instance the effects of separation from the land and its stories could be directly observed by mental health professionals, who reported abnormal rates of violence, crime, alcoholism, depression and suicide, and a consequent eightfold increase in utilisation of psychiatric services. The fate of the Dineh represents a very clear example of the link between social and political change on the one hand, and the possibility of achieving meaningful narrative unity at the level of individual lives on the other. Reflecting on this process, Lassiter concludes that:

> . . . the modern self views the external world as existing primarily to be manipulated and exploited for personal gain. For the Dineh, however, as for most premodern peoples, there cannot be a whole, healthy self apart from the larger ecological community – the Great Self. To disrupt the balance of any part of the community is to hurt one's self. For the Dineh, to take from the Earth without reciprocating, without first having become part of the life of the place, is to disrupt a sacred balance and ultimately to grow ill. (1987: 228)

It is my belief, too, that to engage meaningfully in the life issues facing us in these times, psychotherapy and counselling must seek ways of contributing to the re-establishment, somehow, of a 'sacred balance' (Reason, 1993). Can therapy be used as a means of discovering the stories that enable us to connect with each other and with the traditions that make us who we are?

References

Abramovitch, H. (1986) 'There are no words: two Greek-Jewish survivors of Auschwitz', *Psychoanalytic Psychology*, 3: 201–16.

Albee, G.W. (1977) 'The Protestant ethic, sex and psychotherapy', *American Psychologist*, 32: 150–61.

Alcoff, L. and Gray, L. (1991) 'Survivor discourse: transgression or recuperation?', *Signs: Journal of Women in Culture and Society*, 18: 260–90.

Andersen, T. (1992) 'Reflections on reflecting with families', in S. McNamee and K.J. Gergen (eds), *Therapy as Social Construction*. London: Sage. pp. 54–68.

Anderson, H. and Goolishian, H. (1992) 'The client is the expert: a not-knowing approach to therapy', in S. McNamee and K.J. Gergen (eds), *Therapy as Social Construction*. London: Sage. pp. 25–39.

Angus, L.E. (1992) 'Metaphor and communication interaction in psychotherapy: a multi-methodological approach', in S.G. Toukmanian and D.L. Rennie (eds), *Psychotherapy Process Research: Paradigmatic and Narrative Approaches*. London: Sage. pp. 187–210.

Angus, L. (1996a) 'Narrative and psychotherapy: a multiperspectival approach'. Paper delivered to the Annual Convention of the American Psychological Association, Toronto, August 1996.

Angus, L. (1996b) 'An intensive analysis of metaphor themes in psychotherapy', in J.S. Mio and A. Katz (eds), *Metaphor: Pragmatics and Applications*. New York: Erlbaum. pp. 73–84.

Angus, L. and Hardtke, K. (1994) 'Narrative processes in psychotherapy', *Canadian Psychology*, 35 (2): 190–203.

Angus, L. and Rennie, D. (1988) 'Therapist participation in metaphor generation: collaborative and noncollaborative styles', *Psychotherapy*, 25: 552–60.

Angus, L. and Rennie, D.L. (1989) 'Envisioning the representational world: the client's experience of metaphoric expression in psychotherapy', *Psychotherapy*, 26: 372–9.

Ariès, P. (1962) *Centuries of Childhood*. New York: Knopf.

Aveline, M.O. (1986) 'The use of written reports in brief group psychotherapy training', *International Journal of Group Psychotherapy*, 36: 477–82.

Averill, J.R. (1991) 'Emotions as episodic dispositions, cognitive schemas, and transitory social roles: steps toward an integrated theory of emotion', in A.J. Stewart, J.M. Healy, jr. and D. Ozer (eds), *Approaches to Understanding Lives. Perspectives in Personality Vol. 3, Part A*. London: Jessica Kinsley. pp. 139–67.

Bagarozzi, D.A. and Anderson, S.A. (1989) *Personal, Marital and Family Myths: Theoretical Formulations and Clinical Strategies*. New York: Norton.

Bakan, D. (1966) *The Duality of Human Existence: Isolation and Communion in Western Man*. Boston, MA: Beacon Press.

Bakan, D. (1976) 'Politics and American psychology', in K. Riegel (ed.), *Psychology: Theoretical–Historical Perspectives*. New York: Springer. pp. 87–99.

Baker, S.B., Daniels, T.G. and Greeley, A.T. (1990) 'Systematic training of graduate-level counselors: narrative and meta-analytic reviews of three programmes', *Counseling Psychologist*, 18: 355–421.

Bamberg, M. (1991) 'Narrative activity as perspective taking: the role of emotionals, negations, and voice in the construction of the story realm', *Journal of Cognitive Psychotherapy*, 5 (4): 275–90.

Barrett-Lennard, G. (1996) 'Carl Rogers' helping system: journey and substance.' Unpublished manuscript.

Bass, E. and Davis, L. (1988) *The Courage to Heal: A Guide for Women Survivors of Child Sexual Abuse*. New York: Harper and Row.

Basso, K.H. (1984) '"Stalking with stories": names, places, and moral narratives among the Western Apache', in E.M. Bruner (ed.), *Text, Play and Story: The Construction and Reconstruction of Self and Society*. Washington, DC: American Ethnological Society. pp. 19–55.

Baumeister, R.F. (1987) 'How the self became a problem: a psychological review of historical research', *Journal of Personality and Social Psychology*, 52 (1): 163–76.

Baumeister, R.F. (1994) 'The crystallization of discontent in the process of major life change', in T.F. Heatherton and J.L. Weinberger (eds), *Can Personality Change?*. Washington, DC: American Psychological Association. pp. 281–97.

Baumeister, R.F., Stillwell, A.M. and Heatherton, T.F. (1995) 'Interpersonal aspects of guilt: evidence from narrative studies', in J.P. Tangnay and K.W. Fischer (eds), *Self-Conscious Emotions: the Psychology of Shame, Guilt, Embarrassment and Pride*. New York: Guilford Press. pp. 255–73.

Benjamin, W. (1969) *Illuminations*. New York: Schocken.

Berger, P. (1983) 'On the obsolescence of the concept of honour', in S. Hauerwas and A. MacIntyre (eds), *Revisions: Changing Perspectives in Moral Philosophy*. Notre Dame, IN: University of Notre Dame Press. pp. 172–81.

Berger, P., Berger, B. and Kellner, H. (1974) *The Homeless Mind*. Harmondsworth: Penguin.

Bergin, A.E. and Garfield, S.L. (1994) (eds), *Handbook of Psychotherapy and Behavior Change*, 4th edn. New York: Wiley.

Bergner, R.M. (1987) 'Undoing degradation', *Psychotherapy*, 24: 25–30.

Bergner, R.M. and Staggs, J. (1987) 'The positive therapeutic relationship as accreditation', *Psychotherapy*, 24: 315–20.

Berne, E. (1975) *What Do You Say After You Say Hello? The Psychology of Human Destiny*. London: Corgi.

Bernstein, B. (1972) 'Social class, language and socialization', in P.P. Giglioli (ed.), *Language and Social Context: Selected Readings*. Harmondsworth: Penguin. pp. 157–78.

Bettelheim, B. (1976) *The Uses of Enchantment: the Meaning and Importance of Fairy Tales*. Harmondsworth: Penguin.

Birren, J.E. and Birren, B.A. (1996) 'Autobiography: exploring the self and encouraging development', in J.E. Birren, G.M. Kenyon, J.-K. Ruth, J.J.F. Schroots and T. Svensson (eds), *Aging and Biography: Explorations in Adult Development*. New York: Springer. pp. 283–99.

Birren, J.E., Kenyon, G.M., Ruth, J.-K., Schroots, J.J.F. and Svensson, T. (eds) (1996) *Aging and Biography: Explorations in Adult Development*. New York: Springer.

Borden, W. (1992) 'Narrative perspectives in psychosocial interventions following adverse life events', *Social Work*, 37: 135–41.

Bozarth, J.D. (1984) 'Beyond reflection: emergent modes of empathy', in R.F. Levant and J.M. Shlien (eds), *Client-Centered Therapy and the Person-Centered Approach: New Directions in Theory, Research and Practice*. New York: Praeger. pp. 59–75.

Bravo, A., Davite, L. and Jalla, D. (1990) 'Myth, impotence, and survival in the concentration camps', in R. Samuel and P. Thompson (eds), *The Myths We Live By*. London: Routledge. pp. 95–110.

Brewer, W.F. and Lichtenstein, E.H. (1982) 'Stories are to entertain: a structural–affect theory of stories', *Journal of Pragmatics*, 6: 473–86.

Brown, B., Nolan, P., Crawford, P. and Lewis, A. (1996) 'Interaction, language and the "narrative turn" in psychotherapy and psychiatry', *Social Science and Medicine*, 43 (11): 1569–78.

Brown, P. (1993) 'Psychiatric intake as a mystery story', *Culture, Medicine and Psychiatry*, 17: 255–80.

Brown, G.W. and Harris, T.O. (1978) *Social Origins of Depression: a Study of Psychiatric Disorder in Women*. London: Tavistock.

Bruner, E.M. (1986) 'Ethnography as narrative', in V.W. Turner and E.M. Bruner (eds), *The Anthropology of Experience*. Chicago, IL: University of Illinois Press. pp. 139–55.

Bruner, J.S. (1983) *Child's Talk: Learning to Use Language*. Oxford: Oxford University Press.

Bruner, J.S. (1986) *Actual Minds, Possible Worlds*. Cambridge, MA: Harvard University Press.

Bruner, J.S. (1987) 'Life as narrative', *Social Research*, 54 (1): 11–32.

Bruner, J.S. (1990) *Acts of Meaning*. Cambridge, MA: Harvard University Press.

Bruner, J.S. (1991) 'The narrative construction of reality', *Critical Inquiry*, 18: 1–21.

Bruner, J.S. (1993) 'The autobiographical process', in R. Folkenflik (ed.), *The Culture of Autobiography: Constructions of Self-Representation*. Stanford, CA: Stanford University Press. pp. 38–56.

Bruner, J.S., Goodnow, L.L. and Austin, G.A. (1956) *A Study of Thinking*. New York: Wiley.

Bruner, J.S. and Luciarello, J. (1989) 'Monologue as narrative recreation of the world', in K. Nelson (ed.), *Narratives from the Crib*. Cambridge, MA: Harvard University Press. pp. 73–97.

Bucci, W. (1993) 'The development of emotional meaning in free association: a multiple code theory', in A. Wilson and J.E. Gedo (eds), *Hierarchical Concepts in Psychoanalysis: Theory, Research and Clinical Practice*. New York: Guilford Press. pp. 3–47.

Bucci, W. (1995) 'The power of the narrative: a multiple code account', in J.W. Pennebaker (ed.), *Emotion, Disclosure and Health*. Washington, DC: American Psychological Association. pp. 93–124.

Burke, K. (1966) *Language as Symbolic Action*. Berkeley, CA: University of California Press.

Burke, K. (1969) *A Grammar of Motives*. Berkeley, CA: University of California Press.

Burns, R.B. (1979) *The Self Concept: Theory, Measurement, Development and Behaviour*. London: Longman.

Burton, A. (1965) 'The use of written productions in psychotherapy', in L. Pearson (ed.), *Written Communications in Psychotherapy*. Springs, IL: Thomas.

Cain, C. (1991) 'Personal stories: identity acquisition and self-understanding in Alcoholics Anonymous', *Ethos*, 19: 210–51.

Campbell, J. (1949) *The Hero with a Thousand Faces*. New York: Bollinger.

Carlson, R. (1988) 'Exemplary lives: the uses of psychobiography for theory development', *Journal of Personality*, 56 (1): 105–38.

Cath, C. and Cath, S. (1978) 'On the other side of Oz: psychoanalytic aspects of fairy tales', *The Psychoanalytic Study of the Child*, 33: 621–39.

Cheney, J. (1989) 'Postmodern environmental ethics: ethics as bioregional narrative', *Environmental Ethics*, 11: 117–34.

Clarke, K.M. (1989) 'Creation of meaning: an emotional processing task in psychotherapy', *Psychotherapy*, 26: 139–48.

Clarkson, P. (1995) *The Therapeutic Relationship*. London: Wurr.

Cohen, L.H., Sargent, M.H. and Sechrest, L.B. (1986) 'Use of psychotherapy research by professional psychologists', *American Psychologist*, 41: 198–206.

Cohen, L.J. (1994) 'Phenomenology of therapeutic reading with implications for research and practice of bibliotherapy', *The Arts in Psychotherapy*, 21 (1): 37–44.

Craig, C. (1996) *Out of History: Narrative Paradigms in Scottish and British Culture*. Edinburgh: Polygon.

Crites, S. (1971) 'The narrative quality of experience', *Journal of the American Academy of Religion*, 39: 291–311.

Csikszentmihalyi, M. and Beattie, O.V. (1979) 'Life themes: a theoretical and empirical exploration of their origins and effects', *Journal of Humanistic Psychology*, 19 (1): 45–63.

Cushman, P. (1990) 'Why the self is empty: toward a historically-situated psychology', *American Psychologist*, 45: 599–611.

Cushman, P. (1992) 'Psychotherapy to 1992: a historically situated interpretation', in D.K. Freedheim (ed.), *History of Psychotherapy: a Century of Change*. Washington, DC: American Psychological Association. pp. 21–64.

Cushman, P. (1995) *Constructing the Self, Constructing America: A Cultural History of Psychotherapy*. Reading, MA: Addison-Wesley.

Danieli, Y. (1988a) 'Confronting the unimaginable: psychotherapists' reactions to victims of the Nazi Holocaust', in J.P. Wilson, Z. Harel and B. Kahana (eds), *Human Adaptation to Extreme Stress: From the Holocaust to Vietnam*. New York: Plenum Press. pp. 219–38.

Danieli, Y. (1988b) 'Treating survivors and children of survivors of the Nazi Holocaust', in F.M. Ochberg (ed.), *Post-Traumatic Therapy and Victims of Violence*. New York: Brunner/Mazel. pp. 278–94.

Davis, K. (1986) 'The process of problem (re)formulation in psychotherapy', *Sociology of Health and Illness*, 8 (1): 44–74.

de Rivera, J. (1989) 'Choice of emotion and ideal development', in L. Cirillo, B. Kaplan and S. Wapner (eds), *Emotions in Ideal Human Development*. Hillsdale, NJ: Erlbaum. pp. 7–34.

de Rivera, J. (1991) 'The structure and dynamics of emotion', in A.J. Stewart, J.M. Healy, jr. and D. Ozer (eds), *Approaches to Understanding Lives. Perspectives in Personality Vol. 3, Part A*. London: Jessica Kinsley. pp. 191–212.

deShazer, S. (1985) *Keys to Solution in Brief Therapy*. New York: Norton.

de Vries, B. and Lehman, A.J. (1996) 'The complexity of personal narratives', in J.E. Birren, G.M. Kenyon, J.-K. Ruth, J.J.F. Schroots and T. Svensson (eds), *Aging and Biography: Explorations in Adult Development*. New York: Springer. pp. 149–66.

DeWaele, J. and Harre, R. (1976) 'The personality of individuals', in R. Harré (ed.), *Personality*. Oxford: Blackwell.

Docherty, R.W. (1989) 'Post-disaster stress in the emergency rescue services', *Fire Engineers Journal*, August, pp. 8–9.

Dryden, W., Horton, I. and Mearns, D. (1995) *Issues in Professional Counsellor Training*. London: Cassell.

Dryden, W. and Thorne, B. (eds) (1991) *Training and Supervision for Counselling in Action*. London: Sage.

Edelson, M. (1993) 'Telling and enacting stories in psychoanalysis and psychotherapy: implications for teaching psychotherapy', *The Psychoanalytic Study of the Child*, 48: 293–325.

Efran, J.S. (1994) 'Mystery, abstraction, and narrative psychotherapy', *Journal of Constructivist Psychotherapy*, 7: 219–27.

Ehrenhaus, P. (1993) 'Cultural narratives and the therapeutic motif: the political containment of Vietnam veterans', in D.K. Mumby (ed.), *Narrative and Social Control: Critical Perspectives*. London: Sage. pp. 77–96.

Ellenberger, H.F. (1970) *The Discovery of the Unconscious: The History and Evolution of Dynamic Psychiatry*. London: Allen Lane.

Elliott, R. (1991) 'Five dimensions of therapy process', *Psychotherapy Research*, 1: 92–103.

Emde, R.N. and Oppenheim, D. (1995) 'Shame, guilt and the Oedipal Drama: developmental considerations concerning morality and the referencing of critical others', in J.P. Tangnay and K.W. Fischer (eds), *Self-Conscious Emotions: the Psychology of Shame, Guilt, Embarrassment and Pride*. New York: Guilford Press. pp. 413–36.

Enns, C.Z., McNeilly, C.L., Corkery, J.M. and Gilbert, M.S. (1995) 'The debate about delayed memories of child sexual abuse: a feminist perspective', *The Counseling Psychologist*, 23: 181–279.

Epston, D. (1989) *Collected Papers*. Adelaide, South Australia: Dulwich Centre Publications.

Epston, D. and White, M. (eds) (1992) *Experience, Contradiction, Narrative and Imagination*. Adelaide, South Australia: Dulwich Centre Publications.

Epston, D. and White, M. (1995) 'Termination as a rite of passage: questioning strategies for a therapy of inclusion', in R.A. Neimeyer and M.J. Mahoney (eds), *Constructivism in Psychotherapy*. Washington, DC: American Psychological Association. pp. 339–54.

Epston, D., White, M. and Murray, K. (1992) 'A proposal for a re-authoring therapy: Rose's revisioning of her life and a commentary', in S. McNamee and K.J. Gergen (eds), *Therapy as Social Construction*. London: Sage. pp. 96–115.

Etherington, K. (1995) *Adult Male Survivors of Childhood Sexual Abuse*. London: Pitman.

Farson, R. (1978) 'The technology of humanism', *Journal of Humanistic Psychology*, 18: 5–35.

Feldman, C.F. (1989) 'Monologue as problem-solving narrative', in K. Nelson (ed.), *Narratives from the Crib*. Cambridge, MA: Harvard University Press. pp. 98–119.

Finnegan, R. (1992) *Oral Traditions and the Verbal Arts: a Guide to Research Practices*. London: Routledge.

Fisher, W.R. (1985) 'The narrative paradigm: an elaboration', *Communication Monographs*, 52: 347–67.

Fisher, W.R. (1984) 'Narration as a human communication paradigm: the case of public moral argument', *Communication Monographs*, 51: 1–22.

Foucault, M. (1967) *Madness and Civilization: a History of Insanity in the Age of Reason.* London: Tavistock.

Frank, J.D. (1973) *Persuasion and Healing: a Comparative Study of Psychotherapy.* Baltimore, MD: Johns Hopkins Press.

Frank, J.D. (1987) 'Psychotherapy, rhetoric, and hermeneutics: implications for practice and research', *Psychotherapy*, 24: 293–302.

Fransella, F. (1985) 'Individual psychotherapy', in E. Button (ed.), *Personal Construct Theory and Mental Health.* Beckenham: Croom Helm. pp. 86–104.

Freedheim, D.K. (ed.) (1992) *History of Psychotherapy: a Century of Change.* Washington, DC: American Psychological Association.

Freud, S. (1900 [1953]) 'The interpretation of dreams', in *Standard Edition*, vol. 4. London: Hogarth Press. pp. 1–338.

Freud, S. (1905 [1953]) 'Fragment of an analysis of a case of hysteria', in *Standard Edition*, vol. 7. London: Hogarth Press. pp. 7–122.

Gadamer, H. (1975) *Truth and Method.* New York: Continuum.

Ganaway, G. (1989) 'Historical versus narrative truth: clarifying the role of exogenous trauma in the etiology of MPD and its variants', *Dissociation*, 2: 205–20.

Garfinkel, H. (1957) 'Conditions of successful degradation ceremonies', *American Journal of Sociology*, 63: 420–4.

Gee, J.P. (1986) 'Units in the production of narrative discourse', *Discourse Processes*, 9: 391–422.

Gee, J.P. (1991) 'A linguistic approach to narrative', *Journal of Narrative and Life History*, 1 (1): 15–39.

Gendlin, E.T. (1962) *Experiencing and the Creation of Meaning.* New York: Free Press.

Gendlin, E.T. (1969) 'Focusing', *Psychotherapy*, 6: 4–15.

Georges, E. (1995) 'A cultural and historical perspective on confession', in J.W. Pennebaker (ed.), *Emotion, Disclosure and Health.* Washington, DC: American Psychological Association. pp. 11–24.

Gergen, K.J. (1985) 'The social constructionist movement in modern psychology', *American Psychologist*, 40: 266–75.

Gergen, K.J. (1988) 'If persons are texts', in S.B. Messer, L.A. Sass and R.L. Woolfolk (eds), *Hermeneutics and Psychological Theory: Interpretive Perspectives on Personality, Psychotherapy and Psychopathology.* New Brunswick, NJ: Rutgers University Press. pp. 28–51.

Gergen, K.J. (1990) 'Therapeutic professions and the diffusion of deficit', *The Journal of Mind and Behavior*, 11: 353–68.

Gergen, K.J. (1991) *The Saturated Self: Dilemmas of Identity in Modern Life.* New York: Basic.

Gergen, K.J. (1994) *Toward Transformation in Social Knowledge*, 2nd edn. London: Sage.

Gergen, K.J. (1996) 'Beyond life narratives in the therapeutic encounter', in J.E. Birren, G.M. Kenyon, J.-K. Ruth, J.J.F. Schroots and T. Svensson (eds), *Aging and Biography: Explorations in Adult Development.* New York: Springer. pp. 205–23.

Gergen, M.M. and Gergen, K.J. (1993) 'Autobiographies and the shaping of gendered lives', in N. Coupland and J.F. Nussbaum (eds), *Discourse and Lifespan Identity.* London: Sage. pp. 28–54.

Gersie, A. (1991) *Storymaking in Bereavement: Dragons Fight in the Meadow.* London: Jessica Kingsley.

Gersie, A. and King, N. (1990) *Storymaking in Education and Therapy.* London: Jessica Kingsley.

Giddens, A. (1991) *Modernity and Self-Identity: Self and Society in the Late Modern Age.* Cambridge: Polity Press.

Glaser, B. and Strauss, A. (1967) *The Discovery of Grounded Theory.* Chicago, IL: Aldine.

Glaser, S. (1980) 'Rhetoric and psychotherapy', in M.J. Mahoney (ed.), *Psychotherapy Process: Current Issues and Future Directions.* New York: Plenum. pp. 313–34.

Glasgow, R.E. and Rosen, G.M. (1978) 'Behavioral bibliotherapy: a review of self-help behavior therapy manuals', *Psychological Bulletin*, 85: 1–23.

Goncalves, O.F. (1994) 'From epistemological truth to existential meaning in cognitive narrative psychotherapy', *Journal of Constructivist Psychology*, 7: 107–18.

Goncalves, O.F. (1995a) 'Hermeneutics, constructivism and cognitive-behavioral therapies: from the object to the project', in R.A. Neimeyer and M.J. Mahoney (eds), *Constructivism in Psychotherapy*. Washington, DC: American Psychological Association. pp. 195–230.

Goncalves, O.F. (1995b) 'Cognitive narrative psychotherapy: the hermeneutic construction of alternative meanings', in M.J. Mahoney (ed.), *Cognitive and Constructive Psychotherapies: Theory, Research and Practice*. New York: Springer. pp. 139–62.

Goolishian, H. and Anderson, H. (1987) 'Language systems and therapy: an evolving idea', *Psychotherapy*, 24: 529–38.

Graham. H. (1992) *The Magic Shop: an Imaginative Guide to Self-Healing*. London: Rider.

Graham, H. (1995) *Mental Imagery in Health Care*. London: Chapman and Hall.

Greenberg, G. (1994a) *The Self on the Shelf: Recovery Books and the Good Life*. Albany, NY: State University of New York Press.

Greenberg, G. (1994b) 'If a self is a narrative: social constructionism in the clinic', *Journal of Narrative and Life History*, 5: 269–83.

Greenberg, L.S., Rice, L.N. and Elliott, R. (1993) *Facilitating Emotional Change: The Moment-by-Moment Process*. New York: Guilford Press.

Greening, T.C. (1977) 'The uses of autobiography', in W. Anderson (ed.), *Therapy and the Arts: Tools of Consciousness*. New York: Harper and Row. pp. 46–81.

Greenspan, H. (1992) 'Lives as texts: symptoms as modes of recounting in the life histories of Holocaust survivors', in G.C. Rosenwald and R.L. Ochberg (eds), *Storied Lives: The Cultural Politics of Self-Understanding*, New Haven, CT: Yale University Press. pp. 145–64.

Gustafson, J.P. (1992) *Self-Delight in a Harsh World: The Main Stories of Individual, Marital and Family Psychotherapy*. New York: Norton.

Halmos, P. (1965) *The Faith of the Counsellors*. London: Constable.

Harber, K.D. and Pennebaker, J.W. (1992) 'Overcoming traumatic memories', in S. Christianson, (ed.) *The Handbook of Emotion and Memory: Research and Theory*. Hillsdale, NJ: Lawrence Erlbaum. pp. 359–87.

Heikkinen, R.L. (1996) 'Experiencing aging as elucidated by narratives', in J.E. Birren, G.M. Kenyon, J.-K. Ruth, J.J.F. Schroots and T. Svensson (eds), *Aging and Biography: Explorations in Adult Development*. New York: Springer. pp. 187–204.

Hermans, H.J.M. and Hermans-Jansen, E. (1995) *Self-Narratives: The Construction of Meaning in Psychotherapy*. New York: Guilford Press.

Hill, C.E. (1986) 'An overview of the Hill counselor and client verbal response modes category systems', in L.S. Greenberg and W.M. Pinsof (eds), *The Psychotherapeutic Process: a Research Handbook*. New York: Guilford Press. pp. 131–60.

Hill, C.E. (1989) *Therapist Techniques and Client Outcomes: Eight Cases of Brief Psychotherapy*. London: Sage.

Hillman, J. (1975) 'The fiction of case history: a round', in J.B. Wiggins (ed.), *Religion as Story*. New York: Harper and Row. pp. 123–74.

Hillman, J. (1983) *Healing Fiction*. Barrytown, NJ: Station Hill Press.

Hobson, R. (1985) *Forms of Feeling: the Heart of Psychotherapy*. London: Tavistock.

Hoffman, L. (1992) 'A reflexive stance for family therapy', in S. McNamee and K.J. Gergen (eds), *Therapy as Social Construction*. London: Sage. pp. 7–24.

Hogman, F. (1985) 'Role of memories in lives of World War II orphans', *Journal of the American Academy of Child Psychiatry*, 24: 390–6.

Holifield, E.B. (1983) *A History of Pastoral Care in America: From Salvation to Self-Realization*. Nashville, TN: Abingdon Press.

Holland, S. (1979) 'The development of an action and counselling service in a deprived urban area', in M. Meacher (ed.), *New Methods of Mental Health Care*. London: Pergamon. pp. 124–56.

Holmes, J. (1993) *John Bowlby and Attachment Theory*. London: Routledge.

Howard, G.S. (1991) 'Culture tales: a narrative approach to thinking, cross-cultural psychology and psychotherapy', *American Psychologist*, 46: 187–97.

Howe, D. (1993) *On Being a Client: Understanding the Process of Counselling and Psychotherapy*. London: Sage.

Hoyt, M.F. (1996) 'Introduction: some stories are better than others', in M.F. Hoyt (ed.),

Constructive Therapies, vol. 2. New York: Guilford Press. pp. 1–32.

Humphreys, K. (1993) 'Expanding on the pluralist revolution: a comment on Omer and Strenger (1992)', *Psychotherapy*, 30: 176–7.

Hyden, L.-C. (1995) 'The rhetoric of recovery and change', *Culture, Medicine and Psychiatry*, 19: 73–90.

Invernizzi, M.A. and Abouzeid, M.P. (1995) 'One story map does not fit all: a cross-cultural analysis of children's written story retellings', *Journal of Narrative and Life History*, 5: 1–19.

Janoff-Bulman, R. (1991) 'Understanding people in terms of their assumptive worlds', in A.J. Stewart, J.M. Healy, Jr. and D. Ozer (eds), *Approaches to Understanding Lives. Perspectives in Personality Vol. 3, Part A*. London: Jessica Kinsley. pp. 99–116.

Jaynes, J. (1977) *The Origin of Consciousness in the Breakdown of the Bicameral Mind*. Boston, MA: Houghton Mifflin.

Josselson, R. and Lieblich, A. (eds) (1993) *The Narrative Study of Lives*. London: Sage.

Josselson, R. and Lieblich, A. (eds) (1995) *Interpreting Experience: the Narrative Study of Lives, Vol. 3*. London: Sage.

Keen, E. (1995) 'Narrative construction in treating Multiple Personality Disorder', *Journal of Narrative and Life History*, 5: 247–53.

Kenyon, G.M. (1996) 'The meaning/value of personal storytelling', in J.E. Birren, G.M. Kenyon, J.-K. Ruth, J.J.F. Schroots and T. Svensson (eds), *Aging and Biography: Explorations in Adult Development*. New York: Springer. pp. 21–9.

Kiev, A. (ed.)(1964) *Magic, Faith and Healing: Studies in Primitive Psychiatry Today*. New York: Free Press.

Klein, M.H., Mathieu-Coughlan, P. and Kiesler, D.J. (1986) 'The Experiencing scales', in L.S. Greenberg and W.M. Pinsof (eds), *The Psychotherapeutic Process: a Research Handbook*. New York: Guilford Press. pp. 21–72.

Kleinman, A. (1988) *The Illness Narratives: Suffering, Healing and the Human Condition*. New York: Basic Books.

Knights, B. (1995) *The Listening Reader: Fiction and Poetry for Counsellors and Psychotherapists*. London: Jessica Kingsley.

Kovel, J. (1981) 'The American mental health industry', in D. Ingleby (ed.), *Critical Psychiatry: the Politics of Mental Health*. Harmondsworth: Penguin. pp. 72–101.

Krell, R. (1985a) 'Child survivors of the Holocaust: 40 years later', *Journal of the American Academy of Child Psychiatry*, 24: 378–80.

Krell, R. (1985b) 'Therapeutic value of documenting child survivors', *Journal of the American Academy of Child Psychiatry*, 24: 397–400.

Labov, W. (1972) *Language in the Inner City: Studies in the Black English Vernacular*. Philadelphia, PA: University of Philadelphia Press.

Labov, W. and Waletzky, J. (1967) 'Narrative analysis: oral versions of personal experience', in J. Helm (ed.), *Essays on the Verbal and Visual Arts*. Seattle, WA: University of Washington Press. pp. 12–44.

Lahad, M. (1992) 'Story-making in assessment method for coping with stress: six-piece story-making and BASIC Ph', in S. Jennings (ed.), *Dramatherapy: Theory and Practice 2*. London: Routledge. pp. 150–63.

Laird, J. (1989) 'Women and stories: restorying women's self-constructions', in M. McGoldrick, C.M. Anderson and F. Walsh (eds), *Women in Families: a Framework for Family Therapy*. New York: Norton. pp. 127–65.

Landrine, H. (1992) 'Clinical implications of cultural differences: the referential versus the indexical self', *Clinical Psychology Review*, 12: 401–15.

Lange, A. (1994) 'Writing assignments in the treatment of grief and traumas from the past', in J. Zeig (ed.), *Ericksonian Methods: the Essence of the Story*. New York: Brunner/Mazel. pp. 377–92.

Lange, A. (1996) 'Using writing assignments with families managing legacies of extreme traumas', *Journal of Family Therapy*, 18: 375–88.

Langellier, K.M. (1989) 'Personal narratives: perspectives on theory and research', *Text and Performance Quarterly*, 9: 243–76.

Lankton, S.R. and Lankton, C.H. (1986) *Enchantment and Intervention in Family Therapy: Training in Ericksonian Approaches*. New York: Brunner/Mazel.

Lassiter, C. (1987) 'Relocation and illness: the plight of the Navajo', in D.M. Levin (ed.), *Pathologies of the Modern Self: Postmodern Studies in Narcissism, Schizophrenia and Depression*. New York: New York University Press. pp. 221–30.

Lazarus, R.S. (1984) 'On the primacy of cognition', *American Psychologist*, 39: 124–9.

Lee, C.C. and Armstrong, K.L. (1995) 'Indigenous models of mental health intervention: lessons from traditional healers', in J.G. Pomterotto, J.M. Casas, L.A. Suzuki and C.M. Alexander (eds), *Handbook of Multicultural Counseling*. London: Sage. pp. 441–56.

Lewis, H.B. (1989) 'Some thoughts on the moral emotions of shame and guilt', in L. Cirillo, B. Kaplan and S. Wapner (eds), *Emotions in Ideal Human Development*, Hillsdale, NJ: Lawrence Erlbaum. pp. 35–51.

Lewis, J., Clark, D. and Morgan, D. (1992) *Whom God Hath Joined Together: the Work of Marriage Guidance*. London: Routledge.

Lieblich, A. and Josselson, R. (eds) (1994) *Exploring Identity and Gender: the Narrative Study of Lives, Vol. 2*. London: Sage.

Lindsay-Hartz, J., de Rivera, J. and Mascolo, M.F. (1995) 'Differentiating shame and guilt and their effects on motivation', in J.P. Tangnay and K.W. Fischer (eds), *Self-Conscious Emotions: the Psychology of Shame, Guilt, Embarrassment and Pride*. New York: Guilford Press. pp. 274–300.

Lister, E.D. (1982) 'Forced silence: a neglected dimension of trauma', *American Journal of Psychiatry*, 139 (7): 872–6.

Lodge, D. (1995) *Therapy: a Novel*. London: Secker and Warburg.

Logan, R.D. (1987) 'Historical change in prevailing sense of self', in K. Yardley and T. Honess (eds), *Self and Identity: Psychosocial Perspectives*. Chichester: Wiley. pp. 13–26.

Lomas, P. (1981) *The Case for a Personal Psychotherapy*. Oxford: Oxford University Press.

Luborsky, L., Barber, J.P. and Diguer, L. (1992) 'The meanings of narratives told during psychotherapy: the fruits of a new observational unit', *Psychotherapy Research*, 2: 277–90.

Luborsky, L. and Crits-Christoph, P. (eds) (1990) *Understanding Transference: the CCRT Method*. New York: Basic Books.

Luborsky, L., Popp, C., Luborsky, E. and Mark, D. (1994) 'The core conflictual relationship theme', *Psychotherapy Research*, 4: 172–83.

Lukinsky, J. (1990) 'Reflective withdrawal through journal writing', in J. Mezirow (ed.), *Fostering Critical Reflection in Adulthood: a Guide to Transformative and Emancipatory Learning*. San Francisco, CA: Jossey-Bass. pp. 213–34.

Lynch, G. (1996) 'Living in a world of words and silence: counselling and psychotherapy after Wittgenstein'. Unpublished paper. Available from Department of Community Studies, University College Chester, Cheyney Rd, Chester CH1 4BJ, UK.

Lynch, G. (1997) 'Therapeutic theory and social context: a social constructionist approach', *British Journal of Guidance and Counselling*, 25 (1): 5–16.

Lyness, K. and Thomas, V. (1995) 'Fitting a square peg in a square hole: using metaphor in narrative therapy', *Contemporary Family Therapy*, 17 (1): 127–42.

Lyon, D. (1994) *Postmodernity*. Buckingham: Open University Press.

McAdams, D.P. (1985) *Power, Intimacy, and the Life Story: Personological Inquiries into Identity*. New York: Guilford Press.

McAdams, D.P. (1991) 'Self and story', in A.J. Stewart, J.M. Healy, jr. and D. Ozer (eds), *Approaches to Understanding Lives. Perspectives in Personality Vol. 3, Part B*. London: Jessica Kinsley. pp. 133–59.

McAdams, D.P. (1993) *The Stories We Live By: Personal Myths and the Making of the Self*. New York: William Murrow.

McAdams, D.P. (1994) 'Can personality change? Levels of stability and growth across the life span', in T.F. Heatherton and J.L. Weinberger (eds), *Can Personality Change?* Washington, DC: American Psychological Association. pp. 299–313.

McAdams, D.P. (1996) 'Narrating the self in adulthood', in J.E. Birren, G.M. Kenyon, J.-K. Ruth, J.J.F. Schroots and T. Svensson (eds), *Aging and Biography: Explorations in Adult*

Development. New York: Springer. pp. 131–48.

MacIntyre, A. (1981) *After Virtue: A Study in Moral Theory*. London: Duckworth.

McKay, V.C. (1993) 'Making connections: narrative as the expression of continuity between generations of grandparents and grandchildren', in N. Coupland and J.F. Nussbaum (eds), *Discourse and Lifespan Identity*. London: Sage. pp. 173–86.

McKinney, F. (1976) 'Free writing as therapy', *Psychotherapy: Theory, Research and Practice*, 13: 183–7.

McLeod, J. (1993) *An Introduction to Counselling*. Buckingham: Open University Press.

McLeod, J. (1996) 'Qualitative research methods in counselling psychology', in R. Woolfe and W. Dryden (eds), *Handbook of Counselling Psychology*. London: Sage. pp. 65–86.

McLeod, J. and Balamoutsou, S. (1996) 'Representing narrative process in therapy: qualitative analysis of a single case', *Counselling Psychology Quarterly*, 9: 61–76.

Macmurray, J. (1961) *Persons in Relation*. London: Faber.

McNeill, J.T. (1951) *A History of the Cure of Souls*. New York: Harper and Row.

Mahoney, M.J. (1995) 'Theoretical development in the cognitive and constructive psychotherapies', in M.J. Mahoney (ed.), *Cognitive and Constructive Psychotherapies: Theory, Research and Practice*. New York: Springer. pp. 3–19.

Mahrer, A.R. (1989) *The Integration of Psychotherapies: a Guide for Practicing Therapists*. New York: Human Sciences Press.

Mair, J.M.M. (1977) 'The community of self', in D. Bannister (ed.), *New Perspectives in Personal Construct Theory*. London: Academic Press.

Mair, M. (1988) 'Psychology as storytelling', *International Journal of Personal Construct Psychology*, 1: 125–37.

Mair, M. (1989a) *Beyond Psychology and Psychotherapy: a Poetics of Experience*. London: Routledge.

Mair, M. (1989b) 'Psychology as a discipline of discourse'. Paper presented at a Conference on 'Psychology, Psychotherapy and Story-Telling', Psychotherapy Section of the British Psychological Society, Dumfries, Scotland.

Mair, M. (1990a) 'Telling psychological tales', *International Journal of Personal Construct Psychology*, 3: 121–35.

Mair, M. (1990b) 'Speaking the truth'. Paper presented at a Conference on 'Developing a Language for Psychological Research', Psychotherapy Section of the British Psychological Society, University of London.

Mancuso, J.C. (1986) 'The acquisition and use of narrative grammar structure', in T.R. Sarbin (ed.), *Narrative Psychology: The Storied Nature of Human Conduct*, New York: Praeger, pp. 91–110.

Mandler, J.M. (1984) *Scripts, Stories and Scenes: Aspects of Schema Theory*. Hillsdale, NJ: Lawrence Erlbaum.

Markus, H.R. and Kitayama, S. (1991) 'Culture and the self: implications for cognition, emotion and motivation', *Psychological Review*, 98 (2): 224–53.

Martin, W. (1986) *Recent Theories of Narrative*. Ithaca, NY: Cornell University Press.

Masson, J.M. (1985) *The Assault on Truth: Freud and Child Sexual Abuse*. Harmondsworth: Penguin.

Masson, J.M. (1988) *Against Therapy: Emotional Tyranny and the Myth of Psychological Healing*. New York: Atheneum.

Masson, J. (1989) *Against Therapy*. Glasgow: Collins.

Masson, J.M. (1990) *Final Analysis: the Making and Unmaking of a Psychoanalyst*. London: HarperCollins.

Maultsby, M.C. (1971) 'Systematic written homework in psychotherapy', *Psychotherapy*, 8: 195–8.

Mazor, A., Gampel, Y., Enright, R.D. and Orenstein, R. (1990) 'Holocaust survivors: coping with post-traumatic memories in childhood and 40 years later', *Journal of Traumatic Stress*, 3: 1–14.

Meichenbaum, D. (1995) 'Changing conceptions of cognitive behavior modification: retrospect and prospect', in M.J. Mahoney (ed.), *Cognitive and Constructive Psychotherapies: Theory, Research and Practice*. New York: Springer. pp. 20–6.

Michaels, S. (1991) 'The dismantling of narrative', in A. McCabe and C. Peterson (eds), *Developing Narrative Structure*. Hillsdale, NJ: Lawrence Erlbaum. pp. 303–52.

Miller, G.A. (1969) 'Psychology as a means of promoting human welfare', *American Psychologist*, 24: 1063–75.

Minami, M. and McCabe, A. (1991) '*Haiku* as a discourse regulation device: a stanza analysis of Japanese children's personal narratives', *Language in Society*, 20: 577–99

Mishler, E.G. (1986) *Research Interviewing: Context and Narrative*. Cambridge, MA: Harvard University Press.

Mishler, E.G. (1991) 'Representing discourse: the rhetoric of transcription', *Journal of Narrative and Life History*, 1 (4): 255–80.

Mishler, E.G. (1995) 'Models of narrative analysis: a typology', *Journal of Narrative and Life History*, 5: 87–123.

Miyake, K. and Yamazaki, K. (1995) 'Self-conscious emotions, child rearing, and child psychopathology in Japanese culture', in J.P. Tangnay and K.W. Fischer (eds), *Self-Conscious Emotions: the Psychology of Shame, Guilt, Embarrassment and Pride*. New York: Guilford Press. pp. 488–504.

Mollica, R.F. (1988) 'The trauma story: the psychiatric care of refugee survivors of violence and torture', in F.M. Ochberg (ed.), *Post-Traumatic Therapy and Victims of Violence*. New York: Brunner/Mazel. pp. 295–314.

Monk, G., Winslade, J., Crocket, K. and Epston, D. (eds) (1996) *Narrative Therapy in Practice: The Archaeology of Hope*. San Francisco: Jossey-Bass.

Monks, J. (1995) 'Life stories and sickness experience: a performance perspective', *Culture, Medicine and Psychiatry*, 19: 453–78.

Moras, K. (1993) 'The use of treatment manuals to train psychotherapists: observations and recommendations', *Psychotherapy*, 30: 581–6.

Morrow-Bradley, C. and Elliott, R. (1986) 'Utilization of psychotherapy research by practising psychotherapists', *American Psychologist*, 41: 188–97.

Mulhern, S. (1994) 'Satanism, ritual abuse, and multiple personality disorder', *International Journal of Clinical and Experimental Hypnosis*, 42: 265–88.

Murray, H.A. (1938) *Explorations in Personality: a Clinical and Experimental Study of Fifty Men of College Age*. New York: Oxford University Press.

Neimeyer, R.A. (1994) 'The role of client-generated narratives in psychotherapy', *Journal of Constructivist Psychology*, 7: 229–42.

Neimeyer, R.A. (1995) 'Constructivist psychotherapies: features, foundations and future directions', in R.A. Neimeyer and M.J. Mahoney (eds), *Constructivism in Psychotherapy*. Washington, DC: American Psychological Association. pp. 11–38.

Neimeyer, R.A. and Mahoney, M.J. (eds) (1995) *Constructivism in Psychotherapy*. Washington, DC: American Psychological Association.

Neugebauer, R. (1978) 'Treatment of the mentally ill in medieval and early modern England: a reappraisal', *Journal of the History of the Behavioral Sciences*, 14: 158–69.

Neugebauer, R. (1979) 'Early and modern theories of mental illness', *Archives of General Psychiatry*, 36: 477–83.

Ogles, B.M., Lambert, M.J. and Craig, D.E. (1991) 'Comparison of self-help books for coping with loss: expectations and attributions', *Journal of Counseling Psychology*, 38: 387–93.

Omer, H. (1987) 'Therapeutic impact: a nonspecific major factor in directive psychotherapies', *Psychotherapy*, 24: 52–7.

Omer, H. (1990) 'Enhancing the impact of therapeutic interventions', *American Journal of Psychotherapy*, 44: 218–31.

Omer, H. (1993a) 'Quasi-literary elements in psychotherapy', *Psychotherapy*, 30: 59–66.

Omer, H. (1993b) 'Short-term psychotherapy and rise of the life-sketch', *Psychotherapy*, 30: 668–73.

Omer, H. (1996) 'Three styles of constructive therapy', in M.F. Hoyt (ed.), *Constructive Therapies*, vol. 2. New York: Guilford Press. pp. 319–33.

Omer, H. and Strenger, C. (1992) 'The pluralist revolution: from the one true meaning to an infinity of constructed ones', *Psychotherapy*, 29: 253–61.

Ong. W.J. (1982) *Orality and Literacy: the Technologizing of the Word*. London: Routledge.

Orlinsky, D., Grawe, K. and Parks, B.K. (1994) 'Process and outcome in psychotherapy – noch einmal', in A.E. Bergin and S.L. Garfield (eds), *Handbook of Psychotherapy and Behavior Change*, 4th edn. Chichester: Wiley. pp. 270–378.

Paivio, A. (1986) *Mental Representation: a Dual Coding Approach*. New York: Oxford University Press.

Palumbo, J. (1992) 'Narratives, self-cohesion, and the patient's search for meaning', *Clinical Social Work Journal*, 20: 249–70.

Parker, I., Georgaca, E., Harper, D., McLaughlin, T. and Stowell-Smith, M. (1995) *Deconstructing Psychopathology*. London: Sage.

Parry, A. and Doan, R.E. (1994) *Story Re-Visions: Narrative Therapy in the Post-Modern World*. New York: Guilford.

Parson, E.R. (1985) 'Ethnicity and traumatic stress: the intersecting point in psychotherapy', in C.R. Figley (ed.), *Trauma and its Wake. Vol. 1*. New York: Brunner/Mazel. pp. 211–37.

Payne, M. (1996) 'Person-centred and systemic models', in S. Palmer, S. Dainow and P. Milner (eds), *Counselling: the BAC Counselling Reader*. London: Sage. pp. 15–22.

Penn, P. and Frankfurt, M. (1994) 'Creating a participant text: writing, multiple voices, narrative multiplicity', *Family Process*, 33: 217–32.

Pennebaker, J.W. (1988) 'Confiding traumatic experiences and health', in S. Fisher and J. Reason (eds), *Handbook of Life Stress, Cognition and Health*. Chichester: Wiley.

Pennebaker, J.W. (1993a) 'Putting stress into words: health, linguistic and therapeutic implications', *Behaviour Research and Therapy*, 31: 539–48.

Pennebaker, J.W. (1993b) 'Social mechanisms of constraint', in D.W. Wegner and J.W. Pennebaker (eds), *Handbook of Mental Control*. Englewood Cliffs, NJ: Prentice-Hall. pp. 200–19.

Pennebaker, J.W., Barger, S.D. and Tiebout, J. (1989) 'Disclosure of traumas among Holocaust survivors', *Psychosomatic Medicine*, 51: 577–89.

Pennebaker, J.W., Colder, M. and Sharp, L.K. (1990) 'Accelerating the coping process', *Journal of Personality and Social Psychology*, 58: 528–37.

Pennebaker, J.W. and Harber, K.D. (1993) 'A social stage model of collective coping: the Loma Prieta earthquake and the Persian Gulf War', *Journal of Social Issues*, 49 (4): 125–45.

Pennebaker, J.W., Kiecolt-Glaser, J.K. and Glaser, R. (1988) 'Disclosure of traumas and immune function: health implications for psychotherapy', *Journal of Consulting and Clinical Psychology*, 56: 239–45.

Polanyi, L. (1982) 'Linguistic and social constraints on storytelling', *Journal of Pragmatics*, 6: 509–24.

Polkinghorne, D.E. (1988) *Narrative Knowing and the Human Sciences*, Albany, NY: State University of New York Press.

Polkinghorne, D.E. (1991) 'Narrative and the self-concept', *Journal of Narrative and Life History*, 1: 135–53.

Polkinghorne, D.E. (1992) 'Postmodern epistemology of practice', in S. Kvale (ed.), *Psychology and Postmodernism*. London: Sage. pp. 146–65.

Polkinghorne, D.E. (1996) 'Narrative knowing and the study of lives', in J.E. Birren, G.M. Kenyon, J.-K. Ruth, J.J.F. Schroots and T. Svensson (eds), *Aging and Biography: Explorations in Adult Development*. New York: Springer. pp. 77–99.

Polonoff, D. (1987) 'Self-deception', *Social Research*, 54 (1): 45–54.

Polster, E. (1987) *Every Person's Life is Worth a Novel*. New York: Norton.

Prince, R. (1981) 'Variations in psychotherapeutic procedures', in H.C. Traindis and J.G. Draguns (eds), *Handbook of Cross-Cultural Psychopathology*, vol. 6. Boston, MA: Allyn and Bacon. pp. 291–349.

Progoff, I. (1975) *At a Journal Workshop*. New York: Dialogue House.

Rainer, T. (1980) *The New Diary*. London: Angus and Roberston.

Rappaport, J. and Simkins, R. (1991) 'Healing and empowering through community narrative', *Prevention in Human Services*. 10: 29–50.

Reason, P. (1993) 'Reflections on sacred experience and sacred science', *Journal of Management*

Inquiry, 2 (3): 273–83.

Rennie, D.L. (1990) 'Toward a representation of the client's experience of the psychotherapy hour', in G. Lietaer, J. Rombauts and R. Van Balen (eds), *Client-Centered and Experiential Therapy in the 90s*. Leuven, Belgium: Leuven University Press. pp. 155–72.

Rennie, D.L. (1992) 'Qualitative analysis of the client's experience of psychotherapy: the unfolding of reflexivity', in S.G. Toukmanian and D.L. Rennie (eds), *Psychotherapy Process Research: Paradigmatic and Narrative Approaches*. London: Sage. pp. 211–33.

Rennie, D.L. (1994a) 'Storytelling in psychotherapy: the client's subjective experience', *Psychotherapy*, 31: 234–43.

Rennie, D.L. (1994b) 'Human science and counselling psychology: closing the gap between research and practice', *Counselling Psychology Quarterly*, 7: 251–86.

Rennie, D.L. and Toukmanian, S.G. (1992) 'Explanation in psychotherapy process research', in S.G. Toukmanian and D.L. Rennie (eds), *Psychotherapy Process Research: Paradigmatic and Narrative Approaches*. London: Sage. pp. 234–51.

Rice, L.N. and Kerr, G.P. (1986) 'Measures of client and therapist vocal quality', in L.S. Greenberg and W.M. Pinsof (eds), *The Psychotherapeutic Process: a Research Handbook*. New York: Guilford Press, pp. 73–106.

Richardson, L. (1992) 'The consequences of poetic representation: writing the other, rewriting the self', in C. Ellis and M.G. Flaherty (eds), *Investigating Subjectivity: Research on Lived Experience*. New York: Sage.

Riessman, C.K. (1988) 'Worlds of difference: contrasting experience in marriage and narrative style', in A.D. Todd and S. Fisher (eds), *Gender and Discourse: The Power of Talk*. Norwood, NJ: Ablex. pp. 151–73.

Riessman, C.K. (1993) *Narrative Analysis*. New York: Sage.

Rinsley, R. and Bergmann, E. (1983) 'Enchantment and alchemy: the story of Rumplestiltskin', *Bulletin of the Menninger Clinic*, 47: 1–13.

Rogers, C.R. (1951) *Client-Centered Therapy: Its Current Practice, Implications and Theory*. London: Constable.

Rorty, R. (1980) *Philosophy and the Mirror of Nature*. Oxford: Blackwell.

Rosch, E. and Mervis, C.B. (1975) 'Family resemblances: studies in the internal structure of categories', *Cognitive Psychology*, 7: 573–605.

Rosen, S. (ed.) (1982) *My Voice Will Go with You: the Teaching Tales of Milton H. Erickson*. New York: Norton.

Rosenbaum, R. (1994) 'Single-session therapies: intrinsic integration', *Journal of Psychotherapy Integration*, 4 (3): 229–52.

Rubin, R.J. (ed.) (1978) *Bibliotherapy Sourcebook*. Phoenix, AR: Oryx Press.

Runyan, W.M. (1980) 'Alternative accounts of lives: an argument for epistemological relativism', *Biography*, 3: 209–24.

Runyan, W.M. (1991) '"Progress" as an approach to epistemological problems in the study of lives', in A.J. Stewart, J.M. Healy, jr. and D. Ozer (eds), *Approaches to Understanding Lives. Perspectives in Personality Vol. 3, Part B*. London: Jessica Kinsley. pp. 17–33.

Russell, R.L. (1991) 'Narrative in views of humanity, science and action: lessons for cognitive therapy', *Journal of Cognitive Psychotherapy*, 5: 241–56.

Russell, R.L. and Luciarello, J. (1992) 'Narrative, Yes; Narrative ad infinitum, No!', *American Psychologist*, 47: 671–2.

Russell, R.L. and van den Broek, P. (1992) 'Changing narrative schemas in psychotherapy', *Psychotherapy*, 29: 344–54.

Russell, R.L., van den Broek, P., Adams, S., Rosenberger, K. and Essig, T. (1993) 'Analyzing narratives in psychotherapy: a formal framework and empirical analyses', *Journal of Narrative and Life History*, 3 (4): 337–60.

Ruth, J.-K. and Kenyon, G.M. (1996) 'Biography in adult development and aging', in J.E. Birren, G.M. Kenyon, J.-K. Ruth, J.J.F. Schroots and T. Svensson (eds), *Aging and Biography: Explorations in Adult Development*. New York: Springer. pp. 1–20.

Ryle, A. (1990) *Cognitive–Analytic Therapy: Active Participation in Change: a New Integration in Brief Psychotherapy*. Chichester: Wiley.

Sacks, O. (1985) *The Man who Mistook his Wife for a Hat*. London: Duckworth.

Sarbin, T.R. (1986) 'The narrative as a root metaphor for psychology', in T.R. Sarbin (ed.), *Narrative Psychology: the Storied Nature of Human Conduct*. New York: Praeger, pp. 1–37.

Sarbin, T.R. (1989a) 'Emotions as situated actions', in L. Cirillo, B. Kaplan and S. Wapner (eds), *Emotions in Ideal Human Development*. Hillsdale, NJ: Erlbaum. pp. 77–99.

Sarbin, T.R. (1989b) 'Emotions as narrative emplotments', in M.J. Packer and R.B. Addison (eds), *Entering the Circle: Hermeneutic Investigation in Psychology*. Albany, NY: State University of New York Press. pp. 185–201.

Sarbin, T.R. (1995a) 'A narrative approach to "repressed memories"', *Journal of Narrative and Life History*, 5: 51–66.

Sarbin, T.R. (1995b) 'On the belief that one body may be host to two or more personalities', *International Journal of Clinical and Experimental Hypnosis*, 43: 163–83.

Sass, L.A. (1987) 'Schreber's Panopticon: psychosis and the modern soul', *Social Research*, 54: 101–47.

Sass, L.A. (1990) 'The self and its vicissitudes: an "archaeological" study of the psychoanalytic avant-garde', *Social Research*, 57: 551–607.

Schafer, R. (1976) *A New Language for Psychoanalysis*. New Haven, CT: Yale University Press.

Schafer, R. (1980) 'Narration in the psychoanalytic dialogue', *Critical Inquiry*, 7: 29–53.

Schafer, R. (1992) *Retelling a Life: Narration and Dialogue in Psychoanalysis*. New York: Basic Books.

Scheff, T.J. (1977) 'The distancing of emotion in ritual', *Current Anthropology*, 18: 483–505.

Scheff, T.J. (1981) 'The distancing of emotion in psychotherapy', *Psychotherapy: Theory, Research and Practice*, 18: 46–53.

Scheff, T.J. (1990) *Microsociology: Discourse, Emotion and Social Structure*. Chicago: University of Chicago Press.

Scheibe, K.E. (1986) 'Self-narratives and adventure', in T.R. Sarbin (ed.), *Narrative Psychology: the Storied Nature of Human Conduct*, New York: Praeger. pp. 129–51.

Scogin, F., Jamison, C. and Davis, N. (1990) 'Two-year follow-up of bibliotherapy for depression in older adults', *Journal of Consulting and Clinical Psychology*, 58: 665–7.

Scull, A. (1979) *Museums of Madness: the Social Organization of Insanity in Nineteenth Century England*. London: Allen Lane.

Scull, A. (ed.) (1981) *Mad-houses, Mad-doctors and Madmen*. Pennsylvania, PA: University of Pennsylvania Press.

Scull, A. (1989) *Social Order/Disorder: Anglo-American Psychiatry in Historical Perspective*. London: Routledge.

Sheinberg, M. (1992) 'Navigating treatment impasses at the disclosure of incest: combining ideas from feminism and social constructionism', *Family Process*, 31 (3): 201–16.

Shortt, J.W. and Pennebaker, J.W. (1992) 'Talking versus hearing about Holocaust experiences', *Basic and Applied Social Psychology*, 13: 165–79.

Shotter, J. (1975) *Images of Man in Psychological Research*. London: Methuen.

Sluzki, C.E. (1992) 'Transformations: a blueprint for narrative changes in therapy', *Family Process*, 31 (3): 217–30.

Smith, M.B., Bruner, J.S. and White, R.W. (1956) *Opinions and Personality*. New York: Wiley.

Snyder, M. (1996) 'Our "other history": poetry as a meta-metaphor for narrative therapy', *Journal of Family Therapy*, 18: 337–59.

Sollod, R.N. (1978) 'Carl Rogers and the origins of client-centered therapy', *Professional Psychology*, 9: 93–104.

Sollod, R.N. (1982) 'Non-scientific sources of psychotherapeutic approaches', in P.W. Sharkey (ed.), *Philosophy, Religion and Psychotherapy: Essays in the Philosophical Foundations of Psychotherapy*. Washington, DC: University Press of America. pp. 47–73.

Spanos, N.P., Burgess, C.A. and Burgess, M.F. (1994) 'Past-life identities, UFO abductions and Satanic ritual abuse', *International Journal of Clinical and Experimental Hypnosis*, 42: 433–46.

Spence, D.P. (1982a) *Narrative Truth and Historical Truth: Meaning and Interpretation in Psychoanalysis*. New York: Norton.

Spence, D.P. (1982b) 'Narrative persuasion', *Psychoanalysis and Contemporary Thought*, 6:

457–81.

Spence, D.P. (1986) 'Narrative smoothing and clinical wisdom', in T.R. Sarbin (ed.), *Narrative Psychology: the Storied Nature of Human Conduct*. New York: Praeger. pp. 211–32.

Spence, D.P. (1987) *The Freudian Metaphor: Toward Paradigm Change in Psychoanalysis*. New York: Norton.

Spence, D.P. (1989) 'Rhetoric vs. evidence as a source of persuasion: a critique of the case study genre', in M.J. Packer and R.B. Addison (eds), *Entering the Circle: Hermeneutic Investigation in Psychology*. New York: Addison-Wesley. pp. 201–21.

Spence, D.P. (1994) 'Narrative truth and putative child abuse', *International Journal of Clinical and Experimental Hypnosis*, 42: 289–303.

Spera, S.P., Buhrfeind, E.D. and Pennebaker, J.W. (1994) 'Creative writing and coping with job loss', *Academy of Management Journal*, 37: 722–33.

Stacey, J. (1996) 'Conquering heroes: the politics of cancer narratives', in P. Duncker and V. Wilson (eds), *Cancer: Through the Eyes of Ten Women*. London: Pandora. pp. 1–34.

Starker, S. (1988) 'Do-it-yourself therapy: the prescription of self-help books by psychologists', *Psychotherapy*, 25: 142–6.

Stein, N.L. (1982) 'The definition of a story', *Journal of Pragmatics*, 6: 487–507.

Stein, N.L. and Glenn, C.G. (1979) 'An analysis of story comprehension in elementary school children', in R.O. Freedle (ed.), *Advances in Discourse Processes: New Directions in Discourse Processing Vol. 2*. Norwood, NJ: Ablex.

Stein, N.L. and Policastro, M. (1984) 'The concept of a story: A comparison between children's and teachers' viewpoints', in H. Mandl, N.L. Stein and T. Trabasso (eds), *Learning and Comprehension of Text*. Hillsdale, NJ: Lawrence Erlbaum. pp. 113–55.

Steiner, C. (1974) *Scripts People Live: Transactional Analysis of Life Scripts*. New York: Grove Press.

Stiles, W.B. (1995) 'Disclosure as a speech act: is it psychotherapeutic to disclose?', in J.W. Pennebaker (ed.), *Emotion, Disclosure and Health*. Washington, DC: American Psychological Association. pp. 71–92.

Stiles, W.B. and Shapiro, D.A. (1989) 'Abuse of the drug metaphor in psychotherapy process–outcome research', *Clinical Psychology Review*, 9: 521–43.

Strupp, H., Wallach, M. and Wogan, M. (1964) 'Psychotherapy experience in retrospect: questionnaire study of former patients and their therapists', *Psychological Monographs: General and Applied*, 78 (11), Whole No. 588.

Strupp, J.H. and Binder, J.L. (1984) *Psychotherapy in a New Key: A Guide to Time-Limited Dynamic Psychotherapy*. New York: Basic Books.

Sugarman, J. and Martin, J. (1995) 'The moral dimension: a conceptualization and empirical demonstration of the moral nature of psychotherapeutic conversations', *The Counseling Psychologist*, 23: 324–47.

Taylor, C. (1989) *Sources of the Self*. Cambridge, MA: Harvard University Press.

Thorne, B. (1985) *The Quality of Tenderness*. Norwich: Norwich Centre Publications.

Tomkins, S.S. (1979) 'Script theory: differential magnification of affects', in H.E. Howe and R.E. Dienstbier (eds), *Nebraska Symposium on Motivation*, vol. 26. Lincoln, NE: University of Nebraska Press. pp. 201–36.

Tomkins, S.S. (1987) 'Script theory', in J. Aronoff, A.I. Rubin and R.A. Zucker (eds), *The Emergence of Personality*. New York: Springer. pp. 147–216.

Trevarthen, C. (1995) 'The child's need to learn a culture', *Children and Society*, 9 (1): 5–19.

Tseng, W. and Hsu, J. (1972) 'The Chinese attitude toward parental authority as expressed in Chinese children's stories', *Archives of General Psychiatry*, 26: 28–34.

Turner, V. (1964) 'An Ndembu doctor in practice', in A. Kiev (ed.), *Magic, Faith and Healing: Studies in Primitive Psychiatry Today*. New York: Free Press. pp. 230–63.

Turner, V. (1982) *From Ritual to Theatre: the Human Seriousness of Play*. New York: Performing Arts Society Publications.

van den Broek, P. and Thurlow, R. (1991) 'The role and structure of personal narratives', *Journal of Cognitive Psychotherapy*, 5: 257–73.

van Langenhove, L. and Harré, R. (1993) 'Positioning and autobiography: telling your life', in

N. Coupland and J.F. Nussbaum (eds), *Discourse and Lifespan Identity*. London: Sage. pp. 81–100.

Viney, L. (1990) 'Psychotherapy as shared reconstruction', *International Journal of Personal Construct Psychotherapy*, 3: 437–56.

Viney, L. (1993) *Life Stories: Personal Construct Therapy with the Elderly*. Chichester: Wiley.

Vogel, D. (1994) 'Narrative perspectives in theory and therapy', *Journal of Constructivist Psychology*, 7: 243–61.

Vygotsky, L. (1978) *Mind in Society*. Cambridge, MA: Harvard University Press.

Wallas, L. (1986) *Stories for the Third Ear*. New York: Norton.

Wallas, L. (1991) *Stories that Heal: Reparenting Adult Children of Dysfunctional Families Using Hypnotic Stories in Psychotherapy*. New York: Norton.

Walter, T. (1996) 'A new model of grief: bereavement and biography', *Mortality*, 1 (1): 7–25.

Weber, A.L. (1992) 'The account-making process: a phenomenological approach', in T.L. Orbuch (ed.), *Close Relationship Loss: Theoretical Approaches*. New York: Springer. pp. 174–91.

White, M. (1989) *Selected Papers*. Adelaide, South Australia: Dulwich Centre Publications.

White, M. (1992) 'Deconstruction and therapy', in D. Epston and M. White (eds), *Experience, Contradiction, Narrative and Imagination*. Adelaide, South Australia: Dulwich Centre Publications. pp. 109–52.

White, M. and Epston, D. (1990) *Narrative Means to Therapeutic Ends*. New York: Norton.

Widdershoven, G.A.M. (1993) 'The story of life: hermeneutic perspectives on the relationship between narrative and life history', in R. Josselson and A. Lieblich (eds), *The Narrative Study of Lives*. London: Sage. pp. 1–21.

Wiener, W. and Rosenwald, G.C. (1993) 'A moment's monument: the psychology of keeping a diary', in R. Josselson and A. Lieblich (eds), *The Narrative Study of Lives*, London: Sage. pp. 30–58.

Wiggins, J.B. (ed.) (1975) *Religion as Story*. New York: Harper and Row.

Wigrem, J. (1994) 'Narrative completion in the treatment of trauma', *Psychotherapy*, 31: 415–23.

Williams, R. (1961) *The Long Revolution*. London: Chatto and Windus.

Wilson, J.P. (1988) 'Treating the Vietnam veteran', in F.M. Ochberg (ed.), *Post-Traumatic Therapy and Victims of Violence*. New York: Brunner/Mazel, pp. 254–77.

Wurf, E. and Markus, H. (1991) 'Possible selves and the psychology of personal growth', in A.J. Stewart, J.M. Healy, jr. and D. Ozer (eds), *Approaches to Understanding Lives. Perspectives in Personality Vol. 3, Part A*. London: Jessica Kinsley. pp. 39–62.

Yalom, I.D., Brown, S. and Bloch, S. (1975) 'The written summary as a group psychotherapy technique', *Archives of General Psychiatry*, 36: 605–13.

Young, D.M. and Beier, E.G. (1982) 'Being asocial in social places: giving the client a new experience', in J.C. Anchin and D.J. Kiesler (eds), *Handbook of Interpersonal Psychotherapy*. New York: Pergamon.

Young, K. (1986) *Taleworlds and Storyrealms: the Phenomenology of Narrative*. Dordrecht: Martinus Nijhoff.

Zhu, S.H. and Pierce, J.P. (1995) 'A new scheduling method for time-limited counseling', *Professional Psychology: Research and Practice*, 26 (6): 624–5.

Zipes, J. (1979) *Breaking the Magic Spell: Radical Theories of Folk and Fairy Tales*. New York: Routledge.

Index